# POVERTY AND VULNERABILITY IN DHAKA SLUMS

# Poverty and Vulnerability in Dhaka Slums
## The Urban Livelihoods Study

**JANE A. PRYER**
*Royal Free and University College Medical School,
University College London*

LONDON AND NEW YORK

First published 2003 by Ashgate Publishing

2 Park Square, Milton Park, Abingdon, Oxon OX14 4RN
711 Third Avenue, New York, NY 10017, USA

*Routledge is an imprint of the Taylor & Francis Group, an informa business*

First issued in paperback 2016

Copyright © 2003 Jane A. Pryer

The author has asserted her moral right under the Copyright, Designs and Patents Act, 1988, to be identified as the author of this work.

All rights reserved. No part of this book may be reprinted or reproduced or utilised in any form or by any electronic, mechanical, or other means, now known or hereafter invented, including photocopying and recording, or in any information storage or retrieval system, without permission in writing from the publishers.

Notice:
Product or corporate names may be trademarks or registered trademarks, and are used only for identification and explanation without intent to infringe.

**British Library Cataloguing in Publication Data**
Pryer, Jane A.
  Poverty and vulnerability in Dhaka slums : the urban livelihoods study
  1 Poor - Bangladesh - Dhaka 2.Dhaka (Bangladesh) - Social policy
  I.Title
  362.5'0954922

**Library of Congress Cataloging-in-Publication Data**
Pryer, Jane A., 1958-
  Poverty and vulnerability in Dhaka slums : the urban livelihoods study / Jane A. Pryer.
     p. cm.
  Includes bibliographical references and index.

  1. Poor--Bangladesh--Dhaka. 2. Poverty--Bangladesh--Dhaka. 3. Slums--Bangladesh--Dhaka. 4. Dhaka (Bangladesh)--Social conditions. 5. Dhaka (Bangladesh)--Economic conditions. I. Title.

HV4140.6.D43 P79 2002
362.5'095492'2--dc21

2002028123

ISBN 13: 978-0-7546-1864-5 (hbk)
ISBN 13: 978-1-138-26394-9 (pbk)

# Contents

| | | |
|---|---|---|
| *List of Figures* | | *vii* |
| *List of Tables* | | *ix* |
| *Preface* | | *xiii* |
| *Acknowledgements* | | *xv* |
| Introduction | | 1 |
| 1 | Poverty and Vulnerability | 7 |
| 2 | Study Design and Methods | 17 |
| 3 | Livelihood Clusters | 33 |
| 4 | Marital Instability | 43 |
| 5 | Child Labour | 59 |
| 6 | Female Workforce and the Family | 71 |
| 7 | Investing in Health | 83 |
| 8 | Work Disabling Morbidity | 95 |
| 9 | Strategies for Coping with Costs of Work Disabling Ill Health among Household Heads | 103 |
| 10 | Women's Negotiation Control and Well-being within the Households | 111 |
| 11 | Factors Affecting Adult Body Mass Index | 123 |
| 12 | Investing in Children's Nutritional Status | 137 |
| 13 | Intra-household Distribution of Nutritional Vulnerability | 149 |
| 14 | Managing Financial Shocks and Stresses | 161 |
| 15 | Policy Implications | 173 |
| *Bibliography* | | *187* |
| *Index* | | *197* |

# List of Figures

| | | |
|---|---|---|
| 2.1 | Conceptual framework of the urban livelihoods study | 21 |
| 4.1 | Factors increasing marital discord, insecurity and breakdown | 48 |
| 11.1 | Seasonal variations in the percentage distribution of low BMI in adults (BMI≤18.5) | 131 |
| 12.1 | Seasonal variation in the percentage distribution of the stunted, wasted and underweight children | 142 |
| 12.2 | Prevalence of stunted, wasted and underweight children as observed in Bangladesh | 144 |

# List of Tables

| | | |
|---|---|---|
| 1.1 | Shocks faced by urban households in Dhaka slums | 11 |
| 1.2 | Mechanisms for managing shocks | 12 |
| 2.1 | Demographic characteristics of household heads | 25 |
| 2.2 | Percentage distribution of marital status among men and women by age group | 26 |
| 2.3 | Percentage distribution of various indicators of marital behaviour among men and women | 27 |
| 2.4 | Percentage distribution of household structures by sex of household head | 28 |
| 2.5 | Mean household size by household characteristics | 29 |
| 2.6 | Percentage distribution of household structures by household characteristics (Poverty line = Taka 518 per consumption unit) | 30 |
| 3.1 | Socio-economic variables by cluster | 36 |
| 3.2 | Work participation and occupational groups by cluster | 37 |
| 3.3 | Demographic and occupational characteristics by cluster | 38 |
| 4.1 | Percentage distribution of various indicators of marital behaviour among men and women | 44 |
| 4.2 | Various indicators of well-being in female headed and male headed houscholds | 53 |
| 5.1 | Percentage of children performing income generating work by age and sex | 60 |
| 5.2 | Percentage of children (5–16 years) currently attending school by worker status | 60 |
| 5.3 | Percentage distribution of reasons reported among children not attending school | 61 |
| 5.4 | Percentage of children (5–16 years) currently attending school by household characteristics | 62 |
| 5.5 | Percentage of children (5–16 years) in different occupational groups (main occupation) | 64 |
| 5.6 | Percentage of children (5–16 years) performing income generating work in the past month | 65 |
| 5.7 | Children's (aged 5–16 years) contribution to household income | 66 |
| 5.8 | Regression analysis for children under 16 years with height as the dependent variable and other economic variables as independent variables | 67 |
| 6.1 | Percentage of the population performing income generating work by age and gender | 72 |
| 6.2 | Percentage of women working by various factors (aged 15 years or more) | 73 |

| | | |
|---|---|---|
| 6.3 | Mean number of days and hours worked in the past month among working women by occupational category (15 years and above) | 74 |
| 6.4 | Daily wage rates for various occupational groups by gender (aged 15 and over) | 75 |
| 6.5 | Mean percentage of total household income and workdays contributed by women to their households | 76 |
| 6.6 | Reasons reported for not currently working among wives of male heads | 76 |
| 6.7 | Percentage of women reporting that they perform household tasks and women reporting that they had received help | 78 |
| 6.8 | Child death and family planning by gender | 79 |
| 7.1 | Major health indicators for rural and urban populations in Bangladesh | 84 |
| 7.2 | Self reported illness and injury (14 day period prevalence) by broad population categories and gender | 85 |
| 7.3 | Self reported illness (14 day period prevalence) among adults (15–64) by area | 86 |
| 7.4 | Self reported illness by gender and other factors | 87 |
| 7.5 | Reported number of days (mean and standard deviation) suffered by the adult population over the last 14 days due to fever, headache, abdominal pain and other illnesses by gender | 88 |
| 7.6 | Household's adult illness by headship and poverty line | 88 |
| 7.7 | Logistic regression of prevalence of reported illness with socio-demographic characteristics of adult both sexes and female adults | 89 |
| 7.8 | Logistic regression of prevalence of reported cough and cold and fever with socio-demographic characteristics of adults | 91 |
| 8.1 | Socio-economic variables by cluster | 97 |
| 8.2 | Demographic characteristics by cluster | 98 |
| 8.3 | The cost of ill health | 99 |
| 9.1 | Self reported illness and injury (14 day period prevalence) among male and female adults (16–64 years old) | 104 |
| 9.2 | Self reported illness (14 day period prevalence) among adults (15–64 years) by relation to household head | 104 |
| 10.1 | Intra-household negotiations around food, medical treatment, education and clothes | 113 |
| 10.2 | Women's socio-economic variables among female controlled households and male controlled households | 114 |
| 10.3 | Women's visiting rights among female controlled households and male controlled households | 116 |
| 10.4 | Men's violence and divorce threats among female and male controlled households | 117 |
| 10.5 | Women's health and children's nutritional status among female and male controlled households | 118 |
| 11.1 | Percentage of malnourished adults (BMI <18.5) by sex and age group | 125 |
| 11.2 | Influence of family structure on the prevalence of adult malnutrition | 125 |
| 11.3 | Influence of area of residence on the prevalence of malnutrition among adults | 126 |

## List of Tables

| | | |
|---|---|---|
| 11.4 | Influence of loan membership involvement of family members on the prevalence of malnutrition in adults | 126 |
| 11.5 | Influence of self-perceived financial situation in households in the last 30 days on the prevalence of adult malnutrition | 127 |
| 11.6 | Influence of monthly income on the prevalence of malnutrition in adults | 128 |
| 11.7 | Influence of household head's occupation on the prevalence of malnutrition in adults | 128 |
| 11.8 | Comparison of per capita floor space in square metres between households having at least one malnourished adult and households with no malnourished adult | 129 |
| 11.9 | Influence of drinking water on the prevalence of malnutrition in adults | 129 |
| 11.10 | Influence of sex of household head on the prevalence of malnutrition in adults | 130 |
| 11.11 | Influence of electricity in the household on the prevalence of adult malnutrition | 130 |
| 11.12 | Logistic regression (unadjusted and adjusted) of malnutrition among adults in relation to different socio-demographic, economic and environmental factors | 131 |
| 12.1 | Percentage distribution of malnourished children classified by Z scores and age group | 139 |
| 12.2 | Influence of father's and mother's literacy on the prevalence of malnutrition in children | 139 |
| 12.3 | Influence of housing construction on the prevalence of malnutrition in children | 140 |
| 12.4 | Influence of latrine use by children in households on the prevalence of malnutrition in children | 140 |
| 12.5 | Comparison of mean gross monthly household income in Taka between households with no malnourished child and households having at least one malnourished child | 141 |
| 12.6 | Influence of self-perceived financial situation in households in the last 30 days on the prevalence of malnutrition in children | 141 |
| 12.7 | Logistic regression (unadjusted and adjusted) of prevalence of malnutrition in children, socio-demographic, economic, health and environmental factors | 142 |
| 13.1 | Patterns of intra-household anthropometry | 150 |
| 13.2 | Intra-household anthropometric patterns by livelihood groups | 153 |
| 14.1 | Self reported financial situation in the past 30 days among all households: September to December 1996 | 162 |
| 14.2 | Self reported financial situation in the past 30 days among male and female headed households: September to December 1996 | 163 |
| 14.3 | Self reported financial situation in the past 30 days among households in three locations: September to December 1996 | 163 |
| 14.4 | Percentage distribution of main reasons reported for deterioration in financial situation among all households: September to December 1996 | 164 |

| | | |
|---|---|---|
| 14.5 | Percentage of strategies to stop deterioration getting worse | 165 |
| 14.6 | Percentage distribution of main reasons reported for improvement in financial situation among all households | 165 |
| 15.1 | Poverty statistics in Bangladesh | 174 |

# Preface

Bangladesh, despite the lowest levels of urbanisation in the developing world, has a remarkably high urban population in absolute terms, being one of the most densely populated countries. The urban population of 22 million in 1990 is expected to increase, according to World Bank estimates, to 57 million by the year 2010. Rapid urbanisation in developing countries brings in its wake numerous problems and challenges. Urban poverty is one important issue and the urban poor, i.e. "those who cannot meet their basic needs with their own incomes" are a vulnerable segment of the urban population. The Urban Livelihoods Study (ULS) funded by the UK Department for International Development (DfID) in Bangladesh investigated many aspects of poverty and vulnerability in Dhaka slums. This important volume summarises the findings of the excellent work carried out by the ULS team and examines a wide range of issues including livelihood clusters, intra-household nutritional vulnerability, work disabling morbidity and coping strategies, the female workforce, women's negotiation control and well-being, marital instability, child labour, investments in health and in children's nutrition, and the management of financial shocks and stresses. It uses the knowledge and information garnered to debate on the policy implications of this study for both governmental and non-governmental organisations in the country.

For Jane Pryer this has been more than a labour of love. It was her enthusiasm following her PhD work in an urban environment in Khulna, Bangladesh, that sparked this study which she has pursued despite encountering tremendous obstacles including serious illness. The published volume is a testimony of her dedication, commitment and tenacity to see things to their fruition. The post-September 11 environment has brought home to us the stark fact that no one is invulnerable – and Jane Pryer, in bringing out this most important book, has shown how one can rise above personal vulnerability. I believe this book has important lessons for a wide spectrum of individuals from academics to policy makers. However, the spirit of how Jane has addressed this challenge is an even more important lesson to us all.

Professor Prakash Shetty
UN Food & Agriculture Organisation
Rome, Italy.

# Acknowledgements

Thanks to Stephen Rogers for his full support in the process of writing this book, and to the Department of Primary Care and Population Sciences for providing me with a refuge where I could assemble my thoughts and get down to work. Last but not least to friends and colleagues on the ULS team who helped create this important piece of work.
Sponsorship: Department of International Health.

**Urban Livelihoods Study (ULS)**
The ULS Team includes:

**ULS Steering Committee**
Dr. Qazi Faruque Ahmed (Proshika Co-Chair), Dr. Jane Pryer (LSHTM Co-Chair), Dr. Geof Wood, Mr. Shahabuddin, Dr. Sarah Salway, Mr. Iqbal Alam Khan, Mr. Matthew Kiggins, Mr. Mahbubul Karim, Professor Nazrul Islam, Dr. Oona Campbell.

**Bangladesh Team Members**
Bangladesh Project Director: Mr. Md Shahabuddin.
Project Coordinator (Qualitative): Mr. Iqbal Alam Khan.
Qualitative Researchers: Ms. Sonia Jesmin, Mr. Azmal Kabir Kazal, Ms. Mottahera Nasrin, Mr. AEA Opel.
Quantitative Research Officers: Dr. Ataur Rahman, Ms. Shahana Rahman.
Database Manager: Mr. Mostafa el Helal.
Supervisors: Mr. S M Zubair Ali Khan, Mr. Akramul Islam.
Interviewers: Mr. Shahajahan Hossain, Ms. Rifat Aara, Mr. Md Salim, Ms. Dilafroze, Ms. Rezina Khan Ratna, Ms. Rafeza Shaheen, Mr. Patrick Rozario, Ms. Afsari Begum, Mr. Tasbir-ul-Hasnain, Mr. Moniruzzaman, Mr. Md Ataul Islam, Mr. Dayal Chandra Das, Mr. Golam Firoz, Ms. Nurun Nahar, Ms. Namita Chakravarti, Mr. Chandon Banik, Mr. Mustafiz Ali Khan, Ms. Shahina Khan, Ms. Asma Begum, Mr. Mahbubal Alam.
Data Entry Clerks: Mr. Md Helaluddin Farid, Ms. Nargis Akter, Mr. Md Sohel Ahmed Tarafder, Ms. Monira Islam.
Mapping Team: Ms. Rifat Aara, Mr. Arif Hossain Khan, Mr. Md Mainul Islam.

**London Team Members**
Team Leader: Dr. Jane Pryer.
Project Coordinator: Dr. Sarah Salway.
Project Co-ordinator: Mr. Matthew Kiggins.
Epidemiology Adviser: Dr. Oona Campbell.

**Bath Team members**
Qualitative Adviser: Dr. Geof Wood.
Student Placement: Ms. Emily Delap.

**The Slum Environment**

# Introduction

Twenty percent of the population of Bangladesh live in urban areas. The urban poor are at risk of any number of financial and environmental stresses, which combine to make them vulnerable to the effects of poor nutrition and ill health. In order to target interventions towards the most vulnerable, it is necessary both to be able to identify such households and to understand the interplay of factors that place them at risk. The Dhaka Urban Livelihoods Study is a prospective cohort study of a slum population of around 850 households in Dhaka City. The study integrates a social science analysis of livelihoods with a detailed epidemiological investigation of the interrelationships of the social, economic and material conditions of poverty, nutritional status, and morbidity. The complex database of qualitative and quantitative information will provide detailed profiles of vulnerable households and identification of the factors that place them at risk.

The association between poverty and ill health is well documented (Feachem et al., 1992; World Bank, 1996; World Bank, 2000–2001; Pryer, 1993). It has also been recognised that the relationship is two-way, so that reductions in poverty and improvements in health tend to reinforce each other (World Bank, 1996). At the individual level, among communities dependent on physical labour, health and nutritional status can be viewed as both an input into the process of impoverishment and an outcome of poverty (Pryer, 1990). Health and nutritional status are thus important dimensions of vulnerability (Pryer, 1990; Osmani, 1993; Payne, 1992) and nutritional status can be viewed as a unique index of the impact on individuals of the whole socio-economic and political system of production, utilisation and exchange (Pryer, 1990).

Having said this, it is evident that the links between socio-economic status and poor health and nutrition are inadequately understood, and potential points of effective intervention have yet to be identified. The failure to acknowledge the complex interrelations between poverty and ill health means that many conventional interventions do not have the expected effect (Harpham and Tanner, 1995).

This book is about poverty and vulnerability in many facets of life, including livelihood strategies, marital instability, child labour, ill health and poor nutritional status and the impact of shocks and stresses. We also propose policies to reduce poverty and vulnerability in Dhaka, Bangladesh.

## Summary of each chapter

*Chapter 1* examines poverty and vulnerability. "Absolute poverty" is now prevalent as a means of conceptualising poverty in most countries around the world. In this chapter we explain the measurement of poverty using income and expenditure, and the advantages and disadvantages of this approach. We then move on to entitlement and capability theory as an alternative to poverty measurement.

*Chapter 2* presents the study design and methods, including the setting of Bangladesh and topography, economy and demographic characteristics of the slum population. We explain the livelihoods approach which provides the theoretical perspective for the study.

*Chapter 3* describes livelihood clusters. Four livelihoods groups were identified. The first cluster, self-employed, was the richest cluster with land, animals, business assets and savings. Loans as well as income were higher which shows that this group was creditworthy. The group was mainly self-employed and worked more days per month than in other groups. The dependent self-employed group was a poor cluster. This group had the least land and the least animals. Loans and savings were the lowest across the groups. Group 3 was mainly female headed households and was the most vulnerable group. This group were mainly casual unskilled and 40 percent were female headed households. Total income and expenditure were lowest of the groups. Group 4 was the casual skilled (n=67) which was the second richest cluster. This group was comprised mainly of skilled workers. In conclusion, cluster analysis has identified four groups which differed in terms of socio-economic variables and demographic variables. We suggest the technique could be a practically useful tool of relevance to the development, monitoring and targeting of vulnerable households, by public policy in Bangladesh.

*Chapter 4* presents information on marital instability. The changing slum society has provided greater options for women, compared to their rural counterparts. Flexibility of social control against divorce, dysfunction of the lineage, weaker familial ties, and increased options for female labour participation are working as positive forces which give women greater freedom. Slum women are more likely to be able to avoid serious domestic violence, like homicide and suicide, by rejecting unfavourable marital ties or re-partnering. Despite these factors, overall, women appear to be suffering from the increasingly unstable and uncertain nature of marriage. Children, too, are faring badly. The impact of marital instability on children may also be severe. Slum stepchildren are often treated poorly, receiving inadequate food, health care and education. Moreover, if their mothers are living alone without taking another partner, they are forced to become one of the household's economic contributors and to forgo educational opportunities. If they have been adopted by other elderly relatives, they may also be treated badly compared to those relative's own children. These situations may severely hamper their social and human development. Thus the negative consequences of marital instability and family breakdown are far-reaching, affecting not only the husband and wife, but also the next generation – their children.

*Chapter 5* explores child labour. It examines the determinants of child work in Bangladesh. Nearly half of girls and boys aged 10–14 years were involved in income generating work. More girls and boys who are working came from female headed households. Most boys came from households where there was unemployment. More boys from male headed households went to school compared to those from female headed households. Girls and boys from the area of Beri Badh had the least percentage attending school compared to other areas. Thirty percent of female headed households had income below the poverty line, but when children's income was left out 48 percent of female headed households were below the poverty line, showing that child income was an important part of the household income.

*Chapter 6* examines female workforce and family. Using quantitative and qualitative data, factors affecting women working include age, marital status, household head and income status. Persistent inequalities in women's wages, which were lower than men's wages for similar types of occupation. Among households with female earners, women contributed 34 percent of total income and 58 percent of total work days by women. Fifty three percent of husbands do not allow women to work at all, which supports male control over female labour. This reinforces women's subordination within and outside the household. For example, as well as working full time, women have the responsibility for domestic and child care work.

*Chapter 7* examines the prevalence of illness in the study population. Children under five had the highest prevalence of illness, followed by female adults. Beri Badh had the highest prevalence compared to other areas. Over 80 percent of households reported at least one adult member ill over the previous 14 days. Female adults had a higher prevalence of illness compared to male adults, and female household heads had a higher prevalence of fever, abdominal pain and any illness compared with male household heads. Female earners also had a higher prevalence of illness compared to male earners. The odds of illness was greater in females, female heads, married or divorced individuals and in non-workers. The likely impact of the high rates of adult ill health and the factors affecting observed gender differentials are discussed.

*Chapter 8* examines work disabling illness. Four livelihoods groups emerged in our cluster analysis which may be summarised as "self employed", "casual unskilled", "female headed" and "casual skilled" households on the basis of their socio-economic, demographic and occupational characteristics. The "self employed" and "casual skilled" groups were better off in terms of income, assets and creditworthiness. The greatest burden of adult illness fell in the "casual unskilled" and "female headed" households. In any month, 30–40 percent of these households reported loss of labour days due to illness. On average, about four days per month were lost in casual unskilled households and over seven days per month in female headed households, on account of illness. The income lost due to illness far exceeded household expenditure to treat the illness. Programmes which mitigate the adverse effects of adult ill health on household economies, might help break the cycle of ill health and poverty which characterise many urban slum households, and could help reduce inequalities between livelihood groups.

*Chapter 9* describes coping followed by slumdwellers when household members are struck with illness. Strategies include borrowing money, diversifying income sources, women going to work, reducing expenditure, use of savings, sale of assets, merging households, movement of family members, movements to rural areas, use of gifts and other help. A particular purpose of this chapter is to illustrate the range of strategies taken and their possible effects, positive and negative.

*Chapter 10* examines women's negotiation control and wellbeing in households. The overall management of material resources has been traditionally the responsibility of the head of household. However, a close examination of the data suggests that women are often playing a significant role in the management of material resources within the household. In households where the head of household manages the budget, the spouse earns more, but has fewer assets and less savings compared to female controlled households, where women work more days and have a common fund. Violence against women within marriage is frequent and is tolerated in order to gain some protection from other men. Women's health and children's nutritional status was better in female controlled households compared to male controlled households. In Sen's terminology, though working for an income enables women to secure a better fall-back position, their rights still remain weak, and the broader social, economic and political structures continue to weigh against women. With support from the policy community, it seems likely that working women could lead to favourable changes in gender inequalities, with greater options for their control of their lives.

*Chapter 11* examines factors affecting body mass index. Anthropometric data of adults aged 20–59 was analysed to assess their nutritional status. Body mass index (BMI) was the measure used. Undernutrition was related to demographic, economic, social and environmental factors. More females were undernourished than males. Female headed households had worst nutritional status than male headed households. Logistic regression results show 50–59 year olds were the most undernourished. Beri Badh was the most undernourished area. Families with deficit financial situations, casual wage workers, unskilled and dependent self employed were the most likely to suffer low BMI. Families without involvement with credit organisations and those with poor environmental facilities were more likely to have a poor BMI.

*Chapter 12* explores investing in children's nutritional status. Wasting was more prevalent among older girls compared to older boys. Logistic regression results show that females are better nourished than boys. Female headed households have less stunted children, but more wasting compared to male headed households. Children in the age group 24–59 months are more likely to be stunted, but show less wasting and more underweight children compared to the younger age group (3–23 months). Beri Badh had the worst stunting and underweight children of areas covered. Financial deficit households are more likely to be stunted, and more likely to be wasted and more likely to be underweight. In conclusion, undernourished children were related to demographic, economic, social and environmental factors.

*Chapter 13* looks at intra-household distribution of nutritional vulnerability. The utility of nutritional indicators may be enhanced by extending the unit of measurement from the individual to the household. Such a classification may enable patterns of intra-household undernutrition to be identified and to characterise different problems and causes. Female headed households were the most vulnerable with more household members undernourished compared to other groups. We also provide two detailed profiles; one about a female headed household and how the household became undernourished, and secondly, how ill health in a main earner causes households to become undernourished.

*Chapter 14* describes managing financial shocks and stresses. 30 percent of households suffered a severe deficit, with female headed households and the area of Beri Badh facing the highest percentage of severe deficit. The main reason for deterioration in financial status was income earning members being incapacitated, followed by decreased earning and inability to work. The coping strategies for the slum households included changed work, reduced expenditure, and taking loans, with little households taking out mortgages, or selling assets, family migrated or begging. There was no evidence of the moral economy in Dhaka slums – for example, hardly any financial exchange relationships were found.

*Chapter 15* examines policy implications. In this chapter we describe the setting of Dhaka and poverty alleviation in Bangladesh. We then examine the policy implications for child labour, marital instability, work disabling morbidity and coping strategies, child and adult undernutrition and morbidity, intra-household distribution of nutritional vulnerability, women's negotiation control and well-being within household, female workforce and family, and lastly, managing shocks and stresses.

## References

Feachem, R.G.A., Kjellstrom, T., Murray, C.J.L., Over, M. and Phillips, M.A. (1992), *The Health of Adults in the Developing World*, Oxford University Press, Oxford.
Harpham, T. and Tanner, M. (1995), *Urban Health in Developing Countries: Progress and prospects*, Earthscan Publications, London.
Osmani, S.R. (1993), 'On some controversies in the measurement of undernutrion', in Osmani, S.R. (ed.) *Nutrition and Poverty*, University Press Limited, Dhaka.
Payne, P.R. (1992), 'Assessing undernutrition: the need for reconceptualisation', in Osmani, S.R. (ed.) *Nutrition and Poverty*, Clarendon Press, Oxford.
Pryer, J.A. (1990), 'Socio-economic and environmental aspects of undernutrition and ill health in an urban slum in Bangladesh', unpublished PhD thesis, London School of Hygiene and Tropical Medicine.
Pryer, J.A. (1993), 'Nutritionally vulnerable households in the urban slum economy: a case study from Khulna, Bangladesh', in Schell, L.M., Smith, M., Bilsborogh, A. (eds), *Urban Ecology and Health in the Third World*, Cambridge University Press, Cambridge.
World Development Report (1994), *Infrastructure for Development*, The World Bank, Oxford University Press, New York.
World Development Report (2000/2001), *Attacking Poverty*, Oxford University Press, New York.

# Chapter 1
# Poverty and Vulnerability

*In this chapter we explain the measurement of poverty using income and expenditure, and the advantages and disadvantages of this approach. We then move on to entitlement and capability theory as an alternative to poverty measurement.*

## Measurement of poverty using income and consumption

Income poverty has a long history. "Absolute poverty" is now prevalent as a means of conceptualising poverty in most countries around the world, and is usually traced back to the work of Seebohm Rowntree. Rowntree's method was to conduct a survey covering nearly every working-class family in York in 1901, to collect information on earnings and expenditure. He then defined poverty as a level of total earnings insufficient to obtain the minimum necessities for maintenance of "merely physical efficiency" including food, rent and other items. He calculated that for a family of five (father, mother and three children) the minimum weekly expenditure to maintain physical efficiency was 21 shillings and 8 pence; he proposed different amounts for families of different size or composition. Comparing these poverty lines with family earnings, he arrived at the poverty estimate (Rowntree, 1901).

The same principles underpin the current World Bank approach. A key building block in developing income or consumption measures of poverty is the poverty line. In principle, this tests for the ability to purchase a basket of commodities that are roughly similar across the world. In Bangladesh for instance, in 1995–6, 36 percent of people nationally, 40 percent of rural people and 14 percent of urban people were below the National Poverty Line, while 29 percent survived on less than $1.00 a day and 78 percent on less than $2.00 a day (World Bank, 2000–2001). But such a universal line is not suitable for analysis of poverty within a country. For that purpose, a country-specific poverty line needs to be constructed, reflecting the country's economic and social circumstances. Similarly, the poverty line needs to be adjusted for different areas (for example, urban and rural areas) within the country if prices of goods and services differ. The country-specific poverty line is now common practice. In Bangladesh, for instance, 29 percent had less than a $1.00 per day, and 78 percent had less than $2.00 a day. In 1991–2, 42 percent of people nationally, 46 percent of rural people and 23 percent of urban people were below the National Poverty Line. In 1995–6, 36 percent of people nationally, 40 percent of rural people and 14 percent of urban people were below the National Poverty Line (World Bank, 2000–2001).

The most straightforward way to measure poverty is to calculate the percentage of the population below the poverty line. But this has disadvantages; it fails to reflect the fact that among the poor people there may be wide differences in income levels, with some people located just below the poverty line and others experiencing far greater shortfalls. Other poverty measures include the poverty gap, which takes account of the distance of poor people from the poverty line, and the squared poverty gap, which measures the degree of income inequality among poor people (World Bank, 2000–2001). The strengths of the poverty line approach are that it enables governments or the international community to set targets for judging policy options. But there are also a number of limitations. The approach fails to reflect the fact that among the poor people there may be wider differences in income levels, with some people located just below the poverty line and others experiencing far greater shortfalls. Other poverty measures attempt to address this including the poverty gap, which takes account of the distance of poor people from the poverty line and the squared poverty gap, which also measures the degree of income inequality between poor people (World Bank, 2000–2001).

There are also difficulties associated with data collection. Household surveys measure income or consumption, but the design varies between countries, and over time, making comparisons difficult. One month recall data tends to result in higher poverty estimates compared to a one week recall. Then we must decide how to allow for household size and composition into measures for individuals, as well as measurement error. Moreover, income or consumption at the household level has a basic shortcoming in that neither can reveal inequality within the household, so they can underestimate overall inequality and poverty. Haddad and Kanbur (1990) desegregated household consumption by individual members and found that relying on household information could lead to an underestimate of inequality and poverty by 25 percent. In particular, the conventional household survey approach does not allow direct measurement of income or consumption of poverty among women.

## Poverty measurement and the within-household distribution

People, not households, experience poverty. Yet it is standard practice to measure poverty at the household level. Household members are assumed to receive equal shares of their household income. The equal sharing concept has long been questioned (Chippori, 1997). The World Bank approach does not account for the fact that some parents make sacrifices to maintain their children's living standards, and some neglect their children.

The discussion of risk management has viewed the household as the unit of impact and decision making. Yet risk sharing within the household may not be equal, and the burden of the household's response may fall dispropriationately on the weakest members – children and women. A shock affecting a household as a whole may have different effects on different household members (Udry, 1999). Because poor households have many children, children are more exposed to poverty and vulnerability than other groups. Children in poor households are especially vulnerable to fluctuations in household income and consumption. They are more likely to be underweight, and further declines in food consumption can cause irreversible harm. In Bangladesh, children's growth suffered during major floods (Foster, 1995). Studies in Bangladesh show that girls' nutritional status is worse than boys' in poor households (Pryer, 1992). Price changes also affect girls' consumption more than it affects boys' consumption (Behrman and Deolalikar, 1990).

Women suffer more than men from adverse shocks. Rising food prices led to larger reductions in nutrient intake for women than for men in India (Dercon and Krishman, 2000). Divorced and widowed women in South Asia often face higher health risks and are more likely than married women to be poor, because they lose access to their husband's property (Lanjouw and Stern, 1999). A study in Pakistan found evidence that gender bias in health expenditure decreases with rising income (Alderman and Gertler, 1997). In south Asia, lower value is assigned to women and girls, which translates into excess mortality – 4 percent of girls under five years old are missing (Klasen, 1994).

Gender inequality has strong repercussions for human capital in the next generation, because the burden of bearing and rearing children falls largely upon women. Women deprived of education and decision making power face serious constraints in rearing healthy and productive children. Studies from India find that even controlling for education, household income and other socio-economic characteristics, low domestic autonomy is associated with higher infant and child mortality rates (Das Gupta, 1995), while giving income generating loans to women improves the nutritional status of their children.

In conclusion, it is obvious that incorporating within-household aspects in poverty measurement raises difficult issues of allocation and valuation. Theoretical work can play a role. It may be, for example, that a range of indicators better capture the experience of individuals within-household than estimates of income do. We need more research on how to summarise experience and formulate poverty lines using multi-dimensional measures. There is a burgeoning economic literature on household decision making which is theoretical, as well as proving useful models which have been used (Hoddinott, Alderman, Haddad, 1997; Haddad, Hoddinott, Alderman, 1997).

## Entitlement and capability theory as an alternative to poverty measurement

Both entitlement and capability theories were developed as part of Sen's long-term project of moving the analysis of poverty and hunger away from a focus on commodities and food availability, and towards the idea of the individual as an economic factor. "Commodity fetishism" according to Sen, attempts to define well-being in terms of commodities owned or needed. In capability theory the focus is on what human beings are capable of achieving, rather than what they possess, or think and believe. The capability approach continues to concentrate on human beings – on their education, skills, social skills, and health. The "Entitlement approach" has two dimensions: *endowment* and *exchange*. Firstly, a household is considered to be endowed with a set of resources which conditions the range of economic options available to it. These resources include:

1. *Material resources*: These include assets and stores of value as well as money.
2. *Human resources*: The skills and capabilities of people within the household, including the age, gender, educational, skills, health and nutritional status of household members.
3. *Social resources*: These include the set of relationships which a household has with other individuals, households and organisations which may be used to maintain or improve their situation. Such "claims" to assistance may include claims on food, credit, labour or productive resources or services from kin, neighbours, labour groups, patrons, landlords and employers, from government, or from NGOs and the international community.
4. *Environmental and common property resources*: Natural resources may be used by different kinds of households. These can be defined by clear property rights, or may be notionally common property. Within the urban context, common property resources may include water, grazing land, fodder materials, fuel, trees, natural vegetation and garbage.
5. *Cultural resources*: Those resources which are available to households due to their cultural or ethnic origin. These may be experienced as a negative resource in the sense that certain ethnic groups may be marginalised and excluded.
(Sen, 1981, 1987, 1997; Swift, 1989.)

The exchange entitlements provide the household with the potential to obtain food, income, and other needs upon transfer or exchange of these assets. This may be through wage labour, sale of household products or other commodities, or taking out loans. The sum of household endowments and exchanges constitutes the total income of the household and this is then translated into the ability of the household to sustain itself. The extent to which the household is able to achieve this has a direct effect upon the health and nutritional status of household members, which in turn affects the resource bundle (endowments) at the household's disposal to attain future livelihoods (Sen, 1981, 1987, 1997).

Vulnerability and the extent of the ability of an individual or household to recover from shocks are linked to the resources or assets that the household holds, so the relationships between vulnerability, assets and poverty are important to understand. Vulnerability is not synonymous with poverty but means defencelessness, insecurity, and exposure to risk, shocks and stress. It is linked with assets such as human investment in health and education, and also productive assets such as houses, domestic equipment, access to community infrastructure, stores of money, jewellery and gold, and claims on other households, patrons, governments and the international community for resources at times of need (Chambers, 1989; Swift, 1989).

While poverty (measured by income) can be reduced by borrowing, such debts make the poor more vulnerable. Poverty is a static concept, but insecurity and vulnerability are dynamic; they describes the responses to change over time. Insecurity is exposure to risk; vulnerability the resulting possibility of decline in well-being. The event that triggered the decline is often related to a shock which can affect an individual (illness, unemployment or death) or a community or region, or even an entire country (natural disasters or macroeconomic crisis).

Risk and risk exposure are related but not synonymous. Risk refers to uncertain events which can damage – the risk of becoming ill, or risk of floods that will occur. The uncertainty can pertain to the timing of the magnitude of the event. For example, seasonal fluctuations in income is an event known in advance, but the severity is not always predictable. Risk exposure measures the probability that a certain risk will occur. Vulnerability measures the resilience against the shock, and the likelihood that a shock will result in a decline in well-being. Vulnerability is primarily a function of a household's assets, endowments and exchange, and the insurance mechanisms, and the true characteristics (severity, frequency) of the shocks. If the household has low income this means that they are less able to save and accumulate assets. This restricts their ability to deal with a crisis.

Table 1.1  Shocks faced by urban households in Dhaka slums

| Event | Percentage of households where deterioration in financial situation was reported |
|---|---|
| Income earning member ill or incapacitated | 21.6 |
| Wage/earnings decreased | 19.3 |
| Unable to find work | 18.1 |
| Unable to work due to a strike | 9.2 |
| Expenditure for medicine and/or treatment | 3.8 |
| Visitors came | 3.2 |
| Repayment of loans | 3.0 |
| Small profits in business | 1.5 |
| Increase in the number of non earning family members | 1.4 |
| Unable to work because of illness of other family members | 1.1 |
| Loss of employment | 1.1 |
| N | 2373 |

As can be seen from Table 1.1, the most important shocks in the Urban Livelihoods Study were the incapacitation of an income earning member, reductions in earnings, and inability to find work. Shock mitigation aims to reduce the impact of shocks as shown in Table 1.2. Households mitigate risk through income diversification, from wage income, self-employed income, and investments in physical and human capital.

**Table 1.2  Mechanisms for managing shocks**

|  | Household and Individual | Group based | Publicly provided |
|---|---|---|---|
| Mitigating risk |  |  |  |
| Diversification | Income diversification | Occupational associations | Public Health policy<br>Labour Market policies |
|  | Investment in physical capital | Rotating saving and credit associations | Protection of property rights |
|  | Investment in human capital |  | Education and training policy |
| Insurance | Marriage and extended family | Investments in social capital (networks, associations, rituals, reciprocal gift giving) | Pension systems |
|  | Tenancy agreements |  | Mandated insurance for unemployment, illness, disability and other risks |
|  | Buffer stocks |  |  |
| Coping with shocks | Changes in work patterns | Transfers from networks of mutual support | Social assistance |
|  | Reduction in expenditure |  | Public works |
|  | Taking loans |  | Subsidies |
|  | Leasing or mortgaging of any assets |  | Social funds |
|  | Sale of any assets |  | Cash transfers |
|  | Movement of family members (to or from the household) |  |  |
|  | Receipt of help from others |  |  |
|  | Begging |  |  |

## The poverty trap and long-term consequences of inadequate risk management

Poor people have to rely largely on self-insurance. Households insure themselves by accumulating assets in good times, and then drawing on them in bad times. But poor households do not have many assets in good times, so they are very vulnerable. In informal insurance, households use group-based mechanisms of risk sharing that rely on social capital of groups or households. Typically, informal insurance involves a mutual support network of members of a community or extended household, or among members of the same occupation. In another Bangladesh slums, there was a successful informal insurance among a work group. The members of this group would pool their wages and divide the sum by one more than the number of workers participating. The remaining share was used to provide income to support a worker who could not work because of illness (Pryer, 1990). In addition, several recent experiences have underscored the great demand by poor households for safe savings accounts (Desmet, Chowdhury and Islam, 1999).

When a shock hits, households cope by changing work patterns – moving more members into the labour force, or working more hours – or by reducing expenditure, taking loans, leasing assets, or in the extreme by selling assets. Members of households may migrate to the village while earners stay in the slums, or families may move in together. If this doesn't work, then members will beg or ask for help.

As households move closer to extreme poverty and destitution, they become very risk adverse: any drop in income could push them below the survival point. The poorest households try to avoid this even if it means forgoing a large future gain in income. Despite facing the highest risk, they have fewer resources for dealing with that risk, and are forced into marginal lands (flood plains) and into areas with poor infrastructure. They are most at risk from natural disasters and are usually far from health facilities (World Bank, 2000/2001). Extreme poverty deprives people of almost all means of managing risk by themselves. With few or no assets, self-insurance is impossible. With poor health and bad nutrition, working more or sending out more household members to work is difficult. With high default rates, group insurance mechanisms are often closed off. The poorest households thus face extremely unfavourable trade-offs. When a shock occurs they must obtain immediate increases in income or cut spending, but in doing this they incur a high long-term cost by jeopardising their economic and human development prospects. These are situations that lead to child labour and malnourishment, with lasting damage to children and the breakdown of families. In the lean season in Bangladesh children work on farms, tend cattle or carry out household tasks in exchange for food.

Poverty reduction strategies can lessen the vulnerability of poor households through a range of approaches that can reduce volatility, provide the means for poor people to manage risks themselves, and strengthen markets or public institutions for risk management. Supporting the range of assets of poor people – human, material, financial, and social – can help them to manage the risks they may face (Chambers, 1989). Supporting the institutions that help poor people manage risk can enable them to pursue higher risk, higher return activities that can lift them out of poverty. Improvement risk-management institutions should be a permanent feature of poverty reduction strategies. The tools include health insurance, old age assistance and pensions, unemployment insurance, public works, social funds, micro-finance programmes, and cash transfers (Holzmann and Jorgensen, 2000). Safety nets should be designed to support immediate consumption, and to protect the accumulation of human, material, financial and social assets by poor people (Dercon, 1999).

Empowerment means enhancing the capacity of poor people to influence the State institutions that affect their lives, by strengthening their participation in the political process and local decision making. It means removing the barriers – political, legal and social – that work against particular groups in society and building the assets of poor people to enable them to engage effectively in markets. Expanding economic opportunities for poor people indeed contributes to their empowerment. Efforts are needed to make State and social institutions work in the interests of poor people. The State's most important task in fostering poor people's organisations is to remove legal and other barriers to forming associations and to provide an administrative and judicial framework supportive of such associations (World Bank, 1994). Without this, it is very difficult for poor people's associations to flourish and to influence public policy.

In Bangladesh, Ain-O-Salish Kenra (ASK) was established in 1986 and seeks to reform the law through its representation of poor women and children, organised groups of workers, the rural poor and slum dwellers. It provides legal aid primarily on family matters, including violence against women. Litigation on behalf of victims is undertaken in criminal cases and when legal rights are violated. ASK investigates and monitors violations of the law and human rights, including police torture, murder, and rape and death in the garment factories. It also monitors police stations to collect information on violence against women and children and to track cases reported at the stations. The work by ASK is significant because of the substance of what it does – work on basic issues for disenfranchised people – and because of the way it does it through mediation, discussion groups, legal awareness training, individual court cases, administrative and legal lobbying, group representative, and public interest litigation (Manning, 1999).

In Bangladesh also there is an umbrella organisation which consists of poor people's organisations. This umbrella organisation was successful at lobbying MPs. The MPs listened and acted to turn the slums on government land into plots for houses, the purchase of which was made possible by the provision of government loans.

Sen's model of entitlement and capability seeks to bring a multi-dimensional view onto poverty and vulnerability. Within this it is possible, in addition, to examine the impact of intra-household distribution on human capital. It is against the backdrop of poverty, vulnerability and need for effective policy described in this chapter that we have framed the Urban Livelihoods Study.

## References

Alderman, H., Gertler, P. (1997), 'Family resources and gender differences in human capital investments', in Haddad, L., Hoddinott, J. and Alderman, H. (eds), *Intra-household Resource Allocation in Developing Countries*, The John Hopkins University Press, Baltimore.

Barret, C., Carter, M. (1999), *Can't get ahead for falling behind: new directions for development policy to escape poverty and relief traps*, US Agency for International Development, Washington DC.

Behrman, J.R. and Deolikar, A. (1990), 'The intra-household demand for nutrients in rural south Asia: Individual estimates, fixed effects and permanent income', *Journal of Human Resources*, 24(4), pp. 655–96.

Chambers, R. (1989), 'Vulnerability, coping and policy', *IDS Bulletin*, 20(2), pp. 1–8.

Chippori, P.A. (1997), '"Collective" models of household behaviour: The haring rule approach', in Haddad, L., Hoddinott, J. and Alderman, H. (eds) *Intra-household Resource Allocation in Developing Countries*, The Johns Hopkins University Press, Baltimore.

Das Gupta, M. (1995), 'Lifecourse perspectives on Women's autonomy and health outcomes', *American Anthropologist*, 97(3), pp. 481–91.

Dercon, S. (1999), 'Income risk, coping strategies and safety nets', Katholike Universiteit, Leuven, Oxford University, Centre for the study of African Economics and World Bank, in World Development Report (2000/2001), *Attacking Poverty*, Oxford University Press, Washington DC and London.

Dercon, S., Krishnan, P. (2000), 'In Sickness and in Health: Risk sharing within households in rural Ethopia', *Journal of Political Economy*, 108(4), pp. 58–75.

Desmet, M., Chowdhury, A.Q., Islam and Md K. (1999), 'The potential for social mobilisation in Bangladesh: The organisation and functioning of two health insurance schemes', *Social Science and Medicine*, 48, pp. 925–938.

Foster, A. (1995), 'Prices, credit markets and child growth in low income rural areas', *Economic Journal*, 105, pp. 551–70.

Haddad, L., Hoddinott, J. and Alderman, H. (1997), 'Policy Issues and intra-household allocation: Conclusions', in Haddad, L., Hoddinott, J. and Alderman, H. (eds), *Intra-household Resource Allocation in Developing Countries*, The Johns Hopkins University Press, Baltimore.

Haddad, L., Kanbur, R. (1990), 'Are better-off households more equal or less equal?', Policy Research and External Affairs Working Paper 373, World Bank, Washington DC.

Hoddinott, J., Alderman, H., Haddad, L. (1997), 'Introduction: the scope of intra-household resource allocation issues', in Haddad, L., Hoddinott, J. and Alderman, H. (eds), *Intra-household Resource Allocation in Developing Countries*, The Johns Hopkins University Press, Baltimore.

Holzmann, R., Jorgensen, S. (2000), 'Social risk management: a new conceptual framework for social protection and beyond', *Social Protection*, Discussion Paper 0006, World Bank, Human Development Network, Washington DC.

Jacoby, H., Skoufias, E. (1997), 'Risk, financial markets and human capital in a developing country', *Review of Economic Studies*, 64(3), pp. 311–35.

Kabir, Md A., Rahman, A., Salway, S. and Pryer, J. (2000), 'Sickness among the urban poor: a barrier to livelihood security', *Journal of International Development* (12), pp. 707–772.

Khandker, S.R. (1998), *Fighting Poverty with Microcredit: Experience in Bangladesh*, Oxford University Press, New York.

Klasen, S. (1994), '"Missing women" reconsidered', *World Development*, 22(7), pp. 1061–71.

Lanjouw, P., Stern, N. (1999), 'Poverty in Palanpur', *World Bank Review*, 5(1), pp. 23–56.
Manning, D.S. (1999), *The role of legal services organisations in attacking poverty*, in World Development Report, 2000/2001, Oxford University Press, Oxford.
Narayan, D., Chambers, R., Shah, M.K. and Petesch, P. (2000), *Voices of the Poor: crying out for change*, Oxford University Press, New York.
Pryer, J.A. (1990), 'Socio-economic and environmental aspects of undernutrition and ill health in an urban slum in Bangladesh', unpublished PhD thesis, London School of Hygiene and Tropical Medicine.
Pryer, J.A. (1993), 'Nutritionally vulnerable households in the urban slum economy: a case study from Khulna, Bangladesh', in Schell, L.M., Smith, M. and Bilsborogh, A. (eds), *Urban Ecology and Health in the Third World*, Cambridge University Press, Cambridge.
Rowntree, B.S. (1901), *Poverty: A Study of Town Life*, Macmillan, London.
Sen, A.K. (1981), *Poverty and Famines: an essay on entitlement and deprivation*, Clarendon Press, London.
Sen, A.K. (1987), *Resources, Values and Development*, Blackwell, Oxford.
Sen, A.K. (1997), *Inequality re-examined*, Harvard University Press, Cambridge, Massachusetts.
Swift, J. (1989), 'Why are rural people vulnerable to famine?', *IDS Bulletin*, 20(2), pp. 8–15.
Udry, C. (1999), 'Poverty, risk and households', paper presented to World Bank Workshop, July 2000, Washington DC.
World Development Report (1994), *Infrastructure for Development*, Oxford University Press, New York.
World Development Report (1999/2000), *Entering the 21$^{st}$ Century*, Oxford University Press, New York.
World Development Report (2000/2001), *Attacking Poverty*, Oxford University Press, New York.

Chapter 2

# Study Design and Methods

*In this chapter we describe the setting – Bangladesh – and the history of Dhaka and the slum settlements. We then go on to the livelihoods approach and describe the methodology in detail. Population structure, marital patterns and family structure are also included. We then go on to the Livelihoods Approach and describe the methodology in detail.*

## Setting

*Bangladesh*

The population of Bangladesh was nearly 128 million in 1999, making it the most densely populated country in the world. Officially, Bangladesh is the second poorest country after Bhutan. There are over 80 voluntary aid agencies. Foreign aid provides 90 percent of their development budget. Infant mortality was 73 per 1,000 births in 1998, which has improved from 132 per 1,000 births in 1980. Fifty six percent of children were malnourished in 1999.

The Gross National Product (GNP) in 1999 was nearly 47 million dollars (per capita 370 dollars), and the rate of growth between 1998 and 1999 was 3.3 percent. Despite economic growth, wealth is not evenly distributed. The Gini Index in 1996 was 33.6 which was higher than in 1992 when it was 23.7. In 1999, the lowest 20 percent earned only 8.7 percent of the national income, and the richest 20 percent earned 42.8 percent of the national income. In 1996 30 percent of the Bangladeshi population were below the poverty line and 77 percent were below $2 a day (World Bank, 2000/2001). In 1999 the General Domestic Product (GDP) was nearly 46 million dollars. Agriculture accounted for 21 percent of the GDP; industry accounted for 27 percent and manufacturing accounted for 39 percent. Export of goods and services accounted for 14 percent of the GDP. Bangladesh has a total area of 143,998 square km.

The topography is characterised by alluvial plains, bound to the north by the Himalayas, and to the north-east the fringes of Assam, Tripura and Myannmar. These are broken by the forested hills of Mymensingh, Sylhet, and Chittagong. The great rivers, Ganges and Brahmaputra, which divide the land into four regions: north-west, south-west, central and eastern. The alluvial river plains which dominate 90 percent of the country, are very flat and never rise more than 10 metres above sea level. The only relief from the plains occurs in the north-east and south-east corners of the country where the hills rise to an average of 240 metres and 600 metres respectively. Most of Bangladesh's coastline forms the mouths of the Ganges. This is the largest estuarine delta in the world. The coastal strip from the western border to Chittagong is a shifting river course and little islands. The Sundarbans, a vast area of coastal forest, rises only a metre above sea level. The south-eastern coast, south from Chittagong, is backed by wooded Arakan Hills which overlooks 120 km of sandy coast. Bangladesh is affected, on average 16 times in a decade by cyclones which form in the Bay of Bengal during the monsoon season which is from mid-June to mid-October. It is then that the plains flood and bring chaos and death to the poorest people.

*Dhaka as a city*

At the beginning of the Mughal rule, Dhaka attained great commercial importance, and became a trading centre for the whole of South East Asia. The greatest development took place under Shaiska Khan (1662–1679). The city stretched for 12 miles in length and 8 miles in breath, and had nearly one million people living there. The business area was Royal Market (Badshahi Bazaar). This was rich in merchandise and colourful in appearance. The Burhiganga River serves as a means of communication. The cottage industries were very important; gold and silver, weave cloth, pottery, fishermen, shell cutters and betel leaf. At the end of the Mughal rule (1608–1764) 900,000 people lived in Dhaka. At the inception of British Power around 1765, Dhaka began to decline in importance and contracted in size. The city experienced disastrous famine, floods and fire. Calcutta was growing in importance, and it was difficult for Dhaka to compete with Calcutta which, as the capital of British India, enjoyed the patronage of the rulers.

In 1800, the population was about 200,000, but it fell to around 68,000 in 1838 and then to around 58,000 in 1868. The city was described as a wreck of its ancient grandeur (Islam, 1996). Two-thirds of Dhaka were filled with ruins and were overgrown with jungles.

With the transfer of power from the East India Company to the Crown in 1858, Dhaka started to grow more rapidly. The railways connected Dhaka to other towns in Bangladesh, electricity began in 1878, and water facilities were offered to residents.

Bengal was partitioned and a new province of East Bengal and Assam came into being in July 1905. Dhaka was declared a provincial capital with new responsibilities. The city of less than 100,000 inhabitants started to expand rapidly. The increase between 1901–1911 was 21 percent. But Dhaka's phase as a capital of Bengal was short-lived. In 1911, the partition of Bengal was annulled, and Dhaka lost its administration function. During this period, a small number of large scale factories were established; a glass factory and a pharmaceutical industry. At the end of British Rule the population rose to nearly 335,000 (Islam, 1996). Pakistan was created on the 14th August 1947, and Dhaka was made the capital of the province of East Pakistan. Dhaka was suddenly called upon to shoulder many responsibilities. The problem was how to house the increasing number of government offices, firms, industrial establishments and government employees. Muslim migrants from India and other parts of the province caused the population to rise from 336,000 in 1951 to 557,000 in 1961. After Independence in 1971,

Dhaka had a phenomenal industrial growth. Business was booming, eventually totalling over 100 industries (Islam, 1996).

In 1999, 30 million people, around 20 percent of the total population of Bangladesh, live in urban areas. By the year 2005 this figure will have risen to 46 million, and by 2015 projections indicate that 68 million (more than a third of the total population of Bangladesh) will live in urban areas (Task Force, 1992; World Development Report 1999/2000).

Fourteen percent of the urban population live below the national poverty line and the largest gap between the rich and poor is in the urban areas (World Bank, 2000–2001). The number of slum settlements has grown rapidly in recent years and the urban poor are now estimated at around 11 million, or 37 percent of the urban population (Government of Bangladesh, 1990; World Bank, 2000–2001). The Urban Livelihoods Study is based in the slum settlements of Mohammadpur thana. Agargoan includes the biggest slum in Mohammadpur. The land is owned by the government but has been occupied informally by squatters for over 20 years. Central Mohammadpur includes slums in Rayer Bazaar, Jafrabad, Pisciculture, Adabar and Pulpar Bottola areas. Most of the slums in this area consist of poor housing within middle and lower-middle class residential housing settlements. Private landlords own most, though some are on disputed land. Finally, Beri Badh is the peripheral area of Mohammadpur. The settlements have been developed along the embankment of the Dhaka City Flood Protection, alongside the Buri Ganga River. The embankment is government owned land, with slums adjacent to the embankment situated on privately owned land.

**The livelihoods approach**

The livelihood approach is a powerful tool through which to examine the social and material conditions of livelihoods and hence the command a household has over food and other basic needs. The approach is based on the work of authors such as Sen (1981), Swift (1989), Kabeer (1995) and Pryer (1990).

Sen uses the term "entitlement" to cover a set of resources and relationships determining the control a household has over food and other basic needs. A household "entitlement" has two dimensions: endowment and exchange.

*Endowments* have been classified into five groups. Thus material resources cover money, assets and stores of value while human resources include the age, gender, education, skills, health and nutritional condition of household members. The relationship a household has with other individuals, households and organisations is also important and constitutes their social resources. (Such relationships may be used to make "claims" to assistance, include claims on food, credit, labour, productive resources or services from kin, neighbours, labour groups, patrons, landlords, employers, government or non governmental organizations.) A related concept is the idea of cultural resources including status, restrictions and norms that govern behaviour.

Finally, the environment in which the household lives is associated with a set of endowments. Environmental resources cover facilities like housing, water, and sanitation, and also common property resources which include natural resources that may be shared by households; these may be defined by clear property rights, or notionally may be common property. Within the urban context, common property resources might include water, grazing land, fodder materials, fuel, trees, natural vegetation and garbage.

The "entitlement" model is dynamic and potential is provided by the *exchange* of any part of what is owned (for money or kind) to provide for food and other basic needs. For example, human labour may be sold for a wage, commodities produced may be used for domestic production or sold onto the market, and other commodities procured may be traded. A household may therefore have a large range of possible sources of "entitlement", which together may be seen as constituting its livelihood.

Using this model, a *livelihood strategy* is defined as the way in which a household combines and utilises its various forms of entitlement to maintain its members on a daily basis. A culturally determined *livelihood standard* could be derived to define culturally determined minimal needs. *Vulnerable livelihoods* could then be considered as those forms of livelihoods that are unable to fulfill culturally determined minimal needs over the annual cycle. Such households can be considered vulnerable to extremes of climate, illness and disease, loss of earnings or income as a result of adjustments in markets for goods and labour and to adverse treatment in the socio-political system. When such households are unable to cope with difficulties of this kind, they may be reduced to starvation and beyond. Within this framework analyses of ownership and/or access to different resource or entitlement bases can be undertaken both at a household level and at the level of characteristics of individuals such as by age and gender.

An important dimension of the livelihood framework is that the health and nutritional status is seen simultaneously as an *outcome* and an *input* into the processes of production and reproduction of a household's livelihood. The anthropometric and morbidity profile of all household members has been collected. Information on incapacitating earner ill health will also be used to ascertain the constraint ill health places on the pattern and level of livelihoods pursued over the annual cycle.

The livelihoods approach seeks to be of practical as well as analytical value. It is intended to allow development organisations to recognise which groups are socio-economically and nutritionally vulnerable and why, and which groups are being made particularly vulnerable to change and why. It is also intended to assist in a clearer identification of possible interventions in support of vulnerable livelihoods. Types of interventions can be categorised in terms of the level at which they seek to have greatest impact.

At the level of the *individual and household*, vulnerability reducing interventions may include the need to increase the strength of the household and individuals within it – either in terms of material resources, skill training and education, or health and nutritional status.

At the level of the *community*, interventions may include strengthening and supporting already existing or potential networks of exchange or access to services, or to common property resources which households can utilise during periods of stress. Examples may include mutual aid societies, labour and trade union organisations, savings and credit organizations, health insurance, access to services, asset protection schemes, community child care, etc.

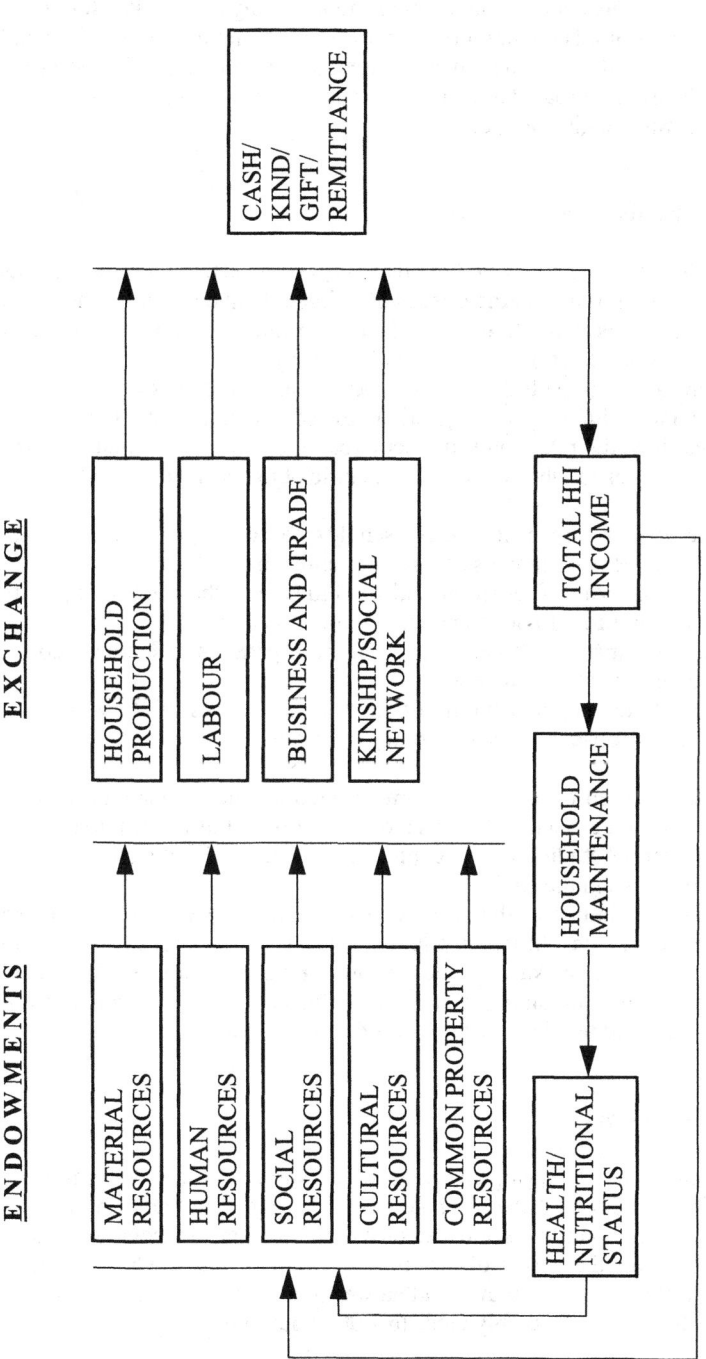

**Figure 2.1** Conceptual framework of the urban livelihoods study

At the level of the *State*, actions may include strengthening of state institutions to which individuals/households/communities can turn to for support, eg. services and amenities. Actions may also include advocacy for protective policies for the urban poor such as policies on urban land, housing and amenities, equal opportunity policies, minimum wage legislation, etc.

**The Urban Livelihoods Study**

The rationale for the Dhaka Urban Livelihoods Study (ULS) is that there is a serious gap in our understanding of the characteristics of vulnerable livelihoods in the urban economy, and that this is a limiting factor in the design and implementation of effective programmes aimed at reducing this vulnerability.

The overall aim of the study is to integrate social science analysis of livelihoods of poor urban people with epidemiological investigation to explore how socio-economic and health status relate and interact over time. To identify and describe the patterns of livelihoods in Dhaka slums the specific objectives will include:

1. To profile the economic capacity of households based on patterns of labour, household income, expenditure, assets, savings and debt.
2. To describe the patterns of nutrition and morbidity and the relationship with social, economic, intra-household, and environment factors.
3. To document the impact of ill health on household patterns of labour income, expenditure, assets, savings and debt.
4. To describe the frequency and timing of shocks and periods of stress periods, and to describe the consequences and coping strategies.

Data collection is based on two sets of interrelated activities; quantitative data collection on a panel of around 850 households – termed the quantitative panel survey – and qualitative studies which explore the same study objectives within selected slum settlements in the study area.

The work is focused in one of the seven thanas (administrative units) of Dhaka City, Mohammadpur thana. Mohammadpur thana has the largest total slum population of any thana in Dhaka City and the entire range of slum settlements are represented, including peri-urban and waterside settlements, with the proportion of slums built on private and public land similar to the city as a whole.

**Quantitative Panel Survey**

Sample size calculations for the quantitative panel survey were made based on planned tests of hypothesised differences between both child and adult nutritional levels in different livelihood groups and also on a desire to detect seasonal variations in nutritional status over the period of the study. The calculations, which included adjustments for cluster sampling, indicated that we should aim to select a sample of at least 700 households and preferably close to 1,000 households.

Panel households were selected through a random cluster sample of all slum areas in Mohammadpur, with stratification for geographical area. To maintain consistency we used the definition of slum (or bustee) used by Centre for Urban Studies and the Bangladesh government as follows:

> Bustees (slums and squatters) are authorised or unauthorised areas of very high area density, as well as very high room crowding, and poor housing fabrics. The areas have inadequate water supply, poor sewerage and drainage facilities, little paved streets and lanes and irregular clearance of garbage. Bustees are inhabited by very poor and poor people who are mostly engaged in various types of "informal sector activities" (CUS 1989).

As a result of this process 117 slum areas were identified and mapped, then subdivided into primary sampling units (PSU) of 20–50 households. The PSUs (around 540 of them) were stratified into five groups based upon geographical location, and a stratified random sample of 25 PSUs (or clusters) were selected. Detailed maps were drawn and a population census undertaken in each of the clusters.

The 25 clusters were estimated to contain around 1,000 households. By the nature of the cluster sampling process, there is uncertainty surrounding the final sample size and in actuality only 907 households were selected. At the outset we had decided that households entering our sample should have resided within the slum for at least one month – that entry criterion eliminated a further 57 households resulting in a final sample size of 850 households.

A registration book, revised and updated monthly, was used to record basic information on household composition including in- and out-migrants, residency status, births and deaths together with summary socio-economic information. As such, the registration book describes the household membership, which is fundamental descriptive information for the livelihoods approach.

In deciding upon the operational definition of "household" and "household member" it was necessary to balance a need for operational feasibility with analytical desirability.

We devised a scheme to go beyond a simple de facto definition of a household member, to include individuals who may not actually sleep and eat together, but who are household members in the sense that they have access to and/or contribute to a common set of assets and resources. We also wanted to be able to distinguish between individuals for whom the present household is the main or primary set of resources to which an individual has access, as compared to a secondary set, with a primary set of resources elsewhere. To make the assessments, we asked each household to name its own head of household and to provide a list of people who were:

1  regarded as members of the immediate family, regardless of place of residence;
2  unrelated individuals resident in the same structure(s);
3  other relatives contributing money to the household's budget.

Households were followed up on a monthly basis. The monthly questionnaire was administered to the head of household and spouse and enquiries were made into work participation, sources of income, changes in financial status, shocks, stresses and coping strategies, and food expenditure. Acute and work disabling morbidity was recorded for a two-week recall period and anthropometry was carried out on household head, spouse and children under five.

Every third month a more extensive data collection interview took place, this time involving head of household, spouse and all resident family members. At this interview detailed information was recorded on employment and employment status; education and skills; income from all sources; debts and savings; asset ownership, sale and purchase; food supply and food stocks; child feeding practices; common property resource use; social relations (Trades Union group/committee/Non governmental organisation membership and activities); use of amenities and environmental situation. Again, changes in financial status, self reported morbidity and anthropometry were documented.

The cohort was also subject to one-off special surveys addressing migration and mobility; birth and marriage history and decision making on desired family size and family planning; intra-household decision making, domestic task allocation and domestic time use. Inevitably, some households moved during the eighteen months of the cohort study. Follow-up of individuals was restricted to the household head and spouse, plus individuals who moved with them, but such households were followed up wherever they moved in Dhaka City. In addition, households moving into the selected 25 clusters were registered to the study and followed up so the ULS includes two cohorts or panels. The household cohort comprises all households who had resided for at least one month in the selected 25 baseline clusters and the geographic cohort comprises all households who reside within the selected 25 clusters at each round of follow up.

**Population sample**

Table 2.1 presents some basic characteristics of the households heads of 732 households in round 4 (September–December 1996). Overall, 11 percent of households reported a female household head. Whereas male household heads were almost all currently married, female household heads were mainly single (either widowed, divorced or separated). However, 27 percent of female heads reported themselves as currently married (18–22) and the husband was reported as a household member. In eight of these cases the husband was a resident family member (see this chapter for details), and in another four cases, he had performed income generating work in the past month. In the other four cases the husband was reported to be disabled or engaged only with household work. In the case of the female headed households where the husband was reported as a non-resident family member, four of the ten had received some kind of remittance in the past month from this absent husband. Thus the majority of female headed households do have an adult male member who is contributing to the household livelihood in some form.

In 5 percent of households where the head was reported to be male, this individual was non-resident in the month prior to data collection. In 55 percent of the cases, the male head was reported to be polygamously married, suggesting that his non-resident status may be the norm rather than a temporary phenomena. This table also indicates that male headed households are more likely to be the main earner in the household than are female headed.

### Table 2.1 Demographic characteristics of household heads

|  | Male % | Female % |
|---|---|---|
| **Marital Status** | | |
| Currently married (monogamous) | 83.1 | 26.5 |
| Currently married (polygamous)[1] | 5.7 | 0.0 |
| Deserted/divorced | 0.5 | 22.9 |
| Widowed | 0.0 | 49.4 |
| Never married | 0.8 | 1.2 |
| **Age (years)** | | |
| <20 | 0.6 | 0.0 |
| 20–29 | 23.4 | 12.1 |
| 30–39 | 39.0 | 43.4 |
| 40–49 | 24.7 | 26.5 |
| 50–59 | 7.7 | 14.5 |
| 60+ | 4.6 | 3.6 |
| Mean age | 36.9 | 39.1 |
| (s.d.) | (10.4) | (9.7) |
| **Residency status[2]** | | |
| Resident Family Member | 95.2 | 100.0 |
| Non-resident Family Member | 4.8 | 0.0 |
| Main earner in the household | 83.7 | 48.2 |
| Overall percent | 88.7 | 11.3 |
| N | 649 | 83 |

*Notes:*

1. Here, the category "polygamously married men" includes both those who were currently maintaining a marital relationship with more than one wife as well as those who were married to more than one woman but only maintaining a marital relationship with one wife. In fact, the latter group accounted for just 19 percent of all polygamously married men.
2. See this chapter for the definition of resident and non-resident members.

**Table 2.2** Percentage distribution of marital status among men and women by age group

| Age (years) | N | Never married | Currently monogamous | Currently polygamous | Divorced Deserted | Widowed |
|---|---|---|---|---|---|---|
| Men | | | | | | |
| 10–14 | 219 | 99.5 | 0.5 | 0.0 | 0.0 | 0.0 |
| 15–19 | 108 | 89.8 | 9.3 | 0.0 | 0.9 | 0.0 |
| 20–29 | 239 | 21.3 | 71.8 | 5.2 | 1.2 | 0.4 |
| 30–39 | 272 | 1.1 | 85.3 | 13.6 | 0.0 | 0.0 |
| 40–49 | 177 | 0.0 | 71.8 | 28.2 | 0.0 | 0.0 |
| 50–59 | 56 | 0.0 | 87.5 | 10.7 | 0.0 | 1.8 |
| 60+ | 41 | 0.0 | 73.2 | 21.9 | 0.0 | 4.9 |
| Total N | 1113 | | | | | |
| Women | | | | | | |
| 10–14 | 201 | 95.0 | 5.0 | 0.0 | 0.0 | 0.0 |
| 15–19 | 160 | 34.4 | 60.6 | 0.0 | 5.0 | 0.0 |
| 20–29 | 401 | 2.2 | 93.0 | 0.3 | 3.8 | 0.8 |
| 30–39 | 225 | 0.0 | 87.6 | 0.0 | 7.5 | 4.9 |
| 40–49 | 86 | 0.0 | 63.9 | 0.0 | 2.3 | 34.9 |
| 50–59 | 44 | 0.0 | 45.5 | 0.0 | 9.1 | 45.5 |
| 60+ | 25 | 0.0 | 32.0 | 0.0 | 0.0 | 68.0 |
| Total N | 1142 | | | | | |

Table 2.2 presents the percentage distribution of marital status among men and women in different groups. The universality of marriage in this context is apparent with no individual remaining never married beyond 40 years of age. The younger age of marriage for women is apparent in the low percentages of individuals never married in the age-groups 15–19 and 20–29 just 34 percent and 2 percent compared to 90 percent and 21 percent for men.

Polygynous marriages increase with age among men, up to 22 percent among the oldest age-group. The prevalence of divorced or deserted women increases with age and is higher than among men, reflecting the fact that remarriage following divorce is easier for men, particularly in later life, than for women.

As expected, the prevalence of widowed individuals is higher among older age-groups, and all ages beyond 30 years. Women are more likely to be widowed than men. This tendency for men to marry younger women than themselves is the cause, and the fact that men find it easier to remarry should their wife die before them.

Overall, Table 2.2 shows striking differences in marital patterns between men and women in all age groups. As can be seen from this table, women get married earlier than men, men are more likely to be currently polygamously married than women, and women are more likely to be divorced, deserted or widowed than men.

**Table 2.3    Percentage distribution of various indicators of marital behaviour among men and women**

|  | Men (%) | Women (%) |
|---|---|---|
| Number of times married: | | |
| Once | 70.9 | 83.0 |
| Twice | 23.0 | 16.7 |
| Three or more times | 6.1 | 0.3 |
| Number of times divorced/separated: | | |
| None | 84.9 | 88.6 |
| Once | 10.0 | 10.0 |
| Two or more times | 5.1 | 1.4 |
| Out of individuals divorced once: | | |
| Respondent initiated | 39.1 | 54.4 |
| Spouse initiated | 50.7 | 41.8 |
| Mutual | 10.2 | 3.4 |
| Polygyny: | | |
| Have been polygynously married | 13.7 | – |
| Have been married to a polygynously married man |  | 21.2 |
| N | 557 | 705 |

Table 2.3 indicates that the percentage of individuals who have more than one spouse is high for both men and women. However, men are more likely than women to have been married more than once. This reflects both the fact that men are more likely than women to have been divorced several times, and that large numbers of men maintain polygamous unions. However, as many as 12 percent of all ever married women reported that they have been divorced. A lack of comparative data mean that that it is difficult to compare this figure for the rural settings or earlier time periods.

There is evidence that divorce is more likely among less educated women. Fourteen percent of uneducated women reported that they had been divorced, compared to 8 percent of women with up to five years of education, and just 4 percent of women who have six or more years of education ($X^2=6.8, p=0.03$). However, for men no such educational differentials were found.

Table 2.4 Percentage distribution of household structures by sex of household head

|    |                                                                             | Male Head | Female Head | Overall |
|----|-----------------------------------------------------------------------------|-----------|-------------|---------|
|    | **Nuclear**                                                                 |           |             |         |
| 1  | Head and spouse only                                                        | 7.1       | 2.4         | 6.6     |
| 2  | Head, spouse and children only                                              | 76.7      | 15.7        | 69.8    |
| 3  | Head and children (no spouse, no other immediate relatives)                 | 0.2       | 54.8        | 5.7     |
|    | **Extended**                                                                |           |             |         |
| 4  | Head, unmarried children, parent(s)                                         | 3.5       | 1.2         | 3.1     |
| 5  | Head spouse, unmarried children, spouse's parent(s)                         | 1.9       | 0.0         | 1.6     |
| 6  | Head, unmarried children, parent(s) (no spouse)                             | 0.0       | 2.4         | 0.3     |
| 7  | Head, son(s), son's wife or son's children                                  | 2.6       | 4.8         | 2.9     |
| 8  | Head, daughter(s), daughter's husband or daughter's children                | 1.7       | 8.4         | 2.5     |
| 9  | Unmarried head, head's parents (with or without siblings)                   | 0.9       | 0.0         | 0.8     |
|    | **Joint**                                                                   |           |             |         |
| 10 | Head, head or spouse's sibling(s) (with or without sibling's family)        | 1.7       | 7.2         | 2.3     |
|    | Extended and joint                                                          |           |             |         |
| 11 | Head, head's parents and head's siblings with spouse/children               | 0.8       | 0.0         | 0.7     |
|    | **Other**                                                                   | 2.3       | 2.4         | 2.3     |
| 12 | N                                                                           | 649       | 83          | 732     |

*Notes:*

1. Only resident and non-resident family members considered.
2. The category 'Head and children only' includes four cases of female headed households where the head herself was the only family member in the month of data collection.
3. Categories 2 and 3 largely consists of households with children under age 16, though five households had only adult offspring of the head as members along with the head.

## Table 2.5 Mean household size by household characteristics

|  | N | All household members | t-test marked category | Resident and non-family members | t-test marked category | Children aged< 16 years | t-test marked category |
|---|---|---|---|---|---|---|---|
| **Sex of household head:** | | | | | | | |
| male | 649 | 4.7[1] | | 4.6[1] | | 2.2[1] | |
| female | 83 | 3.7[1] | P<0.001 | 3.7[1] | P<0.001 | 1.6[1] | P<0.001 |
| **Location of household:** | | | | | | | |
| Agargoan | 340 | 4.8 | | 4.6[1] | | 2.3[1] | |
| Central Mohammadpur | 280 | 4.5 | | 4.3[1] | P<0.023 | 2.0[1] | P<0.009 |
| Beri Badh | 106 | 4.6 | | 4.5 | | 2.3 | |
| **Occupational category of head:** | | | | | | | |
| Regular salaried worker | 48 | 4.8 | | 4.6 | | 2.1 | |
| Skilled wage worker | 52 | 4.4 | | 4.3 | | 2.0 | |
| Unskilled wage worker | 129 | 4.4 | | 4.3[1] | | 2.1[1] | |
| Dependent self-employed | 227 | 4.4 | | 4.3 | P<0.003 | 2.0 | P<0.027 |
| Self-employed | 194 | 5.1 | | 4.9[1] | | 2.5[1] | |
| Unemployed own housework | 37 | 4.4 | | 4.2 | | 1.5 | |
| Non-resident family member | 31 | 4.8 | | 4.6 | | 2.4 | |
| **Poverty Line (TK 518 per cu)** | | | | | | | |
| Below | 138 | 5.1 | | 4.9[1] | | 2.7[1] | |
| Above | 590 | 4.5 | P<0.001 | 4.4[1] | P<0.002 | 2.1[1] | P<0.001 |
| Missing information | 4 | | | | | | |
| N | 732 | | | | | | |

It is also interesting to note that there is evidence that women are often initiating divorce or separation. Reports from men and women who have been divorced once in the past indicate that divorce was initiated by the female partner in over 50 percent of cases. It should be remembered that some of these divorces or separations may have taken place in the village area, prior to migration to Dhaka. There is some evidence that marital dissolution is often a precursor to migration by women. However, there is some suggestion that the urban environment allows women greater freedom to leave unfavourable marital circumstances in the rural setting.

Among both female and male headed households more than 70 percent can be considered "nuclear" (categories 1, 2 and 3). Female heads were more likely to be single than male heads and a minority of households were extended or joint. Table 2.5 also shows that female headed households were smaller than male headed households, and had fewer children. Households were bigger where the household head was classified as self employed and households below the poverty line were larger and with more children than those above the poverty line. There were no differences in household size by slum area.

Table 2.6 Percentage distribution of household structures by household characteristics (Poverty line = Taka 518 per consumption unit)

|  | Head & spouse only | Head, spouse & children | Head, children, no spouse | Complex/ joint/ extended | $X^2$ |
|---|---|---|---|---|---|
| **Head's sex** | | | | | |
| male | 7.1 | 77.4 | 0.2 | 15.4 | |
| female | 2.4 | 15.7 | 55.4 | 26.5 | $P<0.001$ |
| **Location** | | | | | |
| Agargoan | 6.7 | 66.8 | 5.6 | 18.8 | |
| Central Mohammadpur | 7.5 | 71.4 | 5.0 | 16.1 | |
| Beri Badh | 3.8 | 71.7 | 12.3 | 12.3 | $P<0.09$ |
| **Poverty line (male headed)** | | | | | |
| Below | 0.0 | 86.5 | 0.0 | 13.5 | |
| Above | 8.3 | 75.9 | 0.2 | 15.7 | $P<0.012$ |
| **Poverty line (female headed)** | | | | | |
| Below | 4.2 | 16.7 | 58.3 | 20.8 | $P<0.43$ |
| Above | 0.0 | 16.4 | 54.6 | 29.1 | |

Table 2.6 shows that 55 percent of female headed households were single parents with children. However, 26 percent of households of female households were complex/joint or extended compared to 25 percent of male headed households. This may reflect different living arrangements in the absence of adult males.

Comparing household structure by area, Beri Badh had the most female headed households, and those without children being more common in Central Mohammadpur.

Male headed households showed significant differences among household types with more households with children below the poverty line, compared to those without children. Among female headed households single parents with children were the most below the poverty line compared to households without children.

## Qualitative studies

The qualitative component of the ULS was conducted in five of the QPS clusters, selected to represent a range of settlement patterns:

1   two illegal settlements (including a section of the largest in Dhaka);
2   two legal settlements (1 peri-urban);
3   one water-side flood prone settlement.

Locally determined, rather than geographical boundaries were used to define the settlements for the qualitative work. Initial work was carried out to explore some of the study objectives with slum participants, to learn more of local definitions and terminology (household, crises, stress, vulnerability, and malnutrition), and to support QPS field staff in the development and piloting of questionnaires.

The second phase was one of background ethnographic mapping. This involved household census, mapping of resource ownership and control of settlements, social and geographical mapping, and then the development of a local index of vulnerability. Households within the settlement were subsequently ranked on vulnerability criteria in order to support selection of key informant from households located at the top, bottom and middle of the locally defined vulnerability index. In-depth interviews with key informants covered resource profiles and social networks for major entitlements and exchanges.

Subsequent interviews were carried out to explore key themes emerging from the settlements, namely:

1   food procurement and management strategies;
2   intra-household negotiations (household financing; decisions on livelihood strategies; claims of individuals on resources);
3   domestic work allocation and time use;
4   credit, liquidity and financial transfers;
5   marital/family instability and coping mechanisms;
6   seasonality (employment, environment and health);
7   power structures and implications for different types of households;
8   employment instability.

Finally, a series of case studies to explore and better understand:

1   strategies to cope with work disability morbidity;
2   intra-household distribution of nutrition and food distribution.

## Conclusions

The rapid rate of urban growth in Bangladesh, as elsewhere, has had a serious impact on the physical and socio-economic conditions of the inhabitants, and around 60 percent of the urban population in Bangladesh live below the national poverty line. There has been little work to date on the livelihood and survival strategies of poor people in urban areas, and how they adapt to political, financial and environmental shocks and stresses. The Dhaka Urban Livelihoods Study is a prospective cohort study of a slum population of 850 households in Dhaka City integrating social science analysis of livelihood with a detailed epidemiological investigation of the interrelationships of the material conditions of poverty, nutritional status and morbidity.

## References

Centre for Urban Studies (1989), *The Urban Poor in Bangladesh: Volume 1 comprehensive summary report*, Department of Geography, University of Dhaka.

Kabeer, N. (1995), *Reversed realities: Gender Hierarchies in Development Thought*, Verso, London and New York.

Pryer, J.A. (1990), 'Socio-economic and environmental aspects of undernutrition and ill health in an urban slum in Bangladesh', unpublished PhD thesis, London School of Hygiene and Tropical Medicine.

Sen, A.K. (1981), *Poverty and famines: an essay on entitlement and deprivation*, Clarendon Press, London.

Swift, J. (1989), 'Why are the rural people vulnerable to famine?', *IDS Bulletin*, 20(2), pp. 8–15.

Chapter 3

# Livelihood Clusters

*Here we describe how we identified groups within Dhaka slums that report similar patterns of livelihood. Four livelihood groups were identified. Cluster 1 (n=178) was the richest cluster with land, animals, business assets and savings. Loans as well as income were higher, which shows that this group was creditworthy. The group was mainly self-employed and worked more days per month than in other clusters. Cluster 2 (n=190) was a poor cluster and was mainly dependent self-employed. Savings and loans were lower. Cluster 3 (n=124) was the most vulnerable cluster. This group comprised mainly casual unskilled, and 40 percent were female headed households. Total income and expenditure were lowest of the clusters. Cluster 4 (n=67) was the second richest cluster. This group comprised skilled workers. In conclusion, cluster analysis has identified four groups which differed in terms of socio-economic, demographic variables. The technique could be a practically useful tool of relevance to the development, monitoring and targeting of vulnerable households, by public policy in Bangladesh.*

## Introduction

To date, policy focused research on the livelihood and survival strategies of poor people has largely focused on rural areas (Beck, 1994). There has been little systematic study of the forms of vulnerable livelihoods in urban areas of Bangladesh. Several conceptual frameworks have been proposed for the identification of vulnerable groups (A. de Haan, 1998) within the informal sector labour market (Harris, 1986; Pryer, 1990). However, few have been tested empirically in terms of their ability to identify vulnerable households within urban settlements and rarely have attempts been made to identify groups within the settlements or the types of livelihoods pursued by the most vulnerable households. Indeed, most such studies undertaken in Bangladesh have presented only aggregated data on employment and livelihoods at the level of the settlement or city (Islam, 1997).

Data from a detailed ethnographic study of an inner-city slum in Khulna, Southern Bangladesh, provides important information on the considerable heterogenity of economic activities of the poor, but also demonstrates the possibility that there are broadly homogeneous groups in terms of the level and form of livelihood (Pryer, 1990; 1993). The Khulna study also illustrates the complex factors that differentiates the urban poor into those who are relatively better off and those who are more vulnerable. For the slum as a whole, ownership of productive assets and the value of productive loans (reflecting creditworthiness and capacity to invest) were important variables. Among the asset-less labouring poor, who comprised around half of the slum households, are female headship and male earners incapacitated by ill health. As in rural Bangladesh, resource poor households headed or supported by women face the dual vulnerability associated both with class and gender (Kabeer, 1995) (de facto female supported households). Supporting evidence comes from another more recent cross-sectional squatter study in Dhaka which found that those in the lowest income group were dependent upon female and child labour (Siddiqui et al., 1990).

In this chapter we will analyse the livelihoods by economic and demographic variables by livelihoods groups.

## Data analysis

We used cluster analyses to identify livelihoods groups within the slum households participating in the study. The clustering technique used was a hierarchical agglomerative (or stepwise) technique available on SPSS for windows. Ward's method was used as suggested by Everitt (1980). In Monte Carlo studies, Ward's method has been found to be the most robust clustering method using a similarity matrix based upon squared Euclidean distances (Blashfield, 1979; Aldenderfer and Blashfield, 1984).

A number of economic and demographic variables were entered into the cluster including: land, animals, labour days worked per month, savings, and debts, income, business assets, occupational group, days off because of illness, household type, household size, earner: dependency ratio. Continuous variables were standardised by converting to the standard normal deviate. A matrix of distances then a step-wise fusion of cases based on squared Euclidean distances was computed. The clustering coefficient was then used to indicate the stage on the agglomeration schedule where large changes between fusions were evident as compared to immediately preceding stages (Everitt, 1980). One major advantage of hierarchical clustering algorithms is that results are presented in the form of a dendogram. This aids the investigator in exercising judgements on the number of clusters that exist or are useful for the purpose at hand.

As possible instability of results could be one of the limitations of a cluster analysis, we tested the stability of the cluster solution. Two methods were used: (1) discriminate analysis to test the degree of association between group membership assigned by cluster and that assigned by discriminatory analysis and (2) by randomly splitting the data in two, clustering separately in each subset and comparing cluster membership in the spit sample.

Statistical comparisons were made across the clusters in terms of reported, socio-economic and demographic variables. Parametric one-way analysis of variance (ANOVA) was used to test for between-group differences in mean values, and categorical variables were tested by chi square tests. Where the expected cell size was under five, Fisher's Exact Test was used. Measures of nutritional status and morbidity were available for individuals within clusters. Means and standard errors were calculated for body mass index, morbidity, and nutritional indices of children, and comparisons across clusters were made using ANOVA.

## Results

*Identification of clusters*

Four clusters were identified comprising 90 percent of the households studied. The degree of association between group membership assigned by cluster and by discriminatory analysis using the same variables was 85 percent. There was a good level of agreement between the cluster solutions when the procedure was run on split samples from the original data.

*The clusters*

Table 3.1 presents socio-economic variables by cluster. Cluster 1 (n=178) was the richest group in the Dhaka slums. This group owned more land and animals, by far the most business assets and earned the highest incomes for men and women and girls, but boys' income was the highest in cluster 3 ( female headed households). Savings were highest in this group. Women's business assets were higher than men's as were their savings and their loans. Total expenditure was highest in this group, but not food expenditure, perhaps because they owned land and animals that provided an additional source of food produce (Table 3.1). Men and women in this group worked on average 25 days per month, while boys worked 23 days and girls worked on average 10 days per month (Table 3.2). Men and women in this cluster were mainly self-employed, and hardly any children worked (Table 3.2).

Cluster 2 (n=190) had the least land and animals. Business assets were very low in this cluster. Total expenditure and food expenditure was the second highest after cluster one. Men's savings were more than women's savings. Women's loans were more than men's loans. The loans and savings were amongst the lowest across the clusters. Men's income was more than women's income, boy's income was lower than girl's income. Incomes were lower than in cluster one and lower than in cluster four (Table 3.1). Men and women worked on average 21 days per month while boys worked 25 days and girls worked 22 days per month. In this cluster, men and women were mainly dependent self-employed as were boys and girls (Table 3.2).

Cluster 3 (n=124). This cluster owns some land and animals but less than cluster one. Men and women owned business assets, and these exceed business assets owned by members of cluster 2 or cluster 4. Men's business assets were more than women's. Women's savings were less than men's savings, and women's loans were more than men's loans, but the loans and savings were the least among the clusters. Men's income was more than women's income, but the income was the lowest among the clusters. Total expenditure and food expenditure was the lowest amongst the clusters (Table 3.1). Men worked 20 days per month and women worked 18 days per month, the lowest among the clusters for adults. But boys worked 30 days, and girls worked 26 days per month, the highest among children. Mostly, men and women in this cluster were casual unskilled (Table 3.2).

Table 3.1  Socio-economic variables by cluster

| Variables | C1 (n=178) self-employed | C2 (n=190) dependent self-employed | C3 (n=124) female headed household | C4 (n=67) casual skilled | p |
|---|---|---|---|---|---|
| Land (mean and se) in bhighas | 0.2697 (0.0115) | 0.1526 (0.0412) | 0.2016 (0.051) | 0.2388 (0.0315) | <0.036 |
| Animals (mean and se) | 0.3146 (0.032) | 0.019 (0.011) | 0.1210 (0.031) | 0.1194 (0.019) | <0.0001 |
| Men's business assets (mean and se) Taka | 3090.42 (426.33) | 79.22 (49.04) | 354.84 (154.23) | 179.03 (122.74) | <0.0001 |
| Women's business assets (mean and se) Taka | 6181.48 (1514.94) | 98.04 (45.42) | 333.59 (138.70) | 174.17 (144.87) | <0.0001 |
| Men's savings (mean and se) Taka | 570.66 (163.02) | 369.15 (121.99) | 609.64 (267.54) | 350.72 (124.68) | <0.0001 |
| Women's savings (mean and se) Taka | 820.28 (318.22) | 339.67 (107.42) | 133.77 (41.87) | 473.01 (134.85) | <0.102 |
| Men's loans (mean and se) Taka | 265.62 (38.32) | 225.69 (38.32) | 282.81 (68.47) | 522.03 (124.73) | <0.026 |
| Women's loans (mean and se) Taka | 484.73 (138.82) | 272.28 (68.47) | 214.79 (55.77) | 156.87 (47.94) | 0.030 |
| Men's income cu (mean and se) Taka | 891.63 (75.40) | 740.39 (123.21) | 660.26 (53.65) | 881.29) | <0.0001 |
| Women's income cu (mean and se) Taka | 857.87 (59.80) | 654.70 (55.81) | 563.67 (51.62) | 838.14 (103.94) | <0.0001 |
| Boys' income cu (mean and se) Taka | 545.55 (100.73) | 348.95 (64.94) | 457.18 (323.27) | 159.58 (106.84) | <0.312 |
| Girls' income cu (mean and se) Taka | 553.07 (64.94) | 450.78 (105.97) | 434.90 (175.75) | 250.65 (234.71) | <0.011 |
| Total expenditure cu (mean and se) Taka | 578.35 (37.33) | 572.70 (14.01) | 509.98 (20.90) | 567.74 (23.09) | <0.0001 |
| Food expenditure cu (mean and se) Taka | 466.31 (12.46) | 498.68 (12.55) | 435.95 (16.72) | 535.87 (32.88) | <0.0001 |

Table 3.2  Work participation and occupational groups by cluster

| Variables | C1 self-employed (n=178) | C2 dependent self-employed (n=190) | C3 female headed households (n=124) | C4 casual skilled (n=67) | P |
|---|---|---|---|---|---|
| Male work Days/month (mean and se) | 25.47 (0.61) | 21.08 (0.81) | 20.28 (1.17) | 21.06 (1.63) | <0.0001 |
| Female work Days/month (mean and se) | 25.00 (0.70) | 21.51 (0.67) | 18.31 (1.81) | 20.70 (1.12) | <0.0001 |
| Boys' work Days/month (mean and se) | 23.60 (2.44) | 25.60 (1.43) | 30.00 (1.50) | 21.50 (1.50) | <0.017 |
| Girls' work Days/month (mean and se) | 10.00 (1.95) | 21.83 (1.55) | 26.00 (3.57) | 22.71 (2.89) | <0.0096 |
| **Men's occupational category** | | | | | |
| Permanent work | 10 | 0 | 0 | 0 | |
| Casual skilled | 1 | 0 | 0 | 35 | |
| Casual unskilled | 1 | 0 | 48 | 0 | <0.0001 |
| Self-employed | 63 | 0 | 5 | 0 | |
| Dependent self-employed | 5 | 96 | 5 | 0 | |
| Family worker | 0 | 0 | 0 | 2 | |
| **Women's occupational category** | | | | | |
| Permanent work | 22 | 0 | 0 | 0 | |
| Casual skilled | 1 | 0 | 0 | 27 | |
| Casual unskilled | 0 | 0 | 55 | 0 | <0.0001 |
| Self-employed | 63 | 1 | 2 | 0 | |
| Dependent self-employed | 12 | 93 | 9 | 0 | |
| Family worker | 0 | 0 | 0 | 3 | |

Cluster 4 (n=67) had some land and animals, but less than cluster 1. Business assets were the second lowest (men's business assets were higher than women's) and men's loans were higher than in any other cluster. Women's savings were more than men's, and men's loans were more than women's. Men's and women's income was very close to that in cluster 1, although boy's and girl's income were lowest among all clusters. Total expenditure was second highest after cluster one, and food expenditure was the highest amongst the clusters (Table 3.1). Men worked on average 21 days per month and women worked 20 days per month, while girls and boys worked 22 days and 21 days per month, respectively. Men and women were mainly casual skilled (Table 3.2).

**Table 3.3  Demographic and occupational characteristics by cluster**

| Variables | C1 (n=178) self-employed | C2 (n=190) dependent self-employed | C3 (n=124) female headed households | C4 (n=67) casual skilled | P |
|---|---|---|---|---|---|
| Household size (mean and se) | 5.26 (0.15) | 4.34 (0.12) | 4.63 (0.18) | 4.47 (0.17) | <0.0001 |
| Household type | | | | | |
| Female headed | 2 | 0 | 49 | 0 | <0.0001 |
| Male headed | 176 | 190 | 75 | 67 | |
| Earner: dependency ratio (mean and se) | 2.202 (0.13) | 1.989 (0.098) | 1.579 (0.13) | 2.226 (0.15) | <0.004 |

Table 3.3 presents demographic characteristics by cluster. Cluster 1 had the highest mean household size and household type was mainly male headed. The earner:dependency ratio was second highest after cluster four. Cluster 2 had the smallest household size and household structure was male headed. The earner-dependency ratio was the third highest after cluster 1.

Cluster 3 had the second largest household size after cluster one. The household structure was 40 percent female headed and 60 percent male headed. The earner-dependency ratio was the lowest among the clusters (Table 3.3).

Cluster 4 household size was the third highest among the clusters, and household structure was male headed. The earner-dependency ratio was highest among the clusters and the employment was casual skilled (Table 3.3).

## The labour force and labour market

In a segmented market where the recruitment process is based upon personal connections, graduation in employment status remains restricted at entry. The graduation of slum people is twofold: first, graduation in employment status, that is a progress from insecure job to a secure job through gaining skills, temporary to permanent work through accessing the formal sector of the labour market, or becoming self-employed by managing capital or equipment; and second, graduation in networks, that is becoming a member of a more effective network(s) which ensures progression. The second form of graduation in the urban context, plays the dominant role and usually results in the former type of graduation, since the market operates through informal relations. However, some people are not capable of graduating in the market despite belonging to a strong network. The role of financial resources to gain access to a network which will ensure graduation via the development of skills is increasing. As the financial transaction is increasing and becoming more dominant characteristic of such relationships, many people remain excluded from the mechanism. A number of examples are provided to illustrate these themes.

> Hazat Ali, about 18 years old, migrated about six months ago to join his brother who has been living in Dhaka for the last one and half years. His brother is a labourer and Hazat Ali also intends to do the same type of work. As he looks very young and is not physically strong, it became very difficult for him to find work every day. About three months ago, he joined a neighbouring labour brokers. This new situation gives him certainty of employment, but it costs about 28 percent of his daily income.

People cope with the employment instability in saturated markets by joining labour gangs and secure employment this way despite the financial cost. The rise of labour brokers in the market has both positive and negative implications. As the market operates through informal relations, those who do not belong to a social network or belong to a weak network can gain the opportunity to strengthen them through labour brokers. These middle men can help the resource poor in different ways. In the above example, Hazat Ali and his brother had to depend upon the same labour broker for equipment.

In the urban situation, the prevailing gender notions of out door employment of women has definite implications for existing gender unequalities.

> Rahima and Praveen started their working career soon after they migrated to Dhaka about four years ago. They have been working in the same factory for the whole period. They started as helpers to machine operators and after one year, having gained the required skills, they were themselves promoted to the positions of machine operators. For the last two years, both of them have achieved the status of operator.

> Enus started working about two years ago as a helper in a garment factory. Soon after starting this job he planned to upgrade himself to the next position (machine operator). He managed to learn the operating work in five months with the help of a friend whom he had to entertain with tea and cigarettes. Yet he found no opportunity to upgrade himself into that position and therefore he decided to leave the factory. After one month he managed to secure this position with double the salary of his previous position in a different factory.

He has changed his employment twice so far and now he is trying to graduate to the position of a supervisor, as he is skilled enough. He is sure that he can do that within a short period of time.

The contrast between the two examples indicates how the restriction of mobility of women in the market results in lack of skills and their concentration in the lower levels of the factory workers, while men are upwardly mobile. The examples show how women are losing in the race for graduation and how gender inequality is reproduced in the employment sector with men, but not women, rising to managerial positions.

The contrast between the following examples describes the comparative outcome of social and financial resources in gaining skills and employment.

Twenty-five-year-old Rafique learned to drive a car for which he had to pay Taka 4,000. However, he was unable to find driving work one year later. He tried to work as a van driver with travellers, but lacked the necessary connections in this sphere. Recently he joined as a helper to develop his social networks in this area and he is hoping that it would be easier for him to find driving work in future.

Salim Mia used to pull a rickshaw, when he first migrated to Dhaka. He learnt to drive a car about two years ago with the help of a friend who resided in the same slum. It cost him no money. His friend also gave him information about work and provided a reference.

The first example indicates the weakness of financial resources in the "informalised market" where having a skill does not always ensure one's employment. On the other hand, the second example describes the strength of social resources in both gaining skills and improving one's employment status. This example also indicates a process through which one can get into a social network of connections and therefore utilise a skill which has been acquired through financial resources.

Finally we provide examples of transitions between the labour intensive sector and the business sector.

Abdul Qadir migrated to Dhaka about 26 years ago when he was a seventeen-year-old boy. He began his employment as a rickshaw driver, but only for seven days. It was contrary to his social position. He managed to save 100 Taka and started to sell belel-leaf and cigarettes in the Agargoan area. Within one year, he managed to buy a rickshaw and out of its income he managed to buy a further five rickshaws in five years. He continued the rickshaw renting business for about ten years. He then sold his rickshaws (but not the licences) because the sector became very unstable due to governmental policy. He now works in the salaried sector.

Chan Mia and his wife Rokeya used to do labouring work in the early period of their migration about fifteen years ago. Chan's primary intention was to shift the retail business that he used to do in the village as he is unable to do labour intensive work due to physical problems. He managed to start a shop selling firewood in the slum two years after their migration with the initial capital of Taka 1,000 which they have accumulated through savings from their waged work. For the last thirteen years they have been running the business. Recently the business has came under threat as the slum is under the threat of eviction.

The first step of graduation is similar in both cases as they shifted from the labour intensive sector into the business sector. Qadir's latest movement from capital owning self-employment to the protected salaried sector is a coping mechanism against insecurity, thus securing his economic position. On the contrary, despite the successful move into business by Chan Mia, in the changing situation he is now vulnerable as his business is under threat of closure.

## Discussion

This paper analyses livelihood groups using cluster analysis. A number of economic and demographic variables were entered into the model including: land, animals, labour days worked per month, savings, and debts, income, business assets, occupational group, household type, household size and earner:dependency ratio. Stability of clusters was demonstrated by associated discriminate analysis and by comparing cluster solutions in split samples.

Cluster analysis has not been widely used to guide public policy. Most urban studies with a socio-economic status focus on household socio-economic indicators, such as income or expenditure. From the perspective of public policy a more integrated analysis is important, so that interventions can be designed which strengthen and complement people's own efforts to manage adversity. In particular this will be necessary if people are to participate in the process of change, rather than receiving aid as passive recipients.

Most analysis assumes the slums are homogeneous (Centre for Urban Studies, 1989; Miah et al., 1988; Madjumder et al., 1989). This analysis confirms that there are well-defined livelihood groups within urban slum populations, each with particular economic, demographic and social characteristics. Clusters are closely, but not exclusively, associated with occupational categories. High levels of business assets are a particular feature of one group and relationships between income, loans, savings and expenditure varies across groups, presumably reflecting access to credit and the nature of employment. One cluster comprising casual unskilled workers and characterised by a high proportion of female headed households emerges as a group that may be particularly vulnerable. The group has the lowest level of income and days worked per month and spend less on food than any other group.

Academics have sought to understand how paid employment alters women's roles, rights and responsibilities. In Bangladesh, with its strong patriarchal tradition and sharp gender segregation of work and space, we might expect to find women's wage employment having a relatively limited impact on prevailing gender identities. However, compared to rural areas, in urban areas opportunities for poor women to participate in paid employment are far greater. Kabeer (1995) concludes that women who earn an income do find themselves with an improved bargaining position within the household, and that work enables women to secure a better "fall-back" position. Our data shows that poor women are acting in a number of ways to secure their own well-being. Women seek to accumulate savings and assets. Working and non-working women alike pursue these strategies, but working for money appears to increase women's room for manoeuvre (Kabeer, 1995).

## Conclusion

Cluster analysis has not been widely used in public policy analysis. Most urban studies with a socio-economic status focus relate household socio-economic indicators, such as income or expenditure, without first analysing the social processes through which income is generated. The aim of this paper was to analyse patterns of household economic livelihoods. We suggest that this approach offers new perspectives on vulnerability of likely value to public policy.

## References

Aldenderfer, M.S., Blashfield, R.K. (1994), *Cluster Analysis*, Series: Quantitative applications in social sciences, Sage Publications, London.
Beck, T. (1994), *The Experience of Poverty: Fighting for respect and resources in village India*, Intermediate Technology Publications, London.
Blashfield, R.K. (1979), 'Mixture models tests of cluster analysis: accuracy of four agglomerative hierarchical methods', *Psychological Bulletin*, 83 (3), pp. 377–388.
Centre for Urban Studies (1989), *The Urban Poor in Bangladesh: Volume 1 Comprehensive Summary Report*, Department of Geography, University of Dhaka.
Everitt, B. (1980), *Cluster Analysis*, Heinemann Educational Books, London.
Haan, A. de (1998), 'Social exclusion: an alternative concept for the study of Deprivation?', *IDS Bulletin*, 29(1), pp. 10–19.
Harris, J. (1986), 'Vulnerable workers in the urban labour markets of south and south east Asia: A report to the International Labour Organisation', *Reports in Development*, No. 32, School of Development Studies, University of East Anglia, Norwich.
Islam, N. (1997), *Addressing the urban poverty agenda in Bangladesh*, Asian Development Bank, University Press, Dhaka.
Kabeer, N. (1995), *Reversed Realities: Gender Hierarchies in Development Thought*, Verso, London and New York.
Madjumder, P.P., Mamud, S. and Asfar, R. (1989), *Squatter Life in the Agargoan area*, Bangladesh Institute of Development Studies, Dhaka, Bangladesh.
Miah, M.A.Q., Weber, K.E. and Islam, N. (1998), *Upgrading a Bustee settlement in Dhaka*, Bangkok, Thailand, Division of Human Settlements, Asian Institute of Technology.
Pryer, J.A. (1990), 'Socio-economic and environmental aspects of undernutrition and ill health in an urban slum in Bangladesh', unpublished PhD thesis, London School of Hygiene and Tropical Medicine.
Pryer, J.A. (1993), 'Nutritionally vulnerable households in the urban slum economy: a case study from Khulna, Bangladesh', in Schell, L.M., Smith, M. and Bilsborogh, A. (eds), *Urban Ecology and Health in the Third World*, Cambridge University Press, Cambridge.
Siddiqui, K., Qudir, S.R., Alamgir, S. and Huq, S. (1990), *Social Formation in Dhaka City*, University Press, Dhaka, Bangladesh.

# Chapter 4
# Marital Instability

*The changing slum society has provided greater options for women compared to their rural counterparts. Flexibility of social control against divorce, dysfunction of the lineage, weaker familial ties and increased options for female labour participation are working as positive forces which give women greater freedom. Slum women are more likely to be able to avoid serious domestic violence, like homicide and suicide, by rejecting unfavourable marital ties or by re-partnering. Despite these factors, overall, women appear to be suffering from the increasingly unstable and uncertain nature of marriage. Children, too, are faring badly. The impact of marital instability on children may also be severe. Slum stepchildren are often treated poorly, receiving inadequate food, health care and education. Moreover, if their mothers are living alone without taking another partner, they are forced to become one of the household's economic contributors and to forgo educational opportunities. If they have been adopted by other elderly relatives, they may also be treated badly compared to those relative's own children. These situations may severely hamper their social and human development. Thus the negative consequences of marital instability and family breakdown are far-reaching, affecting not only the husband and wife, but also the next generation – their children.*

**Universality of marriage**

Marriage is near universal in Bangladesh. Both society and religion urge parents to arrange their children's marriage once they reach adulthood. Marriage is the only legitimate union for sexual gratification and the bearing and rearing of children. It also confers social identity to the women.

Despite traditional norms in Bangladesh, it appears that changes are underway in recent years, particularly in the urban poor setting. Kabeer (1995a; Kabeer, 1995b) provides evidence that the insecurity of marriage is increasing. She asserts that women are becoming more vulnerable as men increasingly abandon their families in the face of poverty. From a rural Matlab site the analysis provides an indication that divorce rates among young couples are on the increase (Shaik, 1998). This is associated with childlessness, negatively associated with educational level, and is more likely to occur where the marriage was arranged by the couple (love marriage) (Shaik, 1998). The end of marriage can lead to social rejection, which has serious economic consequences for the individuals and their families. Table 4.1 indicates that the percentage of individuals who have more than one spouse is high for both men and women. However, men are more likely than women to have been married more than once. This reflects both the fact that men are more likely than women to have been divorced several times, and that large numbers of men maintain polygamous unions. However, as many as 12 percent of all ever married women reported that they have been divorced.

**Table 4.1  Percentage distribution of various indicators of marital behaviour among men and women**

|  | Men % | Women % |
|---|---|---|
| **Number of times married:** | | |
| Once | 70.9 | 83.0 |
| Twice | 23.0 | 16.7 |
| Three or more times | 6.1 | 0.3 |
| **Number of times divorced/separated:** | | |
| None | 84.9 | 88.6 |
| Once | 10.0 | 10.0 |
| Two or more times | 5.1 | 1.4 |
| **Out of individuals divorced once:** | | |
| Respondent initiated | 39.1 | 54.4 |
| Spouse initiated | 50.7 | 41.8 |
| Mutual | 10.2 | 3.4 |
| **Polygyny:** | | |
| Have been polygynously married | 13.7 | |
| Have been married to a polygynously married man | | 21.2 |
| N | 557 | 705 |

It is also interesting to note that there is evidence that women are often initiating divorce or separation. Reports from men and women who have been divorced once in the past indicate that divorce was initiated by the female partner in over 50 percent of cases. It should be remembered that some of these divorces or separations may have taken place in the village area, prior to migration to Dhaka. There is some evidence that marital dissolution is often a precursor to migration by women. However, there is some suggestion that the urban environment allows women greater freedom to leave unfavourable marital circumstances in the rural setting.

## Factors influencing marital instability and discord in the slum population

### *Non-payment of dowry*

As elsewhere in South Asia, non-payment of dowry can lead to marital problems.

> Farida is 20 years old. One year after marriage, her husband forced her to ask her parents to pay the promised dowry of 15,000 Taka. Her parents failed to pay the dowry and her husband sent her to her parents' house. While she was away, her husband remarried, this time obtaining a large dowry. On hearing this information, she decided not to return to the husband's home and instead stayed with her parents. However, after six months she decided to return to Dhaka to live with her sister and reduced the financial burden on her parents. She has since remarried and is now working as an earth digger.

### *Polygamy*

As everywhere in Bangladesh, polygamy exists in the slum setting, and causes marital instability and discord. In the slum, these problems are caused by unequal socioeconomic status of wives and resource sharing between family members. Wives are often dissatisfied, as they feel they are not getting sufficient attention from their husbands, or an equal share of resources. In some cases, these problems lead to wives living separately from their husband. A wife's ability to extract more attention and resources from her husband depends upon her tolerance, wisdom, calculated nature or beauty.

> Rehana (30 years old) and Moyna (35 years old) are wives of Rahim. Rehana is Rahim's second wife. She lives with him and receives more attention from him. Moyna is living separately in another room with her new born baby, eight year old son, a daughter who was separated from her husband and her six month grandson. Moyna receives only Taka 35–40 for the daily consumption needs of the entire household. Her husband only pays attention to her when Rehana is away visiting her home. Rahim pays more attention to Rahana because she is a wise and calculated woman in his eyes.

### *Increased interaction between men and women and rising expectations*

In the slum context unrelated men and women have more opportunity for interaction. Slum women are more mobile and can work aside men. This interaction may lead to distrust. Females aged 25–30 years who are engaged in the labour market were divorcing and re-partnering more frequently. This shift of behaviour was particularly prevalent amongst garment factory workers. An increase in social expectations is blamed on this shift in behaviour amongst the younger generations. This shift in attitude is causing cultural conflicts between the older and younger generations in the slum.

### *Alienation and increased deviant behaviour*

Slum society lacks social cohesion, and contributes to feelings of alienation or deviant behaviour among men. Wealthy and rural people blamed the slum dwellers for the dirty and unhygienic environment, and regarded them as criminals. These feelings, combined with a lack of opportunity for recreation, encouraged men to get involved in drugs and gambling. This can lead to a drain on household resources, and become a source of marital discord and insecurity. Protest by wives can lead to violence and divorce.

> Hasan is a mechanic and a gambler. His wife Afanur is a temporary household maid. She earns Taka 700 per month. She is also a member of a PROSHIKA somiti and has borrowed money. However, she is unable to repay her loan and her husband uses her earnings for gambling. Her husband has also physically abused her and threatens divorce when she complains of his behaviour. She has complained to Rahim (an influential figure in the community and her husband's employer) about her husband's behaviour. Rahim failed to respond.

*Factions, rumours and lack of privacy*

Rumour and factions can destroy marital ties in the slum. The slum does not have a strong social solidarity. Factions represent different regions and districts of origin. These factions lead to deliberate spreading of rumours to discredit members of a rival group. These rumours and factions can make an individual's life miserable and can lead to marital discord and breakdown.

> Bashed beat his wife Naz when he heard rumours that she was a prostitute. I was present when he beat her and compelled him to stop. Others from the slum argued that I should not get involved. They said that as they do not have a friendly relationship with Bashed, interference might be taken in the wrong way. Other slum residents argued that the rumours about Naz's prostitution had been started deliberately when Naz rejected a local influential man.

## Factors increasing the likelihood of marital breakdown

*Segmentation and dysfunction of the Goshti*

Perhaps the most important factor contributing to the rising marital instability is the heterogeneity and segmentation of the population and consequent dysfunction of the *goshti* (lineage group). The social solidarity and collective consciousness of village society is absent in the slums. This has led to an erosion of the traditional socio-cultural constraints against divorce and lack of social control. In the urban slum society, the influence of family and the lineage group over the individual is dwindling, and the traditional lineage function is being obstructed. In this context, the control system of the slum society is becoming weaker and an individual can desert or divorce partners with much less fear of stigma or ostracism. The slum setting is relatively anonymous; it may be possible for an individual to leave a marital relationship and start a new one elsewhere, without anybody knowing their marital history. This applies more to men than to women, since women's movements for living remain restricted.

> Why should I tell you alone and confidentially? Everybody knows about the number of my husbands. They tease me, but they also have some experience. I don't bother about any comments made by others about me.

*Decreasing influence of the family and increasing individualism*

The slum setting is characterised by increasing individualism and decreasing control of parents over their children. The decreasing importance of immovable assets and land, and the increasing role of individual, wage labour, in determining a family member's well-being, appears to be of central importance to the rise of individualism. Family ties are becoming looser and children more independent of their parents. Slum dwellers are unlikely to inherit economic security from their parents and this is leading to an alteration in relations between parents and children. Decisions regarding family matters are more likely to be expressed by children, particularly in relation to their marriage. Because of this, love marriages are increasing, family support and prestige is decreasing; and marital breakdown and re-partnering are becoming more common.

> There is no security of property, so the son does not listen to his father; father does not listen to the son.

Caldwell and Caldwell (1992) described a similar pattern in Sri Lanka, with increasing trends towards love marriages, and decreasing involvement of the wider family in marital affairs with increasing urbanisation and wage-labour force participation.

*Increased economic options for women*

Urbanisation has reduced women's dependence on their husbands for economic support. So if she loses her marital tie or if the husband removes the economic support from the household, a woman may enter the labour market. Rahman (1998) has shown that about 85 percent of unmarried women aged above 15 years, 90 percent of divorced or separated women, 60 percent of widows, and only 43 percent of married women are engaged in economic work. Therefore, women are able to contemplate leaving a marriage and their tolerance of abuse and neglect may be less than their rural counterparts.

## Coping with marital instability

In the slum, greater acceptance of divorce and increased options make separation and divorce more common. Individuality and self-dependency are increasing and men, in particular, are benefiting from new freedoms. However, stigma continues to be attached to divorce, and women are still economically and socially dependent upon men. Women's options may be reduced by increasing age, weak support structures, previous experience of divorce, problems of child guardianship, insecure slum life, or infertility.

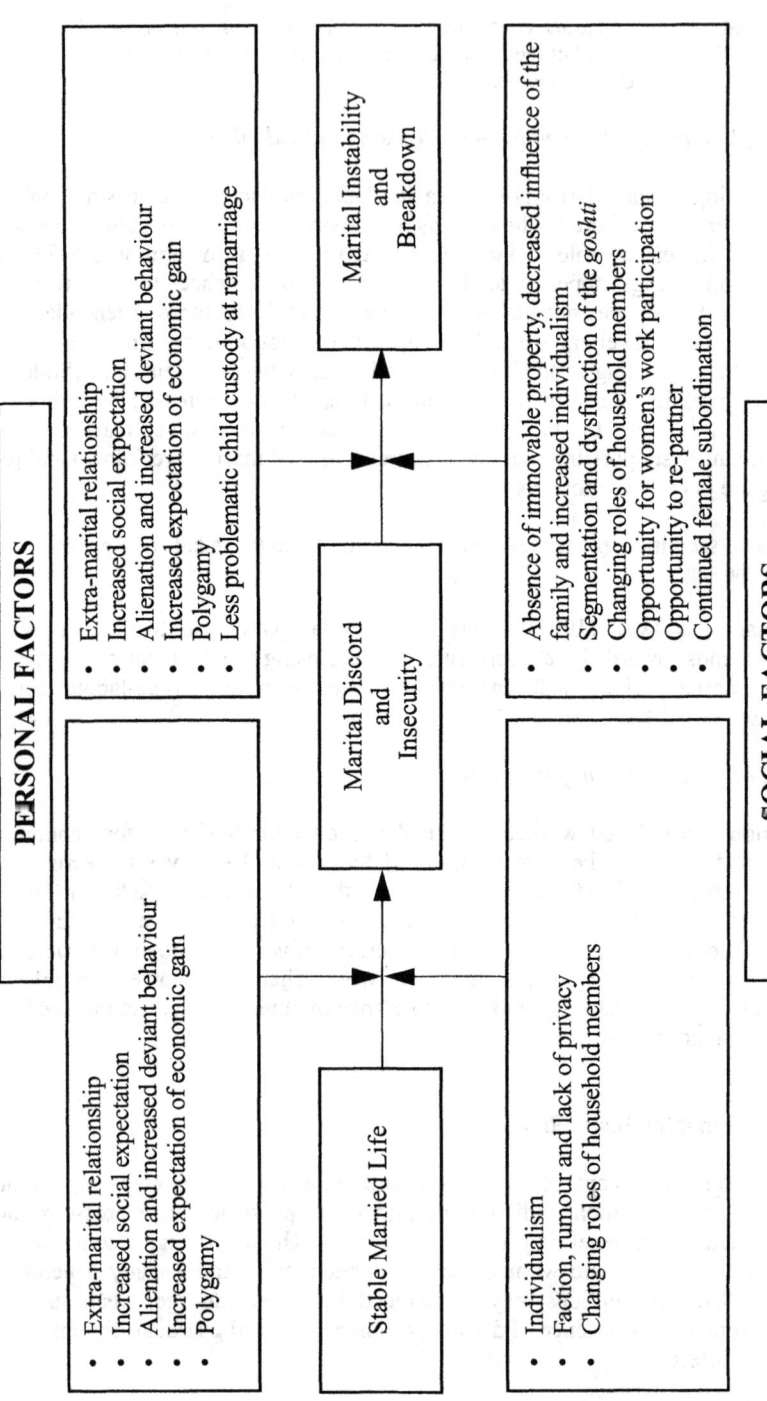

Figure 4.1  Factors increasing marital discord, insecurity and breakdown

Women's lack of alternative options means that strategies designed to prevent marital discord and breakdown are still employed in the slums.

*Compromise and tolerance*

The most common strategy employed by Bangladeshi women in face of marital discord has been compromise and tolerance. Women remain socially and economically dependent on men. Women have limited options, and will often remain married despite physical and psychological abuse, and the absence of emotional support (Goode, 1994).

> Rahana is a 30-year-old woman. Although women of her age would usually expect to remarry after divorce, she has chosen to remain in an unhappy and violent polygamous marriage. She is repeatedly beaten by her husband, but she says, "I don't protest against my husband, and I don't take anything or go anywhere without his permission. I have always served the best pieces of food, thinking, if only I can live in peace. Moreover, I try to save something from the daily expenditure and so help my husband. In spite of my pregnancy I carry water on my own; he does not help me. Nobody, not even he, can say anything against me". She added that domestic violence is a common phenomenon, which every woman should tolerate.

*Acceptance of polygamy*

An extreme form of tolerance on the part of the women is the acceptance of polygamy; either by remarriage or when the husband takes another wife, or by marrying a man who is already married. Polygamy is a revenge for non-payment of dowry, or childlessness. Wives who are treated poorly by their husbands often start paid work for better survival or personal needs.

> Praveen is a 30-year-old woman. She was married for the first time when she was just 12 years old. Her husband beat her constantly for non-payment of dowry. Despite being pregnant, Praveen left her husband and moved to Dhaka. While she was pregnant, she turned to begging. After the birth of the baby, she began to work as a labourer. As there was no-one to look after the child, she would bring the baby with her to work. After a couple of months, the baby died. Praveen remained single for 12 years and then married one of her colleagues. This marriage was also an unhappy experience as Praveen's second husband was already married to someone else. He had not informed Praveen that he had another wife until after they had married. Praveen now lives alone. Her second husband denies the marriage ever happened, and as the marriage was not registered, Praveen does not have proof that it did take place. As Praveen is living alone in the slum, her landlord pressurised her daily to have sexual relations with him. His wife attempted to protect Praveen by giving her shelter in her home, but these attempts failed. Praveen was raped. She left the slum. The landlord was beaten by the local judicial committee for the rape.

*Conformity to husband's and in-law's wishes*

In the slums, women may also adhere to their husband's and in-law's wishes to avoid marital conflict. However, in many cases this adherence may involve entering the workforce. Economic necessity means that many husbands feel that their wives should make a contribution to the household. This is different from middle class women who gave up work to avoid marital conflict (Madjumder, 1992).

*Negotiation and mediation by other family members*

Traditionally, other members and friends of the couple mediate in marital conflicts to avoid separation. However, in the slum context the traditional function of the lineage is absent, and therefore the involvement of wider kin in mediation is rare. It is commonly believed that the wife and her family should make more compromises than the husband and his family. The wife's parents suggest that their daughter should make sacrifices and listen to her husband and in-laws. In some cases, parents will not mediate in marital conflicts, if the marriage was not arranged by the parents and took place against their wishes, then the couple will have to solve their marital conflicts alone.

> Following frequent domestic violence, Taslima left her husband, saying that she would not take her husband's rice anymore (this indicates she wants to be separated). Knowing that her parents would not support her, as she had arranged her own marriage, Taslima went to live with her sister in a nearby slum. Taslima's husband, Maleq, asked the local judicial committee for assistance in getting his wife back. The local judicial committee put pressure on Taslima's father to find his daughter and bring her back.

*Resort to the local judicial system*

In urban slum context, women avoid legal action to prevent conflicts. The lack of certainty of safety during this period of litigation forces them to compromise rather than gain legal help. Women also feel that after litigation, their married life will become more bitter. The following example indicates this type of terrible life for women.

> Sofina, a 40-year-old, is taking help from the Bangladesh Legal Aid Services Centre to demand maintenance costs from her second husband. This marriage was registered. Because of this, she has become a suspected woman in the eyes of women in the community. Some of them rebuke her as a bad woman who does not care about her husband or his religious beliefs. Moreover, they are saying that by her action Sufina will not be benefited but rather adversely affected. For doing this, she may lose the social support of her husband and also the economic support. However, a small number of women were admiring her while the rest of them were silent.

## Preparing for breakdown: contingency plans and protective strategies

*Preserving evidence*

Preserving evidence of a marriage is more important in the slum context due to the heterogeneity and anonymity of residents.

> Mukter's daughter has been recently married. Mukter is anxious about a sudden divorce or separation. He has taken a photograph of the bride-groom as evidence to be used should he face legal problems.

*Forming alliances*

In a few cases, women make alliances with influential people who they believe will protect them at times of desertion.

> Maleq helped a woman who is from his own district. This woman's husband beat her and threatened her with divorce. Maleq threatened the woman's husband and made him promise that he would never beat her again. Malaq said "she calls my mother and asks her to tell me how to help her. That is why I considered her as my own sister. Moreover, she is from our district, so I felt interested in helping her".

In an urban slum setting it is easy for this man to find alternative shelter and live anonymously. Forming alliances in the slum setting is not so easy. Many neighbours are unwilling to become involved in marital discord. Their unwillingness is exacerbated by the implications such involvement may have for the factions that exist within the slum.

*Creating economic independence and strengthening links with kin*

Urban poor women are creating economic independence and securing economic links with kin for their future support. Opel (1998) found that many women contributed money to their parents' household in the hope that their parents would provide them with shelter following divorce. Naved (1997) found that garments factory workers made important contributions to their parents' home, though the motivation was unclear. In other cases, women may start work in the knowledge that their employment will make them more welcome in their parents' home.

> Palash is an 18-year-old separated woman. Her husband left her for not paying the dowry. She is living with her parents. She is working in a nearby garments factory and contributing her income to the natal home. Her mother refuses to pay a dowry as she thinks that if they pay it the son-in-law may become greedy and ask for more money. She also argues that her daughter is bringing money into the household; there is nothing to be gained from reuniting Palash and her husband. She refuses to pay dowry, even in the face of divorce threats from the son-in-law.

## Coping with marital breakdown: responsive strategies

*Re-marriage*

The evidence from the quantitative panel survey indicates that men are more likely to remarry after marital breakdown than women. This is especially true as age increases for women. However, in the slum context, women must remarry in order to survive in an insecure and unstable slum life. Usually women will find work after separation, and then will try to find another partner. This is because women face verbal and physical abuse, including rape and robbery. In the slums, norms and values are changing and it makes re-partnering more acceptable. This makes remarriage easier than elsewhere in Bangladesh. Nevertheless, there are a number of factors which affect women's ability to remarry.

Working women with children in the slum find it easier to find a new partner than infertile or unemployed women. Men will often accept the income of a working women in lieu of dowry. If a woman does not have a dowry or is unemployed, she may have to accept an older man in order to remarry.

> Rohiton Nessa was beaten by her first husband for failing to give him a son and complete household tasks completely. She was a poultry-seller and earned more than her husband. When her husband remarried she left him. They had been married for 23 years. One year after the separation, Rohiton Nessa married one of her colleagues. In this marriage the five daughters were accepted by her second husband. She was then about 35 years old.

*Returning to the natal home and depending on kin*

If women can remarry and chose not to do so, they will often have to rely on their natal kin for support. In some cases they will have to return to the natal home to do this. Many women turn to their married sons for support. However, this option is not always available to them. The urban competitive life and insecure income forces offspring to avoid this burden. Many women who rely on kin for support eventually have to remarry.

> Meherjan was married at the age of seven without any registration. She is now 40 and a mother of five married children. Her husband Jamshed has remarried twice. After four years of marriage he divorced his second wife, Chandravan, as she was too sick to gratify him. His third wife, Ojifa, is 14 years old and still lives with him. Jamshed has accused Meherjan of failing to look after him properly. This has led to conflicts in the marriage. Meherjan attempted to get justice from the local power bodies but failed. During the conflict she had to depend on her two sons for food. She eventually had to compromise with her husband as she was threatened with divorce, and is unable to work owing to her old age.

*Going it alone: forming female headed households*

In a number of cases, divorced, separated, widowed or deserted women have formed households with other women in a similar position. Approximately 10 percent of households in the slum are headed by women.

> Amena lives with her two daughters in the slum. Her husband lives with his first wife in a nearby slum. Amena left her husband as she was often tortured by him and his first wife became too sick to do the household work. She now earns a living by begging.

> Moyna lives separately from her husband with her children. Her husband gives her some money for rent and for food. However, as he does not give her a sufficient income, she had to start work as a housemaid. When she became pregnant, she had to give up work. Although her husband is the father of her baby, he has refused to give her any extra money. She lives at subsistence levels and is forced to feed her baby on rice flour instead of milk.

**Table 4.2 Various indicators of well-being in female headed and male headed households**

|  | Female headed | Male headed | $X^2$ |
|---|---|---|---|
| Percentage of children (5–16 years) performing income generating work in the past month |  |  |  |
| Boys | 55.8 | 26.7 | $P<0.001$ |
| Girls | 32.6 | 21.8 | $P=0.100$ |
| Percentage of children (5–16 years) currently attending school |  |  |  |
| Boys | 29.1 | 46.6 | $P=014$ |
| Girls | 35.9 | 48.0 | $P=0226$ |
| Percentage of households purchasing different types of food in the past 7 days |  |  |  |
| Small Fish | 79.3 | 88.4 | $P=0.018$ |
| Large Fish | 41.5 | 55.9 | $P=0.013$ |
| Beef | 19.5 | 29.6 | $P=0.057$ |
| Lentils | 86.6 | 85.7 | $P=0.823$ |
| Fruit | 30.5 | 44.4 | $P=0.017$ |
| Percentage of households unable to purchase sufficient rice to feed all members on at least one day in the past month | 29.3 | 15.3 | $P=0.002$ |
| Total number of households | 83 | 649 |  |

These examples show that some women in female headed households retain contact with their husbands. In this way, separated women can retain a married identity and be protected from other men. Despite having some economic independence, women in female headed households are worse off on most indicators of well-being, because of multiple forms of discrimination.

As can be seen from Table 4.2 children from female headed households have to take on adult roles earlier than in male headed households. For example, in female headed households, fewer children are attending school, and more children are working.

## Marital instability and its implications for women and children

This section explores the effects of marital instability first on women and then on their children.

### *Competition for men*

Marital instability combined with the continued necessity of marriage for women has caused women to compete with other women for men. In the slum, problems of being a single women are exacerbated by the absence of extended kin networks. This desire to marry forces many women to resort to abusing their relationships with other women by marrying their husbands. Slum residents feel that such tactics are particularly prevalent among the younger generations.

> 25-year-old Saira is infertile. She left the village for Dhaka with her husband in hope of a better life. On arrival in Dhaka, Saira and her husband moved into a slum where they made friends with a neighbouring family. This family had two unmarried daughters, Rashi aged 25 and Razi aged 18. Both of these daughters worked as domestic servants. Saira became very friendly with the girls and discussed her infertility and her search for a job. Saira felt that she needed to work as she and her husband found it hard to survive on his earnings. The sisters suggested to Saira that she should replace Rashi, who had decided to give up her job as a maidservant for personal reasons. The job involved overnight stays away from the slum. A few days after Saira had started work, Razi informed Saira that her sister Rashi had married Saira's husband.

### *Male irresponsibility towards the family*

Frequent divorce and separation means that many in the slum see the family as a short-lived partnership. Marriage is no longer perceived as a life-long commitment. This perception means that men, in particular, are less inclined to be committed to the family. In these circumstances men often make only minimal contributions to the household, choosing instead to spend their money on deviant activities. This irresponsible attitude can cause severe financial hardship for women in the slum. The lack of male contributions can be especially damaging when women become pregnant or lose their jobs. The absence of kin in the slum also means that women are unable to rely on their parents to compensate for the lack of male contributions.

> Mukta is a 30-year-old and the second wife of 30-year-old Bashir. Bashir works as a buyer and seller of iron. Mukta is economically independent and lives separately from her husband. Despite this, Bashir frequently demands money from Mutka. He uses this money to gamble. Bashir also shows an irresponsible attitude to his other wife, Anwara, and their three-year-old son. Bashir does not contribute to their consumption needs. Anwara has to work as a cook to ensure their survival. However, as she only receives Taka 100 per month, she has asked Bashir for additional money. Bashir refused her request and responded to her pleading by beating her.

In the slum, male irresponsibility to the family is exacerbated by the changing role of women. As women make greater contributions to the home, men feel less responsible for meeting family needs. Naved (1997) found similar evidence in the study of female garment workers. It is evident that with reduced economic responsibilities men tend to withdraw from their family responsibilities as well. This makes marriage extremely vulnerable. She also found that many working women continued to be physically and mentally abused and economically exploited. In many cases, men took control of the wives earnings. This evidence contradicts Sen's (1990) argument that women's access to wage income provides women the bargaining chip with which to assert her power in the household decision making process.

*Way out for women*

It should be recognised that, for some women, the slum setting enables them to escape from difficult marriages and start again – something that is not possible for the majority of rural women faced by similar circumstances.

> Rehana's 32-year-old sister was married to Yasin Bepari (40 years). He was a businessman and an influential person involved in the local power bodies. However, the economic security and power wielded by her husband did not provide a happy life for Rahana's sister. Yasin Bepari beat her frequently as she did not become pregnant. The greater acceptability of divorce in the slum and employment opportunities meant that Rehana's sister was able to divorce her husband. She has since found employment, fallen in love with one of her colleagues and remarried. She now has two children and lives happily in the slum.

## Marital breakdown: Implications for children

The effects of divorce on children in Bangladesh is extremely limiting. Research in other settings has highlighted a range of negative effects on children resulting from the divorce of their parents. In America, it has been found that children may suffer emotional scars which can affect their behaviour and personality in later life. Children of divorced parents are often deprived of adequate economic support and have poor educational attainment. Available evidence from the present study suggests that the impact of marital instability on slum children may also be severe.

*Living as a stepchild*

In the slum, stepchildren are often poorly treated. Stepchildren are often accepted by stepfathers in replacement of dowry. These stepfathers see stepchildren purely in terms of their adult earning potential, which will contribute to the household in later years. This perception of stepchildren in purely economic terms can lead to abuse. Stepchildren are often denied adequate food, healthcare and education. Such treatment is likely to have long-term implications for children's physical and psychological development. In the short term, such neglect can mean that children become involved in deviant activities. As children usually have nowhere else to go, they must stay with their step-parents and accept the abuse.

> Ruman is nine years old and lives with his mother Ranu, stepfather Shomser and Shomser's children. Ruman has recently suffered from a fever. Shomser refused to pay to have the fever treated. Shomser will spend money treating his other children when they are

sick. To provide adequate clothing for Ruman, Ranu has to ask her former employers for old clothing. To avoid an angry reaction from Shomser, Ranu has to hide these gifts from him. Ruman has resorted to begging in the streets. He says, my present father is bad and does not love me. My real father visits me occasionally and gives me a little money.

The vulnerable position of stepchildren in the slum is reflected elsewhere in Bangladesh. Stepchildren are rarely accepted by step-parents. This happens even when adoption of a stepchild is part of a verbal agreement between bride and groom before marriage. Children are victimised due to their rights to inherent property. Blanchet (1996) found that children who stayed with their fathers after divorce were the most likely to suffer victimisation from step-parents as men are more likely to remarry than women. Fears about the victimisation of stepchildren can prevent remarriage in some cases (Maloney, Aziz and Sarker, 1981). In other cases, parents will try to persuade relatives to take care of their children so that they can marry. This can also be an unpleasant experience for children.

*Poverty and child labour*

Divorced and separated women often suffer economic hardship. Blanchet (1996) found that poverty affected divorced and separated women all over Bangladesh. For children living with these women, economic necessity can push them into the labour market. Children of divorced parents who live with their mothers are likely to face greater poverty since women generally do not own land, and are highly discriminated against in the labour market having less work opportunity than men, and getting systematically lower salaries when they work. The children are among the poorest and generally enter the labour force early (Blanchet, 1996).

The quantitative panel survey shows that 20 percent of income is earned by children in male headed households, and 35 percent of income in female headed households. Forty-seven percent of boys aged 10–14 years and 44 percent of girls of the same age are engaged in the labour force.

> Amena begs with her three-year-old daughter. Though the child is not directly begging herself, Amena tries to get sympathetic attention of passers-by and so the child is treated as a tool for income generation.

> Jahid is eight years old and sells achar (preserved fruit melted with mustard oil and spices). His mother, Moyna is now unemployed since she has given birth. Moreover, they are getting little attention from Jahid's father. Jahid also has an 18-year-old sister who is separated from her husband and is living with them with her eight-month-old son. So finding no other alternative option, Jahid is working as a substitute earner for the household.

*Adoption or fostering by other relatives, and abandonment*

Fears about mistreatment by stepfathers can mean that women who are remarrying ask relatives to adopt their children. Blanchet (1996) found that adopted or fostered children were often mistreated. Such mistreatment is especially likely to take place if children are poor and/or female. Elderly relatives are often too poor to care for children properly. In some cases, these children receive so little attention and resources from their adoptive parents that they are virtually abandoned. Being abandoned by parents can have serious consequences for children. In an effort to survive, they may enter dangerous and demoralising professions such as child prostitution.

## Conclusions

The changing slum society has provided greater options for women compared to their rural counterparts. Flexibility of social control against divorce, dysfunction of the lineage, weaker familial ties and increased options for female labour participation are working as positive forces which give women greater freedom. Slum women are more likely to be able to avoid serious domestic violence, like homicide and suicide, by rejecting unfavourable marital ties or repartnering. Despite these factors, overall women appear to be suffering from the increasingly unstable and uncertain nature of marriage. Children, too, are faring badly.

Women are faced with a dilemma regarding marriage. Marital discord and instability are high, yet marriage remains a necessity. The unstable slum life, harassment from men, social and economic dependency, the difficulty of returning to the village, and absence of kin networks force women to marry. Married women are protected from harassment of other males, but at the same time may be exploited by their husbands. If they try to escape this exploitation by rejecting the partner or living separately, they may be harassed by others. Even by re-partnering they may or may not escape this exploitation.

In slum society the high incidence of divorce is putting the husband–wife relationship under strain, as men and women become suspicious about extra-marital relationships and other activities. Frequent divorce and separation also means that many slum families are short-lived, and men are less inclined to be committed to their family as a provider. This climate of marital instability leads to compromise by women and also their families in the hope of gaining some security.

The experience of marital discord or breakdown has serious implications for women. Though most of them are becoming child guardians, they lose their maintenance cost from the husband. Men are reluctant to care for children after divorce. This means that women have to bring up children on very limited resources. This problem can be resolved by remarriage but often children are badly cared for by their stepfathers. Thus women face a difficult dilemma: risking the neglect of children after remarriage or continuing to struggle on limited resources.

The impact of marital instability on children may also be severe. Slum stepchildren are often treated poorly, receiving inadequate food, health care and education. Moreover, if their mothers are living alone without taking another partner, they are forced to become one of the household's economic contributors and to forgo educational opportunities. If they have been adopted by other elderly relatives, they may also be treated badly compared to those relatives' own children. These situations may severely hamper their social and human development. Thus the negative consequences of marital instability and family breakdown are far-reaching, affecting not only the husband and wife, but also the next generation – their children.

**References**

Blanchet, T. (1996), *Lost Innocence, Stolen Childhoods*, University Press, Dhaka, Bangladesh.

Caldwell, J. and Caldwell, P. (1992), 'Family systems: their viability and vulnerability', in Berquo, E. and Xenos, P. (eds), *Family Structures and Cultural Change*, Clarendon Press, Oxford.

Goode, J.W. (1994), *The Family*, Prentice-Hall of India (Private) Limited, New Delhi.

Jesmin, S. (1998), *Marital Instability and its Effects on Bustee Women and Children*, Urban Livelihoods Study Monographs 3, Institute for Development Policy Analysis and Advocacy (IDPAA) PROSHIKA, Dhaka, Bangladesh.

Kabeer, N. (1995a), *Reversed Realities: Gender Hierarchies in Development Thought*, Verso, London and New York.

Kabeer, N. (1995b), 'Necessary, sufficient or irrelevant? Women, wages and intra-household power relations in urban Bangladesh', Institute of Development Studies Working Paper, 25, IDS, Sussex.

Madjumder, P.P. (1992), *Marriage, employment and marital adjustment, a case study of educated urban women*, Research Report 132, Bangladesh Institute of Development Studies, Dhaka, Bangladesh.

Maloney, C., Aziz, K.M.A., Sarker, P.C. (1981), *Beliefs and Fertility in Bangladesh*, International Centre for the Diarrhoeal Disease Research, Dhaka, Bangladesh.

Naved, T.R. (1997), 'Female labour migration and its implications for marriage and child bearing in Bangladesh', paper presented at the Population Council Workshop on adolescence and marriage among female garment workers in Dhaka, Bangladesh Institute of Development Studies, Dhaka, Bangladesh.

Opel, A.E.A. (1998), 'The Labour market: where social resources matter', *Discourse*, 2 (1), pp. 49–74.

Rahman, S. (1998), 'Levels and characteristics of female participation in work among the urban poor in Dhaka', Urban Livelihoods Study Working Paper 1, Institute for Development Policy Analysis and Advocacy (IDPAA), Proshika, Dhaka, Bangladesh.

Sen, A.K. (1990), 'Gender and cooperative conflicts', in Tinker, I. (ed.), *Persitent Inequalities: Women and World Development*, Oxford University Press, Oxford and New York.

Shaik, K. (1998), 'The social and demographic correlates of divorce in rural Bangladesh', *Asia Pacific Population Journal*, September.

# Chapter 5
# Child Labour

*This chapter examines the determinants of child work in Bangladesh. Nearly half of girls and boys aged 10–14 years were involved in income generating work. More girls and boys who are working came from female headed households. Most boys came from households where there was unemployment. More boys from male headed households went to school, compared to those from female headed households. Girls and boys from the area of Beri Badh had the least percentage attending school compared to other areas, and 30 percent of female headed households had income below the poverty line. But when children's income was left out, 48 percent of female headed households were below the poverty line, showing that child income was an important part of the household income.*

**Introduction**

According to the national census data, 12 percent of the Bangladesh labour force is constituted of children under 14 years old (BBS, 1994). Attempts to regulate child labour go back to the 19th century. Under British colonial rule, a series of laws on children's work were adopted, but were never seriously applied. Despite new regulations relating to industries, on the whole the State interfered little with child labour.

In the 1970s, there was considerable international concern about Bangladesh's fast growing population. The question was raised as to whether the value of children's work incited parents to have a larger family. In 1977, Cain showed that by the time sons reached 12 years of age, they worked enough to earn their own keep, and by 15 years, they can support other family members as well. Parents reaped a net benefit from their sons' work from age 15 years until they married. Sons were also a security in old age. Before being given away in marriage, daughters participated in housework, but seldom earned. When they married, a dowry had to be provided, which strained the family resources (Cain, 1977).

In the 1980s, children's work was under scrutiny again. This time it was seen to be a major obstacle to the achievement of universal primary education. The importance of universal education was stressed as a means to develop the economy, since "poverty and education move together". Given the interactive relationships between poverty, child work, school enrolment, economic development and population growth, it is not uncommon that many poor countries find themselves in a vicious circle. Bangladesh is a good example, with abysmal poverty, high incidence of child labour, low school enrolment, high population growth, high adult illiteracy, low productivity and low income. Labour that prevents children from going to school should be eliminated to break the vicious circle of poverty.

The debate on child labour was reactivated in 1992, following the bill proposed by the American senator Hankin to boycott imports from countries resorting to child labour. Most commentaries expressed the view that the American senator had a wrong picture of Bangladesh, and was imposing norms that could not apply here. On the whole, there was reluctance to examine critically the multiple causes and circumstances of child labour. Clearly, export industries are not the only ones employing children. Several other industries producing for a national market employ children. Child labour has been challenged by non governmental organisations and United Nations agencies promoting the rights of the child. It is argued that child labour should be eliminated since it "deprives children of their right to a childhood, prevents access to basic needs, undermines development and health, and entails exploitative terms of employment".

In this study we will describe the nature of child work among slum households in Dhaka, and will particularly explore the nature of work being carried out by children under 16 years of age, and the association between child work and a series of indicators of child welfare, as well as the contribution of child work to the household livelihoods of slum dwellers in Dhaka.

**Table 5.1** Percentage of children performing income generating work by age and sex

| Age group | Male % | N | Female % | N | $X^2$ for males vs females |
|---|---|---|---|---|---|
| 5–9 years | 7.1 | 198 | 4.2 | 238 | 1.71 p=0.19 |
| 10–14 years | 47.3 | 169 | 43.9 | 155 | 0.39 p=0.53 |

Table 5.1 shows more girls performing income generating work compared to males, although the sex difference is not significant.

**Table 5.2** Percentage of children (5–16 years) currently attending school by worker status

| | Current school attendance | | | | |
|---|---|---|---|---|---|
| | No | | Yes | | |
| Worker | N | % | N | % | P |
| No | 101 | 47.64 | 111 | 52.36 | |
| Yes | 44 | 86.27 | 7 | 13.73 | <0.0001 |

Table 5.2 shows that the proportion of children who work has a significantly lower proportion who do not currently attend school.

**Table 5.3   Percentage distribution of reasons reported among children not attending school**

|  | Children aged 5–8 years | | Children aged 9–16 years | |
|---|---|---|---|---|
|  | boys | girls | boys | girls |
| Too expensive | 24.2 | 27.5 | 18.3 | 13.0 |
| Busy with income generating work | 5.5 | 5.0 | 57.9 | 54.8 |
| Busy with housework | 0.0 | 1.3 | 1.2 | 7.9 |
| Schooling stopped following marriage | 0.0 | 0.0 | 0.0 | 10.2 |
| Child does not want to attend school | 7.7 | 6.3 | 14.6 | 5.7 |
| Will attend school later | 45.1 | 42.5 | 0.6 | 1.1 |
| Unwell | 2.2 | 1.3 | 0.6 | 1.1 |
| Studying at home | 3.3 | 1.3 | 0.0 | 0.0 |
| No school nearby | 2.2 | 0.0 | 0.0 | 1.1 |
| No place available in school | 5.5 | 8.8 | 1.2 | 0.0 |
| Too old to attend | 0.0 | 0.0 | 2.4 | 2.8 |
| Other reasons | 4.3 | 6.0 | 3.0 | 2.3 |
| Total N | 91 | 80 | 178 | 198 |
| Missing information | (0) | (0) | (14) | (21) |

Parents were asked to mention the main reason why their children were not attending school. Among all children aged 16 years and under who were not currently attending school, the most common reason given was that the child was working (36 percent), followed by "schooling too expensive" (17 percent). The reasons reported did, however, show an interesting pattern by age and sex of the child. Table 5.3 shows the distribution of reasons reported for children not attending school, for both younger children (5–8 years old) and older children (9–16 years).

Among the younger children, the most common reason reported was the child would be sent to school later, followed by "schooling too expensive". However, around 5 percent of younger boys and girls were reported to be busy with income generating work and therefore unable to attend school. In around 8 percent of cases, it was reported that there was no school nearby or no school place available for the child. There was no noticeable difference in reasons reported for boys and girls in this younger age group.

However, when we consider the older children, the reasons reported are quite different and some gender-differentials are apparent. In over 50 percent of cases for boys and girls, income generating work was given as the main reason for not attending school, and the next most common reason for both sexes was "expense".

**Table 5.4 Percentage of children (5–16 years) currently attending school by household characteristics**

|  | Boys | | | Girls | | |
|---|---|---|---|---|---|---|
|  | N | % | $X^2$ | N | % | $X^2$ |
| **Sex of household head** | | | | | | |
| Male | 217 | 46.6 | | 244 | 48.0 | |
| Female | 269 | 29.1 | <0.014 | 277 | 35.9 | P=0.226 |
| **Educational status of household head** | | | | | | |
| No schooling: can sign name only | 287 | 43.9 | | 281 | 45.2 | |
| 1–5 years schooling | 148 | 43.2 | | 182 | 48.4 | |
| 6+ years schooling | 51 | 52.9 | P=0.449 | 48 | 50.0 | P=0.621 |
| **Occupational group** | | | | | | |
| Regular salaried worker | 46 | 63.0 | | 31 | 77.4 | |
| Casual wage worker (skilled) | 30 | 66.7 | | 28 | 46.4 | |
| Casual wage worker (unskilled) | 97 | 33.0 | | 102 | 30.4 | |
| Dependent self-employed | 109 | 38.5 | | 145 | 46.2 | |
| Self-employed | 149 | 49.7 | | 163 | 55.2 | |
| Unemployment/own housework | 34 | 41.2 | <0.003 | 15 | 40.0 | <0.003 |
| **Overall household income last month (Taka)** | | | | | | |
| <2,000 | 85 | 38.8 | | 109 | 43.1 | |
| 2,000–2,499 | 74 | 41.9 | | 79 | 46.8 | |
| 2,500–3,499 | 144 | 41.7 | | 157 | 42.0 | |
| 3,500–4,499 | 73 | 50.7 | | 79 | 55.7 | |
| 4,500+ | 104 | 51.0 | P=0.323 | 92 | 53.3 | P=0.290 |
| **Location of residence** | | | | | | |
| Agargoan | 249 | 47.6 | | 254 | 50.4 | |
| Central Mohammadpur | 146 | 47.3 | | 199 | 51.3 | |
| Beri Badh | 83 | 33.7 | <0.07 | 66 | 21.2 | <0.001 |
| **Child performed income generating work past 30 days** | | | | | | |
| Yes | 121 | 15.7 | | 103 | 4.9 | |
| No | 284 | 56.3 | <0.001 | 340 | 59.7 | <0.001 |
| N | 409 | | | 449 | | |

However, among girls, 10 percent reported to have ceased schooling following marriage; something which was not mentioned for boys. Also, 8 percent of girls were reported to be busy with household work, compared to just 1 percent of boys. For boys, an unwillingness to attend school was reported to be the reason for non-attendance in around 15 percent of cases, compared to 6 percent of girls.

Table 5.4 examines factors associated with school attendance. Among both boys and girls, lower percentages were attending school among female headed than male headed households. However, the difference was larger and statistically significant among boys. There was no evidence of a significant difference in percentage of boys and girls attending school by educational level of the household head. This finding suggests that not having an education oneself is not an important factor in determining whether one's child will attend school or not. There was some indication of a trend towards higher percentages of children attending school with increasing household income. However, the differences were not large and a simple chi-squared test provided no evidence of significant differences between the groups.

When the children were grouped into just two categories, those from households with a monthly income of less than Taka 3,500 and those from households with a monthly income of Taka 3,500 or over, a significant difference was found. Overall, 42 percent of children (boys and girls) were attending school in the lower income group, compared to 53 percent of children in the higher income group ($X^2= 4.45$, $p = 0.035$).

Differentials were apparent in school attendance of children from households with heads working in different occupational groups. Among children from households where the head was working, girls and boys from households where the main head's occupation was "unskilled wage labour" had the lowest levels of participation in schooling (33 percent for boys and 30 percent for girls). However, the highest level of schooling for girls was among those with household heads in "regular salaried" employment, whereas among boys it was those with household heads in "skilled wage work" who are more likely to be attending school. There was a significant difference between boys and girls from different areas, with children from Beri Badh having the least numbers in schools.

Not surprising, a significant difference was found in the percentages of working and non-working children who are currently attending school. The differential between working and non-working children was most striking among girls, with only 5 percent of working girls attending schools, compared to 16 percent for boys. This may reflect the fact that most of the occupations performed by girls are waged and involve long and fixed hours. In contrast, many boys are involved in self-employment; small scale enterprises. Among the children who were reported to be working and attending schools, 58 percent were street hawkers, and 83 percent were reported to be self-employed or unpaid family workers. These results suggest that schooling is recognised as important to both boys and girls, at least up to a certain level. However, it seems clear that income related barriers do play a part in preventing school participation, particularly among older children. Nevertheless, this does not appear to be the whole story. Differentials between girls and boys and between different occupational groupings suggest that cultural and social factors are also at work. In general, the assumption of "adult" roles early in life appears to interfere with schooling of children of both genders.

**Table 5.5 Percentage of children (5–16 years) in different occupational groups (main occupation)**

**Child occupational groups**

| Occupation | NO N | NO % | YES N | YES % | P |
|---|---|---|---|---|---|
| Regular salaried worker | 66 | 81.5 | 15 | 18.5 | |
| Casual wage worker (skilled) | 115 | 89.8 | 13 | 10.2 | |
| Casual wage worker (unskilled) | 192 | 75.6 | 62 | 24.5 | |
| Dependent self-employed | 32 | 84.2 | 6 | 15.8 | |
| Self-employed | 744 | 85.1 | 130 | 14.9 | |
| Family worker | 22 | 78.6 | 6 | 21.4 | <0.003 |

Table 5.5 presents percentages of children aged 5–16 years who perform income generating work. Most children do not work (1171 who do not work, compared to 232 children who do work). Children who work are more likely to be a "casual unskilled wage worker" or a "family worker", and least likely to be a "casual wage worker skilled" or "self-employed".

Bivariate associations between a number of background characteristics and children's work participation are shown in Table 5.6. The percentage of boys and girls who were working was higher in female headed than male headed households, though the difference was larger and significant only for boys. Child's work participation did not appear to vary with the educational status of the household head.

There was some evidence to indicate that levels of children's work do vary between households headed by individuals in different occupational categories. The differentials were larger for girls than for boys. Girls were more likely to be working if they came from households headed by an unskilled wage worker and least likely to be working if their household head was a regular, salaried worker. Among boys, the highest percentage working was among households headed by an unemployed or household worker (mainly female) and the lowest levels of work participation were among those in households headed by dependent self-employed and skilled wage workers. Household income did not show a simple relationship with children's participation. Among girls there was some suggestion that it is those from the middle income households that are most likely to work, and this relationship was even stronger when the analysis was restricted to children aged 5–12 years. The pattern of work participation with location of residence was similar for boys and girls, with the lowest percentage of children resident in the Central Mohammadpur area. However, the differences between the three areas were not statistically significant. Restricting the analysis to younger children, aged 5–12 years, there was evidence of a significantly lower proportion of girls working in Central Mohammadpur area than other areas. Fifteen percent of girls aged 5–12 years in Agargoan were reported to have worked in the last month, compared to just 6 percent in Central Mohammadpur ($p = 0.04$). For boys, these figures were 22 percent and 13 percent ($p = 0.14$).

Table 5.6 Percentage of children (5–16 years) performing income generating work in the past month

|  | Boys | | | Girls | | |
|---|---|---|---|---|---|---|
|  | N | % | $X^2$ | N | % | $X^2$ |
| **Sex of household head** | | | | | | |
| Male | 364 | 26.7 | | 403 | 21.8 | |
| Female | 43 | 55.8 | <0.001 | 46 | 32.6 | P=0.10 |
| **Educational status of household head** | | | | | | |
| No schooling/can sign name only | 249 | 30.1 | | 249 | 21.7 | |
| 1–5 years of schooling | 116 | 25.9 | | 151 | 25.8 | |
| 6+ years of schooling | 42 | 38.1 | P=0.324 | 48 | 20.8 | P=0.591 |
| **Occupational group** | | | | | | |
| Regular salaried worker | 39 | 23.1 | | 25 | 12.0 | |
| Casual wage worker (skilled) | 25 | 20.0 | | 28 | 17.9 | |
| Casual wage worker (unskilled) | 75 | 38.7 | | 85 | 38.8 | |
| Dependent self-employed | 88 | 32.1 | | 124 | 17.7 | |
| Self-employed | 131 | 32.1 | | 150 | 19.3 | |
| Unemployment/own housework | 31 | 45.2 | <0.067 | 10 | 30.0 | <0.011 |
| **Overall household income last month (Taka)** | | | | | | |
| <2,000 | 64 | 26.7 | | 86 | 20.9 | |
| 2,000–2,499 | 59 | 32.2 | | 60 | 18.3 | |
| 2,500–3,499 | 128 | 26.6 | | 147 | 30.6 | |
| 3,500–4,499 | 65 | 38.5 | | 73 | 19.2 | |
| 4,500+ | 87 | 29.9 | P=0.488 | 79 | 16.5 | P=0.080 |
| **Location of residence** | | | | | | |
| Agargoan | 212 | 29.7 | | 224 | 23.2 | |
| Central Mohammadpur | 120 | 23.3 | | 167 | 22.2 | |
| Beri Badh | 69 | 36.2 | P=0.159 | 56 | 25.0 | P=0.905 |
| **Ever been a shomity member (children aged 8+)** | | | | | | |
| Yes | 12 | 38.8 | | 15 | 34.3 | |
| No | 281 | 66.7 | <0.053 | 283 | 26.7 | P=0.544 |
| N | 409 | | | 449 | | |

There was some evidence to suggest that boys who participate in club activities are more likely to be working than those who do not. The assocation was even stronger when younger children were examined (8–12 years) (28 percent vs 83 percent; $p = 0.004$). No association was apparent for girls. Work may well expose children to opportunities for participating in clubs. Being a member of a club may provide access to credit, social contacts and other resources which facilitate employment. Overall, there was some evidence that factors associated with children's work participation differ for boys and girls suggesting that socio-cultural factors may be important.

For all households children contribute on average around 6 percent of household income. However, when only households which include working children are considered, the contribution of children's income is on average 34 percent. If we consider the somewhat artificial scenario where children's contribution were removed from household income, the percentage below the "poverty line" of Taka 532 per consumption unit per month increases from 19 percent to 25 percent. Among female headed households the increase is more dramatic, from 30 percent to almost 50 percent.

Table 5.7   Children's (aged 5–16 years) contribution to household income

|  | Male headed households | Female headed households | All households |
|---|---|---|---|
| Children's contribution to household income |  |  |  |
| Percent of households with child workers | 20 | 35 | 22 |
| Percent of households where child is the main earner | 4 | 11 | 5 |
| Mean percent of total household income contributed by children (across all households) | 5 | 17 | 6 |
| Mean percent of total income contributed by children (in households where children work) | 30 | 49 | 34 |
| Impact of 'removing' children's contribution to household income |  |  |  |
| Percent of households below the 'poverty line' | 17 | 30 | 19 |
| Percent of households below the 'poverty line' if children's income is removed | 22 | 48 | 25 |

*Note*: Poverty line used here was 518 Taka per month per consumption unit.

Earner:dependency ratio and work days off due to illness were both negatively related to height in children under 16 years of age. Home work due to illness and age in months were positively related to height in children aged under 16 years.

**Table 5.8** Regression analysis for children under 16 years with height as the dependent variable and other economic variables as independent variables

| Variables | B | SE | t | 95 % CI | 95% CI | P |
|---|---|---|---|---|---|---|
| Constant | 62.681 | 6.904 | 9.079 | 48.945 | 76.418 | <0.0001 |
| Savings | -2.0000172 | 0.000 | -0.452 | 0.000 | 0.000 | 0.653 |
| Other expenditure | 6.0000403 | 0.003 | 0.213 | -0.005 | 0.007 | 0.832 |
| Household size | 0.791 | 1.006 | 0.786 | -1.212 | 2.793 | 0.434 |
| Earner: dependency ratio | -2.102 | 1.310 | -1.605 | -4.708 | 2.504 | <0.01 |
| Home work days off due to illness/ month | 0.0807806 | 0.028382 | 2.846 | 0.244 | 0.137 | <0.005 |
| Work days off due to illness/month | -0.0414506 | 0.024087 | -1.721 | -0.892 | 0.0063 | <0.088 |
| Area cluster No | -0.234 | 0.459 | -0.509 | -1.146 | 0.679 | 0.612 |
| Total income per CU | -0.390 | 0.718 | -0.542 | -1.819 | 1.040 | 0.589 |
| Total expenditure per CU | 7.000040 | 0.010 | 0.696 | -0.13 | 0.027 | 0.488 |
| Age in months | 0.544 | 0.051 | 10.715 | 0.443 | 0.645 | <0.0001 |

Number of observations: 450
Prop>F=0.0001 R-squared=0.644

## Discussion

In this study, we have described the nature of child work among the slum households in Dhaka, and we have analysed the association between child work and a series of child welfare considerations. We have also analysed the contribution of child work to the household livelihoods of slum dwellers in Dhaka. Seven percent of boys and 4 percent of girls aged 5–9 years were working for money. Forty-four percent of girls and 47 percent of boys aged 10–14 years were performing income generating work. More working girls and boys came from female headed household. Most boys came from families where there was unemployment; most girls came from families where there was a casual wage worker. There was no difference in educational status of the head of households or income for boys, but for girls the most prevalence of girls working was in households with total income from 2,500 to 3,499 Taka. Most boys and girls were from the area of Beri Badh, but the association was not significant. In female headed households, the impact of removing children's contribution to the household income was 48 percent when children's income was left in, and 30 percent when children's income was left out, which was much more in male headed households. In the regression analysis work, days off due to illness, and the earner:dependency ratio, had a negative effect on the height of children, perhaps because there were more dependants, making income less, and for work days off, less income came into the household. But home work days off due to illness had a positive effect, possibly because there was more mother–child contact.

Many children were working, which is against the UN Convention on the rights of the child. There are numerous problems with the application of the UN Convention on the rights of the child. While there should be openness and sensitivity to particular cultures, this should be combined with an acceptance of the desirability of the quest for a universally applicable standard (Alston, 1994). Human Rights are a moral value towards which people, governments and nations in particular make a greater or lesser commitment. The debate around child labour reveals a great deal, not only on the conceptualisations of "children" and "work", but also on the notion of the "poor" and on what is deemed to be essential for social reproduction. The argument that child labour cannot be eliminated because of poverty provides a very convenient excuse to avoid questioning the very unequal social relations in which children's work is embedded. Child labour has been distinguished from child work, which seems to be appropriate and effective (Boydon, 1990) but child labour is a very confused and ill-conceived notion. One of the problems in conceptualising child labour can be attributed to implicit views and a priori judgement on economic activities and the creation of value. Children's labour falls into the category of productive work in a classic sense. Those who are employed for wages to produce marketable goods in the workshops or factories are the most obvious child labourers, and those who do manual labour or who work as self-employed or dependent self-employed are also child labourers. It can be argued that poor children have a right to work, be recognised for what they do, and earn fair wages. This appeal was made by some working children. To them, labouring was not an issue. Rather, they objected to the humiliation, scorn and various abuses they had to endure from their employers and clients. Girls in particular are often denied the right to work for a wage (Blanchet, 1996).

In conclusion, this chapter examines the determinants of child work in Bangladesh. Nearly half of girls and boys aged 10–14 years were involved in income generating work. More girls and boys who are working came from female headed households. Most boys came from households where there was unemployment. More boys from male headed households went to school, compared to those from female headed households. Girls and boys from the area of Beri Badh had the least percentage attending school, compared to other areas. Thirty percent of female headed households had income below the poverty line, but when children's income was left out, 48 percent of female headed households were below the poverty line, showing that child income was an important part of the household income.

**References**

Alston, P. (1994), *The best Interest of the Child: Reconciling culture and human rights*, UNICEF, International Child Development Centre, Florence and Clarendon Press, Oxford.
Bangladesh Bureau of Statistics (1999), *Statistical Yearbook of Bangladesh*, Government of Bangladesh, Dhaka, Bangladesh.
Blanchet, T. (1996), *Lost Innocence, Stolen Childhoods*, University Press, Dhaka, Bangladesh.
Boydon, J. (1990), 'Child work and Policy Makers: A comparative perspective on the globalisation of childhood', in James, A. and Prout, A. (eds), *Constructing and Reconstructing Childhood*, The Farmer Press, London, New York and Philadelphia.
Cain, M. (1977), 'The economic activities of children in a village in Bangladesh', *Population and Development Studies*, September, pp. 20–28.

Chapter 6

# Female Workforce and the Family

*Using quantitative and qualitative data, factors affecting women working include age, marital status, household head and income status. There were persistent inequalities in women's wages, which were lower than men's wages for similar types of occupation. Among households with female earners, women contributed 34 percent of total income and 58 percent of total work days by women. Fifty three percent of husbands do not allow women to work at all, which supports male control over female labour. This reinforces women's subordination within and outside the household. For example, as well as working full time, women have the responsibility for domestic and child care work.*

**Introduction**

The increasing involvement of women in the paid labour force is likely to have important implications for various dimensions of women's lives, for their own and their family members well-being. The most obvious result of women's work is that it offers the possibility of higher family income and greater diversity of income sources. Women's wages can introduce stability to the income flow into the household and so ensure basic subsistence needs (Kabeer, 1995). Research suggests that women's decision making power within the family increases if they are wage-earning members, and this may have positive implications for women's access to resources and personal well-being (Kabeer, 1995; Standing, 1991; Creevy, 1996; Sharma, 1986).

In Bangladesh, with its strong patriarchal tradition and sharp gender segregation of work and space, we might expect to find women's waged employment having a relatively limited impact on prevailing gender norms. Some changes have occurred in women's roles and their degree of subordination, and that expansion of economic opportunities is largely behind the changes. Rahman (1998) argues that the success of interventions by non-governmental organisations such as Grameen Bank and BRAC is clearly due to their promotion of economic opportunities. However, Amin (1995) contends that we cannot expect widespread changes in the position of women due to the efforts of non governmental organisations. She argues that for the majority of women the available options for economic activity do not challenge the pervasive influence of Islam, and she finds little evidence of changes in women's roles in rural areas. In urban areas, opportunities for poor women to participate in paid employment are far greater, and a number of recent studies have explored the implications of these activities for intra-household power relations. Amin et al. (1997) studied garment factory workers, and argued that young women gain new role and life-stage when they participate in this type of employment prior to marriage. They find evidence of increased independence and access to important networks of information and support among these workers.

However, despite some evidence of change, there seems to be a consensus that when women enter into contractual terms of wage employment, their pattern of life does not undergo radical change (Hossain, Johan and Sobhan, 1990). The available evidence suggests that persistent inequalities within the broader social, economic and political structures, combined with resilient gender hierarchies, reinforce women's subordination within and outside the household.

This chapter describes female participation and factors affecting it, and also examines the women's work inside the home, including time taken to do household work and childcare. We also examined leisure time, fertility levels, family planning used, and the power relations related to women's paid work.

Table 6.1  Percentage of the population performing income generating work by age and gender

| Age Group | Male (%) | N | Female (%) | N | $X^2$ test for male vs. females | P |
|---|---|---|---|---|---|---|
| 5–9 | 7.1 | 198 | 4.2 | 238 | 1.7 | 0.19 |
| 10–14 | 47.3 | 169 | 43.9 | 155 | 0.4 | 0.53 |
| 15–59 | 97.3 | 734 | 49.8 | 837 | 436.8 | <0.001 |
| 60+ | 74.3 | 35 | 31.8 | 22 | 10.0 | <0.002 |
| Total | | 1136 | | 1252 | | |

*Notes*: The definition of the working population used here is the same as used to define the market-orientated labour force: persons in paid employment plus persons engaged in activities on a family farm or in a family enterprise/business that sells some or all of its products. The latter group could include employers, own-account workers, unpaid family workers and members of producer co-operatives (Anker, 1983).

Among girls and boys aged 5–9 and 10–14 years there was no significant difference between levels of boys and girls work participation. However, among the adult population a clear gender differential in work participation was apparent. In the age group 15–59 years, the percentage of men's work participation was nearly twice that of women. Among the age group 60 years or more, the percentage of men work participation was also more than twice that of women, though levels in both genders were lower than among younger adults. Despite the apparent gender differential, the level of work participation among slum women was high for Bangladesh.

**Table 6.2 Percentage of women working by various factors (aged 15 years or more)**

| | Agargaon | Central Mohammadpur | Beri Badh | N | Overall (%) | $X^2$ |
|---|---|---|---|---|---|---|
| **Age Group** | | | | | | |
| 15–24 | 43.4 | 39.6 | 34.2 | 325 | 40.6 | |
| 25–34 | 45.3 | 55.9 | 69.1 | 296 | 53.0 | |
| 35–44 | 53.0 | 67.3 | 76.9 | 146 | 63.0 | |
| 55–64 | 51.5 | 46.2 | 80.0 | 56 | 55.4 | |
| 65+ | 22.2 | 33.3 | 0.0 | 13 | 23.1 | P<0.001 |
| **Marital Status** | | | | | | |
| Unmarried | 89.5 | 83.3 | 80.0 | 48 | 85.4 | |
| Married | 38.8 | 43.9 | 55.8 | 698 | 43.4 | |
| Separated/ divorced | 100.0 | 69.2 | 100.0 | 40 | 90.0 | |
| Widowed | 57.9 | 65.2 | 58.3 | 73 | 60.3 | P<0.001 |
| **Education** | | | | | | |
| None | 46.7 | 48.9 | 66.7 | 43 | 51.4 | |
| Up to Class 5 | 44.1 | 54.3 | 27.8 | 253 | 47.4 | |
| Class 6 & over | 37.5 | 34.4 | 66.7 | 556 | 37.2 | P=0.145 |
| **Household Head** | | | | | | |
| Male headed | 41.8 | 45.4 | 54.3 | 736 | 45.1 | |
| Female headed | 71.2 | 79.0 | 81.5 | 117 | 76.3 | P<0.001 |
| **Household Head & other members** | | | | | | |
| Head of household | 67.7 | 80.8 | 81.8 | 83 | 75.9 | |
| Other Members | 43.6 | 46.6 | 55.6 | 776 | 46.5 | P<0.001 |
| **Household income per CU (Taka)** | | | | | | |
| <400 | 68.0 | 72.7 | 85.3 | 157 | 73.3 | |
| 400–599 | 55.3 | 70.0 | 67.9 | 167 | 62.9 | |
| 600–799 | 39.7 | 53.6 | 44.8 | 153 | 45.8 | |
| 800–1099 | 36.9 | 43.9 | 47.4 | 186 | 41.4 | |
| 1100+ | 30.3 | 25.8 | 27.3 | 190 | 28.4 | P<0.001 |
| **Overall** | 45.6 | 49.2 | 60.3 | 859 | 49.4 | |

Table 6.2 presents information on various factors that affect women working. Women's work participation seems to rise as age increases until age was over 55 years old. The pattern is similar among the three areas. It shows large differentials in working participation by marital status. Unmarried women had a higher work participation than married women, but separated/divorced women had the highest work participation (100 percent in two of the areas surveyed) and widowed women were not so far behind. There was no significant difference in educational status in women's work participation by area.

Female headed households had the highest work participation compared to male headed households, which was similar in each area. Heads of household had the greatest work participation compared to other members. As can be seen from Table 6.2, as income rises the work participation among women goes down, which is similar in each area.

Variation in days and hours worked may in part reflect differing availability of work. It may, however, reflect the fact that women in certain types of occupational category have greater flexibility regarding their working hours and choose to work shorter hours and fewer days than those in other occupational groups. We found that hours worked by regular salaried employment was significantly higher than women in the other occupational categories. For example, women who were in casual unskilled work reported an average of 191.6 hours per month, compared to regular salaried workers who worked 254.1 hours per month (t-test=3.37; p<0.001). Comparing working men and women, men appear to work more days and hours on average. The mean total hours worked in the past month was 198 for men and 182 for women (t-test = 2.70; p <0.007).

The number of leisure days taken in the last month differed among working men and women. Among women, 63 percent did not take any leisure days, compared to men at 52 percent. Men taking 1–10 day leisure was more than women (41 percent of men, compared to 27 percent for women). However, the percentage taking 20–30 day leisure was more among women than among men (3.8 percent for women, and 0.6 percent for men). Men and women in Beri Badh took the least days of leisure compared to the other two areas.

Table 6.3  Mean number of days and hours worked in the past month among working women by occupational category (15 years and above)

| Occupational category | N | Mean days worked per month (SD) | Mean hours worked per month (SD) |
| --- | --- | --- | --- |
| Regular salaried worker (skilled) | 54 | 25.6 (5.4) | 254.1 (87.0) |
| Casual wage worker (skilled) | 15 | 19.4 (11.0) | 84.1 (68.7) |
| Casual wage worker (unskilled) | 260 | 23.5 (7.8) | 191.6 (88.6) |
| Dependent self-employed | 11 | 20.1 (9.7) | 92.5 (70.8) |
| Self-employed | 47 | 20.0 (9.3) | 122.8 (100) |
| Unpaid family worker | 23 | 22.0 (8.3) | 127.7 (82.6) |

**Table 6.4  Daily wage rates for various occupational groups by gender (aged 15 and over)**

|  | Male | | Female | | t-test male vs female mean Taka | |
| --- | --- | --- | --- | --- | --- | --- |
|  | N | Mean (Taka) | N | Mean (Taka) | t | p |
| Occupational group | | | | | | |
| Regular salaried worker | 67 | 105 | 50 | 49 | 3.97 | <0.001 |
| Casual wage worker skilled | 60 | 149 | 13 | 21 | 1.85 | <0.070 |
| Casual wage worker unskilled | 120 | 68 | 237 | 28 | 15.50 | <0.001 |
| Dependent self-employed | 264 | 97 | 11 | 20 | 6.63 | <0.001 |
| Self-employed | 198 | 114 | 42 | 71 | 3.19 | <0.001 |

Table 6.4 illustrates large wage level differentials between different occupational categories, and also between gender. Among men, skilled casual wage workers received the highest wages, whereas among women it was self-employed work which has the highest income. Among occupational groups, females face lower income compared to men, for all occupational categories.

All four members of Khaleda's household started working after they migrated to Dhaka. Khaleda and her 12-year-old daughter. Khaleda gets seven Taka a day and one main meal, while her daughter gets three meals a day and no money. Two sons aged 18 and 25 work as day labourers and receive 70 and 50 Taka per day respectively.

Monir Bapir, was working in an office. His salary was Taka 1,400 per month. This was not enough for his family as he had to pay Taka 900 per month for food to his father-in-law and Taka 400 per month for room rent. Recently, he resigned from his job. Now he pulls a rickshaw for half a day and during the rest of the day he receives driving lessons. His wife works in a garment factory, earning Taka 900 per month. Now he pays rent from his wife's income and food expenditure from his income. The father-in-law bears the cost of his training to ensure a secure future for his daughter.

Alam Mia is the only income-earner of a five-member household. He manages the subsistence of the whole family from his small fish trading business, earning Taka 2,500 per month. During the dry season, he cannot afford to continue his business with his small capital. During that time he pulls a rickshaw, which is very harmful to his health. As a result, his income flows are interrupted and household members usually have to starve. But his wife is allowed to be a maidservant for this time, earning 720 Taka per month.

In 43 percent of households, some income is earned directly by female workers. Among all households, the mean percentage of the total household income earned by women was 14 percent. If we consider only the households which have female workers, then on average 34 percent of the total household income is contributed by female workers. Considering the proportion of household total working days, women's contribution was 31 percent. But if we considered those households where women work, it is 58 percent. These data reflect that women's income is lower than men's, and in households where women work they work longer hours.

**Table 6.5   Mean percentage of total household income and workdays contributed by women to their households**

|  | % | N |
|---|---|---|
| Percentage of households receiving some income from women's work | 43.0 | 731 |
| Mean percentage of total household income from women's work (all households) | 14.3 | 731 |
| Mean percentage of total household income from women's work (among households with female earners) | 33.8 | 315 |
| Mean percentage of total household work days worked by women (all households) | 31.0 | 731 |
| Mean percentage of total household workdays worked by women (among households with female earners) | 58.0 | 357 |

**Table 6.6   Reasons reported for not currently working among wives of male heads**

|  | Percentage of all wives currently not working |
|---|---|
| **Main reason for not working** |  |
| Husband does not allow | 38.3 |
| Small child to care for | 26.9 |
| Busy with own household work | 16.1 |
| Own illness/injury | 9.1 |
| Other reasons combined | 9.6 |
| **Would your husband allow you to work?** |  |
| No, not at all | 53.4 |
| Yes, if at home | 11.4 |
| Yes, if respectable | 13.1 |
| Yes, if salary is good | 9.4 |
| Yes, unconditionally | 10.1 |
| Other/ unsure | 2.6 |
| N=298 |  |

Table 6.6 presents findings which support the picture of male control over female labour force participation. Among all wives of male headed households who were not working at the time of interview, almost 40 percent gave their husband's objection as their main reason for not working. When asked, "Would your husband allow you to work?", over half said that he would not under any circumstances. It is perfectly reasonable and natural for a husband to forbid his wife to work if he so chooses. This control over women's participation appears to be motivated by concerns regarding the status of the family and a desire to have a well-maintained household, a responsibility which is firmly placed within the female sphere.

Ful Mia is physically weak and cannot do labour-intensive work. His household gets its main income from his cake business. When his business is doing badly, usually during the hot season when demand is low, he is often forced to consume his capital. When this happens he sends his wife, Ruby, to work as a brick-breaker or a day labourer or to beg for a few days in order to raise the capital to start the business again. Ful Mia only allows Ruby to work outside the home in such emergencies when there is no other option open.

Akari managed to start a business in the slum after she was made destitute by her second husband. Later she remarried again and her new husband tried to stop her from doing business as it lowered his prestige. She stopped for a while but started again when he failed to earn the money required for the household to maintain its subsistence.

Hashem Mollah, a vegetable seller, was unable to walk a lot to sell his items due to his old age. On the other hand, it was not possible for his wife to go out for work as there were no other members to do the household work. Then she found a job, which she could do at home. She started cooking for some boarding house members from where she was able to supplement the household expenditure.

During his work, Harun, a painter, accidentally lost his eyesight and became jobless. Consequently, he agreed that the rest of the family, including his mother, Maya, and his sister who was only 13 years old, become involved in the garments trade to maintain their livelihoods.

Yasmin had been working in a garments factory for five years. After her marriage, her husband forbade her to work, as he would support the household.

Abul migrated one year ago and pulled a rickshaw. Since his income was not enough he tried to find work for his wife in a garments factory, but failed as he had no connections with people who could help her with that opportunity.

Delwar has more than one job. At night he works as a security guard and in the afternoon he pulls a rickshaw. His sister is a maidservant. By working hard he is saving money to get trained as a car driver. After getting a job as a car driver, he will no longer send his sister to work.

Working women were less likely than non-working women to perform domestic tasks every day, and were more likely to receive help for domestic tasks compared to non-working women. Over 60 percent of working women perform domestic tasks apart from shopping for food and washing men's clothing.

**Table 6.7** Percentage of women reporting that they perform household tasks and women reporting that they had received help

|  | Percent of women performing every day | | | Percent of women receiving help | | |
|---|---|---|---|---|---|---|
|  | Worker (n=249) | Non-worker (n=317) | $X^2$ p | Worker (n=249) | Non-worker (n=317) | $X^2$ p |
| Food distribution | 81 | 93 | <0.001 | 32 | 15 | <0.001 |
| Cooking | 77 | 93 | <0.001 | 37 | 17 | <0.001 |
| Food preparation | 74 | 94 | <0.001 | 41 | 25 | <0.001 |
| Washing utensils | 70 | 90 | <0.001 | 40 | 20 | <0.001 |
| Cleaning | 68 | 89 | <0.001 | 41 | 19 | <0.001 |
| Water collection | 66 | 88 | <0.001 | 51 | 34 | <0.001 |
| Washing female/children's clothing | 64 | 74 | <0.003 | 31 | 17 | <0.001 |
| Shopping (food) | 39 | 40 | 0.193 | 73 | 74 | 0.165 |
| Washing male clothing | 18 | 32 | <0.001 | 64 | 59 | 0.356 |
| Washing baby | 73 | 98 | <0.001 | 37 | 8 | <0.001 |
| Feeding baby | 82 | 98 | <0.001 | 52 | 15 | <0.001 |
| Washing a child | 60 | 98 | <0.001 | 40 | 50 | <0.001 |
| Feeding a child | 68 | 98 | <0.001 | 91 | 63 | <0.001 |

Child care was predominantly provided by women. Working women were less likely to do child care compared to non-working women. Working women received more help in child care compared to non-working women. Nevertheless, over 70 percent of working women provided child care every day.

Table 6.8   Child death and family planning by gender

| Variables | Female Mean and sd and numbers | Male Mean and sd and numbers | P |
|---|---|---|---|
| Child deaths Months age of age | 7.41 (5.05) 131 | 5.70 (4.37) 91 | <0.0076 |
| Currently using family planning Yes No | 292 285 | 293 232 | <0.084 |

Table 6.8 provides information on child deaths in this population. Child deaths were higher among girls than among boys. The similar family planning strategies indicate that the differential was not related to whether the births were planned or unplanned.

**Discussion**

Slum households tend to be asset-poor and the opportunities for income generating work are few. In spite of attempts to diversify income sources, most households rely entirely on wage or self-employment of their members in the past month (Pryer et al., 2002). Table 6.8 provides information on child deaths in this population. Child deaths were higher among girls than boys. The similar family planning strategies indicate that the differential was not related to whether the births were planned or unplanned.

Given this heavy reliance on exchange of labour, the number, age, sex and skill of household members available to participate in the workforce will have important implications for the level and security of the income flow into the household.

Overall among slum women aged 15 and above, 49 percent are engaged in earning work, which is very high for Bangladesh. In Bangladesh as a whole, 16 percent of women are categorised as "workers". The urban female employment rate is higher at 29 percent compared to the national rate, but far lower than men's employment rate at 72 percent (BBS, 1996). Despite the gender gap, female employment has shown surprisingly rapid growth in recent years, particularly in the garment factories. Employers in the garment factories discriminated positively in favour of women, in hiring if not in promotions or wages. It has been argued that women are actually more productive than men in certain jobs because of their "nimble fingers" (Stichter, 1990). Area analysis revealed that Beri Badh differs in employment to the other two areas. In Beri Badh manual labour is the most common occupation, compared to domestic service and garment factory workers which are more common in central Mohammapur and Agargoan (S. Rahman, 1998).

Variations in female employment levels and patterns are affected by complex combinations of economic and demographic variables. For example, more women work when income is low; 73 percent compared to 29 percent in the highest income group. In female headed households 76 percent of women work compared to 45 percent of women in male headed households. Female headed households are poorer and more vulnerable (Pryer et al., 2002). Unmarried women are more likely to work than married women, presumably because of their household work responsibilities which are onerous, and because of the gender norms. The observance of these norms grants status and prestige (White, 1992; Amin, 1995). Among the poor of Dhaka, it is clear that women's work participation continues to be considered a sign of poverty and incurs a loss of prestige for the family as a whole. Women's work involves not only a contravening of gender norms, but also implies that the husband has an inability to fulfil his responsibility as a rice winner for the family. This picture is supported by a number of studies among female garment factory workers in urban Bangladesh (Amin et al., 1997; Kibria, 1996; Paul-Majamber and Zohir, 1994). Disapproval of this shift in roles and responsibilities was expressed by men during the present qualitative fieldwork:

> In the village a woman respects her husband but in the city they do not. Often it depends on the husband as well. Some of them want to eat the earnings of their wives and just sit by watching. They are lazy or have bad habits.

The overall level of pay indicates that women are severely disadvantaged. The average monthly income of men was Taka 2,073 compared to just Taka 686 for women. The lower earnings of women is partly due to their shorter hours spent on income generating work. However, when daily rates are compared, women's earnings are still significantly lower than men's, although in households where women work they contributed 34 percent of household income, and 58 percent of total working days in households where women work.

A number of researchers have emphasised the potential costs of maternity and childcare as an important factor in employer discrimination against women. Considering women's family status, it is important to distinguish daughters and childless single women on the one hand from married mothers on the other, since the former are the only ones who do not threaten to cost employers more than men.

Reasons for leaving their jobs are married women who intend to have children or are already pregnant, and the desire to give better attention to children and home. In this case women almost without exception opt for this course of action in response to pressures from the male partner who urges them to leave their job in order to give full time to their homes, which is considered their "normal" or "proper" role.

In contrast, women who are pregnant and are still in their jobs, particularly in the garment industry, are told to leave without notice.

> Yasmin had been working in a garment factory for five years. After her marriage she became pregnant, but she still wanted to continue her work. Because she was pregnant her employment was terminated without notice.

It is striking that employment of young single women fits in so well with the needs of families who are dependent on high fertility reproductive strategy and multiple wage earners by household members. This strategy comes about in the context of low prevailing wages for men and women and low levels of skills (Sticher, 1991).

Domestic work, including childcare, was carried out by women. Working women were less likely to do domestic work compared to non-working women. However, over 60 percent of working women perform domestic work every day, compared to over 80 percent of non-working women. Childcare every day was undertaken by over 70 percent of working women compared to nearly 100 percent of non-working women.

In Bangladesh the national male infant morality is more than females (98 per 1000 live births compared to 91 per 1000 life births for male and females respectively) However in the urban slums the male infant mortality is lower than among females (123 per 1000 live births compared to 146 per 1000 live births, for males and females respectively) (BBS, 1996; Urban Surveillance System, ICDDR,B). We have the same results in our sample: more girls died than among boys from birth to one year old.

## Conclusions

Factors affecting women working include age, marital status, household head and income status. Also, persistent inequalities in women's wages, which were lower than men's wages for similar types of occupation. Among households with female earners, women contributed 34 percent of total income and 58 percent of total work days by women. Fifty three percent of husbands do not allow women to work at all, which supports male control over female labour. This reinforces women's subordination within and outside the household. For example, as well as working full time, women have the responsibility for domestic and childcare work.

## References

Amin, S. (1995), 'The poverty–purdah trap in rural Bangladesh: implications for women's roles in the family', Working Papers No. 75, Population Council Research Division, New York.

Amin, S., Diamond, I., Naved, R. and Newby, M. (1997), 'Transition to adulthood of female factory workers: some evidence from Bangladesh', Working Paper No. 102, Population Council Research Division, New York.

Anker, R. (1983), 'Female labour force participation in developing countries: a critique of current definitions and data collection methods', *International Labour Review* 122 (6), pp. 709–723.

Bangladesh Bureau of Statistics (1996), *Statistical year Book of Bangladesh*, Government of Bangladesh, Dhaka, Bangladesh.

Creevy, I. (1996), *Changing women's lives and work*, UNIFEM, Intermediate Technology, London.

Hossain, H., Johan, R. and Sobhan, S. (1990), *No better option? Industrial women workers in Bangladesh*, University Press, Dhaka, Bangladesh.

Kabeer, N. (1995), *Reversed realities: Gender Hierarchies in Development Thought*, Verso, London and New York.

Kibria, N. (1996), 'Culture, social class and income control in the lives of women garment factory workers in Bangladesh', *Gender and Society* 9(3), pp. 289–309.

Paul-Majamber, P. and S. Chaudhuri Zohir (1994), 'Dynamics of wage employment: a case of employment in the garment industry', *The Bangladesh Development Studies*, 22(2&3), pp. 197–216.

Pryer, J.A., Rogers, S., Normand, C. and Rahman, A. (2002), 'Livelihoods, nutrition and health in Dhaka slums', *Public Health Nutrition*, 5(5), pp. 613–618.

Rahman, H.Z. (1998), 'Poverty issues in Bangladesh: a strategic review', Report commissioned by Department for International Development, UK.

Rahman, S. (1998), 'Levels and characteristics of female participation in work, among the urban poor in Dhaka', Urban Livelihoods Study Working Paper 1, Institute for Development Policy Analysis and Advocacy, Proshika, Dhaka, Bangladesh.

Sharma, U. (1986), *Women's work, class and the urban household*, Tavistock Publications, London.

Standing, H. (1991), *Dependence and Autonomy*, Routledge, London.

Stichter, S. (1990), 'Women, Employment and the family: current debates', in Stichter, S., Parpart, J.L. (eds), *Women, Employment and the Family in the International Division of Labour*, Macmillan, London.

White, S. (1992), *Arguing with the Crocodile: gender and class in Bangladesh*, University Press, Dhaka, Bangladesh.

Chapter 7

# Investing in Health

*In this chapter we examine the period prevalence of illness in the study population. Children under five had the highest period prevalence of illness, followed by female adults. Beri Badh had the highest period prevalence compared to other areas. Over 80 percent of households reported at least one adult member ill over the previous 14 days. Female adults had a higher period prevalence of illness than male adults, and female heads had a higher period prevalence of fever, abdominal pain and any illness compared with male household heads. Female earners also had a higher prevalence of illness compared to male earners. The likely impact of the high rates of adult ill health and the factors affecting observed gender differentials are discussed.*

## Introduction

Ill health is frequently considered a characteristic of poverty. Poor nutrition, inadequate sanitation and water, and insufficient access to health-care are identified in many studies as the underlying causal factors responsible for ill health. Wratten (1995) identifies increased health risks as a special characteristic of urban poverty and draws attention to the spatial juxtaposition of industrial and residential functions, crowded living conditions, inadequate provision of basic amenities, and ineffective pollution control and accident prevention. In the urban settings of developing countries the combined effect of old pathogens and new health risks, including environmental pollution and stress, means that disease burdens are particularly high among the poor. The very poor living conditions and high levels of morbidity have been highlighted in the case of large and rapidly growing cities, like Dhaka (Brockerhoff and Brennan, 1997). As can be seen from Table 7.1, although urban populations overall have lower rates for infant, child and adult mortality, compared with rural populations, the urban poor suffer very high rates indeed compared with either group.

**Table 7.1   Major health indicators for rural and urban populations in Bangladesh**

| Indicator | Unit | Urban | Rural | Total | Urban Poor |
|---|---|---|---|---|---|
| Neo-natal mortality rate | per 1000 live births | 41.0 | 63.0 | 59.0 | – |
| Infant mortality rate | per 1000 live births | 61.0 | 88.0 | 84.0 | 180 |
| Child mortality rate | per 1000 (1 to 4 years) | 8.0 | 12.6 | 12.6 | 114 |
| Crude death rate | per 1000 population | 7.2 | 9.8 | 9.2 | 43.6 |
| Crudebirth rate | per 1000 population | 22.1 | 30.0 | 28.4 | 39.3 |
| Life Expectancy | In 1993 | 60.6 | 56.9 | 57.0 | – |

*Source*: Rahman, 1998 and BBS, 1994.

## Methods

Morbidity measures can be classified either as observed or self-perceived. Observed morbidity (medically defined morbidity) is the assessment by a clinician or other investigators of illness using an examination or a test. Observed morbidity can be classified into four categories: physical sign, physiological or pathological indicator, functional test and clinical diagnosis. Self-perceived morbidity is reported by people about their own illness. If a person says, "I am ill", then by definition he or she is ill. Self-perceived measures of morbidity can be grouped into symptoms, functional disabilities and handicap. It may also be used to assess people's reported utilisation of health services.

It is not possible to say which of these two methods of measuring morbidity is more correct, but there has been a considerable debate as to which is more useful to planners of health services. The proponents of medically defined morbidity argue that this is an objective measure, since it will not be influenced by inter-subject variation, as would self-perceived morbidity. Advocates of medically defined morbidity also tend to appreciate the value of professional diagnosis, over a lay person's opinion. On the other hand, the proponents of self-perceived morbidity argue that, unless the subjects perceive they have a problem, any morbidity will not lead to a demand for health care. Furthermore, it is relatively easy to incorporate questions about health services, either for curative or preventive care, into the questionnaire of health interview survey. In general, surveys of subject perceived morbidity are easier to organise and less costly than surveys of medically defined morbidity, since lay interviewers can be used rather than physicians, and surveys do not need any expensive diagnostic equipment (Ross and Vaughan, 1986; Kroeger, 1983). This project adopted the self-perceived method for morbidity measurement. The illnesses were translated into all possible local terminology of illness in this population.

In this chapter we describe the prevalence of illness in children and adults. Relatively little attention has been paid to adult ill health in such populations

(Feachem et al., 1992). We include a range of analyses including an examination of relationships between adult ill health, household position, occupation, education and area of residence.

## Results

Table 7.2 represents self reported 14 day period prevalence of various illnesses and injury among age groups. Overall, the prevalence of illness was very high. In all age groups, over 40 percent of individuals reported some kind of illness. Among children cough and cold and diarrhoea were the two most commonly reported. In all other age groups cough and cold and fever stand out as the most important illnesses. The broad category of other illnesses also account for a large proportion of illnesses among adults and the elderly.

**Table 7.2 Self reported illness and injury (14 day period prevalence) by broad population categories and gender**

|  | Children (0–4) % | | Older children (5–14) % | | Adult (15–64) % | | Elderly (65+) % | |
|---|---|---|---|---|---|---|---|---|
|  | M | F | M | F | M | F | M | F |
| Diarrhoea | 28.0 | 20.6 | 7.6 | 7.6 | 3.6 | 3.4 | 0.0 | 8.3 |
| Cough & cold | 38.8 | 40.1 | 11.6 | 13.3 | 18.9 | 18.9 | 38.1 | 8.3 |
| Fever | 19.8 | 21.0 | 13.6 | 15.6 | 20.7 | 27.3 | 33.3 | 0.0 |
| Headache | 1.9 | 3.1 | 7.7 | 5.7 | 17.4 | 27.1 | 23.8 | 8.3 |
| Abdominal pain | 4.1 | 3.5 | 4.3 | 5.2 | 7.1 | 9.7 | 9.5 | 8.3 |
| Injury | 1.2 | 0.8 | 4.0 | 0.5 | 2.6 | 2.0 | 0.0 | 0.0 |
| Other illnesses | 10.3 | 13.7 | 6.0 | 11.2 | 12.8 | 23.3 | 18.4 | 19.0 |
| Any illness | 63.8 | 65.0 | 40.4 | 41.5 | 52.4 | 65.9 | 53.8 | 46.2 |
| N | 268 | 257 | 353 | 384 | 720 | 833 | 21 | 12 |

*Notes*: M = male; F = female.

Table 7.3 shows fever was the most common illness in adults in Central Mohammadpur and Beri Badh. In Agargoan headache was the most common illness. Cough and cold was significantly different by area, with Beri Badh faring the worse. The was no significant difference in the prevalence of abdominal pain by area, although Agargoan suffered the worse. There was, however, a significant difference for other illness, with Agargoan suffering the most compared to the other areas.

**Table 7.3  Self reported illness (14 day period prevalence) among adults (15–64) by area**

|  | Agargoan | | Central Mohammadpur | | Beri Badh | | P |
|---|---|---|---|---|---|---|---|
|  | M | F | M | F | M | F |  |
| Fever | 19.8 | 26.0 | 20.6 | 26.5 | 22.5 | 33.0 | NS |
| Headache | 18.6 | 28.6 | 15.7 | 26.2 | 19.1 | 25.4 | NS |
| Cough & cold | 16.8 | 16.6 | 18.9 | 17.6 | 28.1 | 28.8 | <0.001 |
| Abdominal pain | 8.9 | 10.9 | 5.2 | 8.6 | 6.7 | 8.5 | NS |
| Other illness | 15.6 | 29.4 | 10.1 | 19.3 | 10.1 | 13.6 | <0.001 |
| Any illness | 54.0 | 68.8 | 50.4 | 62.3 | 52.8 | 67.0 | NS |
| N | 339 | 385 | 287 | 324 | 89 | 118 |  |

*Note*: M = male; F = female. NS= Not significant at $p<0.05$.

Table 7.4 shows self reported illness among adults by gender, and other factors. Fever was the most common illness. Around 24 percent of the adult population reported having fever over the last 14 days. About 23 percent and 9 percent complained of headache and abdominal pain, respectively. Sixty percent reported some kind of illness over the previous 14 days. Disaggregated by gender, males had the greater prevalence of fever compared with females ($p<0.01$), and females had the greater prevalence of headaches compared with men ($p<0.001$). There was no significant difference in abdominal pain by gender, but overall illness was significantly different by gender with females having a higher prevalence than males.

### Table 7.4  Self reported illness by gender and other factors

|  | Fever | Headache | Pain in Abdomen | Any Illness | N |
|---|---|---|---|---|---|
| **Sex** | | | | | |
| Male | 20.7** | 17.4*** | 7.1 | 52.4** | 720 |
| Female | 27.3 | 27.1 | 9.7 | 65.9 | 833 |
| **Relation with Head** | | | | | |
| Male Head | 21.6 | 18.0 | 7.4 | 54.6 | 584 |
| Female Head | 44.9*** | 29.2 | 4.5* | 79.8** | 89 |
| Wife of male Head | 27.3 | 27.8 | 11.7 | 67.6 | 616 |
| Children, both sexes | 15.4 | 16.5 | 5.5 | 43.0 | 182 |
| Male, other relation | 12.5 | 31.3 | 3.1 | 43.8 | 32 |
| Female, other relation | 20.0 | 18.0 | 4.0 | 54.0 | 50 |
| **Main Occupation** | | | | | |
| Income earner, male | 20.6** | 17.6*** | 6.8 | 52.2 | 693 |
| Income earner, female | 28.0 | 27.3 | 7.5 | 66.2 | 411 |
| Own house work | 26.6 | 27.3 | 12.1 | 66.4 | 414 |
| Jobless | 33.3 | 5.6 | 16.7 | 61.1 | 18 |
| **Education** | | | | | |
| No education | 26.1 | 24.9 | 8.1 | 62.0* | 578 |
| Can sign | 27.1 | 23.9 | 9.1 | 62.9 | 396 |
| Up to 5 years of schooling | 19.9 | 21.3 | 9.9 | 57.4 | 411 |
| 6–12 years of schooling | 22.1 | 15.6 | 4.6 | 50.7 | 154 |
| **Involvement in social organisations** | | | | | |
| Proshika | 22.2 | 22.2 | 14.8 | 66.7 | 54 |
| Other organisations (NGO and local) | 26.7 | 20.4 | 7.9 | 62.8 | 191 |
| No involvement | 23.9 | 23.1 | 8.3 | 59.0 | 1291 |
| Overall percent | 24.2 | 22.7 | 8.5 | 59.6 | |

*Notes*: * <0.05; ** <0.001 $X^2$ was done for male versus female, female head versus male head, male earner versus female earner, and all groups in the education category.

Female headed households had a higher prevalence of fever and also for any illness compared to male headed households. Wives in male headed households had a higher prevalence of pain in the abdomen compared to female headed households.

Female earners had a higher prevalence of fever and headache compared to the male earners. Those with no education had a higher prevalence of illness than those with more education, but there was no relationship between prevalence of illness and involvement in social organisations.

As Table 7.5 shows, female adults reported more days off sick due to illness than males, with this common to fever, headache and other illnesses, but not abdominal pain for which more days off were reported by males than females.

Table 7.5  Reported number of days (mean and standard deviation) suffered by the adult population over the last 14 days due to fever, headache, abdominal pain and other illnesses by gender

| | Mean number of days suffering (SD) | | | |
|---|---|---|---|---|
| | Male Adult | N | Female Adult | N |
| Fever | 4.7 (3.2) | 149 | 5.0 (3.5) | 227 |
| Headache | 3.8 (3.1) | 125 | 4.0 (3.3) | 226 |
| Pain in Abdomen | 6.9 (5.1) | 51 | 5.4 (4.8) | 81 |
| Other Illness | 8.5 (4.9) | 91 | 9.1 (4.7) | 194 |

Table 7.6  Household's adult illness by headship and poverty line

| Characteristics of illness of household adults | Male headed household | Female headed household | Households above the poverty line | Households below the poverty line |
|---|---|---|---|---|
| At least one adult member reported sick | 82.1 | 81.9 | 81.4 | 82.4 |
| Fifty percent and more adult members reported as sick over the last 14 days | 74.2 | 75.9 | 76.3 | 74.3 |
| Percentage of health expenditure as percent of total income | 4.0 | 4.8 | 3.4 | 6.2 |

**Table 7.7  Logistic regression of prevalence of reported illness with sociodemographic characteristics of adult both sexes and female adults**

| | Adult (both sexes) | | | | Adult Female | | | |
|---|---|---|---|---|---|---|---|---|
| | Unadjusted | | Adjusted | | Unadjusted | | Adjusted | |
| | Odds ratio | P | Odds ratio | P | Odds ratio | P | Odds ratio | p |
| Sex | | | | | | | | |
| Male | 1 | | 1 | | | | | |
| Female | 1.75 | 0.0001 | 2.0 | 0.0001 | | | | |
| Head Sex | | | | | | | | |
| Male Headed | 1 | | 1 | | | | | |
| Female Headed | 3.22 | 0.0001 | 3.01 | 0.03 | | | | |
| Age Group | | | | | | | | |
| 15–24 | 1 | | 1 | | 1 | | 1 | |
| 25–44 | 1.51 | 0.0001 | 1.66 | 0.0001 | 1.8 | 0.0001 | 1.69 | 0.002 |
| 45–64 | 1.57 | 0.010 | 1.76 | 0.003 | 2.2 | 0.006 | 2.01 | 0.023 |
| Location | | | | | | | | |
| Agargoan | 1 | | 1 | | 1 | | 1 | |
| Central M'Pur | 0.81 | 0.05 | 0.91 | 0.50 | 0.75 | 0.07 | 0.79 | 0.577 |
| Beri Badh | 0.96 | 0.79 | 0.89 | 0.51 | 0.91 | 0.70 | 0.85 | 0.548 |
| Marital Status | | | | | | | | |
| Unmarried | 1 | | 1 | | 1 | | 1 | |
| Married | 2.19 | 0.0001 | 1.33 | 0.18 | 1.97 | 0.029 | 1.29 | 0.65 |
| Divorced/ Widow/ Separated | 3.25 | 0.0001 | 1.34 | 0.35 | 2.36 | 0.021 | 1.19 | 0.52 |
| Working status | | | | | | | | |
| Worker | 1 | | 1 | | 1 | | 1 | |
| Non-worker | 1.3 | 0.02 | 1.1 | 0.5 | 0.89 | 0.44 | 0.92 | 0.63 |

*Note*:   Adjusted for cluster sampling.

Over 80 percent of households reported at least one adult member sick and in over 70 percent of households at least half of the adult members had been ill in the previous 14 days. Expenditure on health as a proportion of income was about 4 percent, but expenditure on health as a proportion of total income in households below the poverty line was almost double that in households above the poverty line (Table 7.6).

Table 7.7 describes the odds ratios for reported illness. For adults of both sexes, females had a significantly higher odds ratio for reported illness, compared to males which stayed significant when adjusted. Similarly, female headed households had the highest odds ratio for reported illness compared to male headed households which remained significant when adjusted. The older ages, ages 5–22 years and 45–64 years had higher odds ratios for reported illness compared to the younger age group, which remained significant when adjusted. The same result by age was found for female adults. Central Mohaddapur had higher odds ratio for prevalence of reported illness compared to Agargoan, which was significant only until adjusted. Married, divorced, widowed or separated people had higher odds ratios for prevalence of reported illness than unmarried people, but when this was adjusted the results were no longer significant. There was no significant association between working status and prevalence of illness, after adjustment.

Table 7.8 describes logistic regression for the prevalence of reported cough and cold and fever. There was no association between prevalence of cough and cold by gender. There was an association by age group though; 45–64 years had the highest odds ratio for prevalence of cough and cold, compared to younger age groups. However, when this was adjusted, this association was no longer significant. There were also significant differences between areas. Beri Badh had the highest odds ratio for prevalence of cough and cold, compared to other areas, and this remains significant when adjusted. There was no significant association between working status and prevalence of cough and cold. Regarding fever, there was a significant result by gender: female odds ratio for the prevalence of fever was higher than in males, which stayed significant when adjusted. There was also a significant result by age group. 45–65 years had the highest odds ratio for prevalence of fever compared to younger age groups, which remained significant when adjusted. There were no significant differences in the prevalence of fever by area or by working status.

## Discussion

In the 1960s, demographers showed the horrifying magnitude of death rates in childhood in developing countries. Epidemiologists showed that the majority of deaths were attributable to a short list of communicable diseases superimposed upon a background of low birth weight, malnutrition, and environmental squalor. This led to strategies to improve children's health by immunising against selected diseases, reducing exposure to environmental and behavioural risk factors. Development organisations have concentrated their efforts on tropical health and children's health, as well as maternal health. Governments of developing countries, while emphasising the overall development of health services, have tended to target these same areas through special programmes. This strong focus has been both appropriate and effective. As a result, the rates of child death in developing countries has been greatly reduced (Feachem et al., 1992).

**Table 7.8    Logistic regression of prevalence of reported cough and cold and fever with socio-demographic characteristics of adults**

|  | Cough & Cold | | | | Fever | | | |
|---|---|---|---|---|---|---|---|---|
|  | Unadjusted | | Adjusted | | Unadjusted | | Adjusted | |
|  | Odds ratio | P | Odds ratio | P | Odds ratio | P | Odds ratio | P |
| Sex | | | | | | | | |
| Male | 1 | | 1 | | 1 | | 1 | |
| Female | 0.99 | 0.97 | 0.91 | 0.57 | 1.43 | 0.003 | 1.64 | 0.001 |
| Age Group | | | | | | | | |
| 15–24 | 1 | | 1 | | 1 | | 1 | |
| 25–44 | 1.25 | 0.139 | 1.18 | 0.31 | 1.3 | 0.058 | 1.26 | 0.122 |
| 45–64 | 1.52 | 0.049 | 1.28 | 0.27 | 1.44 | 0.066 | 1.52 | 0.056 |
| Location | | | | | | | | |
| Agargoan | 1 | | 1 | | 1 | | 1 | |
| Central M'Pur | 1.1 | 0.712 | 1.15 | 0.38 | 1.04 | 0.775 | 1.12 | 0.43 |
| Beri Badh | 1.98 | 0.0001 | 2.04 | 0.0001 | 1.33 | 0.108 | 1.31 | 0.14 |
| Working Status | | | | | | | | |
| Worker | 1 | | 1 | | | | 1 | 1 |
| Non-worker | 0.95 | 0.70 | 1.12 | 0.53 | | 1.13 | 0.96 | 0.824 |

*Note*:   Adjusted for cluster sampling.

In this study, children under 5 years had the most prevalence of diarrhoea (25 percent) and upper respiratory illness (40 percent) compared to older children (7.6 percent and 12.5 percent). The total period prevalence of any illness for children under 5 years was 64 percent which was more than older children (41 percent). Diarrhoeal morbidity is a severe problem in all ages, but particularly in young children. Diarrhoeal disease is the largest cause of death among children under five years of age (Hoque and Hoque, 1994). Risk for diarrhoea is greater through flooding, and when dirty water was used for drinking. Poverty is the main cause of diarrhoeal disease because of lack of clean water and sanitation (Emach, 1999). The highest prevalence of upper respiratory illness was in children under five. The highest prevalence was in children aged 18–23 months followed by infants aged 6–11 months. Socio-economic variables were not associated with prevalence of upper respiratory illness. The rates were higher in the monsoon and pre-winter months (Zaman et al., 1997).

In this study we were particularly interested in the prevalence of adult ill health. The prevalence of adult ill health is substantial, larger than had been supposed previously. In this study over 80 percent of households reported at least one adult member ill over the previous 14 days and three quarters reported at least half of all household members ill over the previous 14 days. Adults comprise the majority of the labour force and inevitably ill health in adults will have a deleterious effect on productivity and wealth. Adults are the ones on whom other family members depend on and ill health in wage earners and carers will have direct and indirect adverse effects for families as well as for communities. The situation is likely to be most serious in the households where adult earners depend on physical work for wages and have few resources to mitigate the effects of income loss. The effects attributable to adult ill health are likely to be substantial. The effects are difficult to measure. Not only will there be directly observable changes in household economics, but also more subtle changes in labour patterns, which may partially mitigate the adverse effects of adult ill health on the household, but with associated costs. These issues are covered in greater depth in Chapters 8 and 9.

More women reported illness in the preceding 14 days than men. The gender differences in this study are common to findings in many others (Hibbard and Pope, 1996; Wingard et al., 1989; Macintyre et al., 1999).

So are women sicker than men, or are they more likely to report sickness? A number of factors should be considered, including biological risks, risks associated through social roles and illness behaviour, differential access to healthcare treatment and use. Nevertheless higher reported rates of illness and health service use among women are commonly seen to be explicable in terms of gender differences in the way symptoms are perceived, evaluated, and acted upon. Such sex differences are thought to occur as a result of childhood socialisation as well as adult role expectation and obligation. Women may report more illness and adopt the sick role more readily because their roles allow them to pay more attention to symptoms and take curative action. In addition, women's greater responsibilities for their family's health may increase the salience of health matters. The social acceptability of admitting illness, discussing symptoms and seeking help also seem to differ for men and women. At an early age, men are socialised to be stoic and self-reliant, whereas women learn that it is acceptable to seek help. Because of menstruation, child birth, lactation and the menopause, women learn to attend to bodily cues and changes. The work of Kesserler et al. (1981) suggests that women may simply recognise and interpret changes and cues and symptoms more readily than men (Hibbard and Pope, 1986).

In conclusion, children under five had the highest period prevalence compared to female adults. Beri Badh had the highest period prevalence compared to other areas. Over 80 percent of households reported at least one adult member ill over the previous 14 days and three quarters reported at least half of all household members ill over the previous 14 days. Adults comprise the majority of the labour force and inevitably ill health in adults will have a deleterious effect on productivity and wealth. Female adults had a higher period prevalence than male adults did and female household heads had a higher prevalence of fever, abdominal pain and any illness, compared with male household heads. In this study we measured morbidity and suspect that these gender differentials are explained, at least in part, by differences in the way symptoms are perceived, evaluated and acted upon by different sexes.

## References

Bangladesh Bureau of Statistics (1996), *Statistical Year Book of Bangladesh*, Government of Bangladesh, Dhaka, Bangladesh.

Brockerhoff, M., Brennan, E. (1997), 'The poverty of cities in the developing world', Population Council Research Division, Working Paper No. 96, Population Council, New York.

Emach, M. (1999), 'Diarrhoeal disease risk in Matlab, Bangladesh', *Social Science and Medicine*, 49, pp. 519–530.

Feachem, R.G.A., Kjellstrom, T., Murray, C.J.L., Over, M. and Phillips, M.A. (1992), *The Health of Adults in the Developing World*, Oxford University Press, Oxford.

Hibbard, J.H., Pope, C.R. (1986), 'Gender roles and illness orientation and use of medical services', *Social Science and Medicine*, 17, pp. 129–137.

Hoque, B.A., Hoque, M.M. (1994), 'Environment and Health', in Rahman, A.A., Huq, S., Haider, R. and Jansen, E.G. (eds), *Environment and Development in Bangladesh*, University Press, Dhaka, Bangladesh.

Kesserler, R.C., Brown, R.L. and Browan, C.L. (1981), 'Sex differences in psychiatric help-seeking: evidence from four large scale surveys', *Journal of Health and Social Behaviour*, 22, pp. 49–64.

Kroeger, A. (1983), 'Health interview surveys in developing countries: a review of methods and results', *International Journal of Epidemiology*, 12(4), pp. 465–81.

Macintyre, S., Ford, G. and Hunt, K. (1999), 'Do women over-report morbidity? Men's and women's responses to structured prompting on a standard question on long standing illness', *Social Science and Medicine*, 48, pp. 89–98.

Rahman, A. (1998), 'Adult morbidity and its impact on livelihoods of the urban poor in Bangladesh', Urban Livelihoods Study Working Paper 2, Institute for Development Policy Analysis and Advocacy, Proshika, Dhaka, Bangladesh.

Ross, D.A. and Vaughan, J.P. (1986), 'Health interview surveys in developing countries: a methodological review', *Studies of Family Planning*, 17(2), pp. 78–94.

Wingard, D.L., Cohn, B.A., Kaplan, G.A., Cirillo, P.M. and Cohen, R.D. (1989), 'Sex differentials in morbidity and mortality risks examined by age and cause in the same cohort', *American Journal of Epidemiology*, 130(3), pp. 601–610.

Wratten, E. (1995), 'Conceptualizing urban poverty', *Environment and Urbanization*, 7, pp. 11–36.

Zaman, K., Baqui, A.H., Yunus, M., Sack, R.B., Bateman, O.M., Chowdhury, H.R. and Black, R.E. (1997), 'Acute respiratory infections in children: a community-based longitudinal study in rural Bangladesh', *Journal of Tropical Pediatrics* 43(3), pp. 133–7.

Chapter 8

# Work Disabling Morbidity

*Cluster analysis was used to identify relatively homogenous groups within Dhaka slum households, who report similar patterns of livelihood. Four groups emerged which may be summarised as "self employed", "casual unskilled", "female headed" and "casual skilled" households on the basis of their socio-economic, demographic and occupational characteristics. The "self employed" and "casual skilled" groups were better off in terms of income, assets and creditworthiness. The greatest burden of adult illness fell in the "casual unskilled" and "female headed" households. In any month, 30–40 percent of these households reported loss of labour days due to illness. On average, about four days per month were lost in casual unskilled households and over seven days per month in female headed households, on account of illness. The income lost due to illness far exceeded household expenditure to treat the illness. Programmes which mitigate the adverse effects of adult ill health on household economies might help break the cycle of ill health and poverty which characterise many urban slum households, and could help reduce inequalities between livelihood groups.*

## Introduction

There has been a renewal of interest in the consequences of adult illness for households in developing countries (Feachem et al., 1992). The adult population is the productive sector of society and illness or disability will have inevitable adverse consequences for families and communities. Yet with a few notable exceptions (Pryer, 1993) there is very little empirical data on the consequences of adult illness for households in developing countries. The most obvious immediate effects of ill health are the suffering of the individual that is ill or injured. The amelioration of symptoms and the treatment of disease must remain an important goal of health policy. However the full consequences of ill health goes beyond this direct suffering and include direct economic consequences and other long-term effects (Over et al., 1992). Expenditures on health care are likely to increase substantially when an individual becomes ill and income will be forgone if the sick individual is unable to work. Assets may be sold, or loans taken out in order to meet the direct or indirect costs of ill health. Other indirect costs within the household include the withdrawal of a carer from household work, or children from school, where long term repercussions are more likely than immediate adverse effects (Over et al., 1992).

The main focus of this chapter is the direct and indirect economic costs of adult ill health across different livelihoods groups. The hypothesis we test below is that livelihoods groups in the study population differentiate work disabling morbidity and that the cost of ill health is borne disproportionately by the poorest households. We present information on the prevalence of work disabling morbidity, days lost and the costs of ill health including income lost and health expenditure. We will also assess the impact of work disabling ill health on household work and discuss effects across livelihoods groups. Detailed consideration of coping mechanisms employed in the face of adult ill health is presented in Chapter 9.

## Method

Cluster analysis was used to identify relatively homogenous groups within Dhaka slum households, who report similar patterns of livelihoods. The clustering technique used was a hierarchical agglomerative (or stepwise) technique available on SPSS for windows. The aim of the hierarchical agglomerative clustering algorithms is to find the most efficient step at each stage in a progressive synthesis of a population from "n" cases to "N" groups according to predefined criteria, based upon a measure of distance or similarity. One source of variation in the hierarchical clustering techniques is in choice of distance or similarity criteria used. Ward's method was used as suggested by Everitt (1980). Ward's method uses the squared Euclidean distance and is based upon the proposition that at any stage in the analysis the loss of information resulting from the grouping of entities into clusters can be measured by the total sum of squared deviations of each point from the mean of the cluster to which they belong. At each step of the analysis the union of every possible pair of clusters is considered and the two clusters whose fusion results in the minimum increase in the error sum of squares are combined (Everitt, 1980). In Monte Carlo studies, Ward's method has been found to be the most robust clustering method using a similarity matrix based upon squared Euclidean distances (Blashfield, 1976; Aldenderfer and Blashfield, 1984). Continuous variables were standardised by converting to the standard normal deviate. This is to ensure that clusters are not influenced by high specific gravity. A matrix of distance coefficients based upon the squared Euclidean distance was computed. A step-wise fusion of cases based upon the distance coefficient matrix was then produced. The clustering coefficient was used to indicate the stage on the agglomeration schedule where large changes between fusions were evident as compared to immediately preceding stages (Everitt, 1980).

A number of economic and demographic variables were entered into the cluster including: land, animals, labour, days worked per month, savings, debts, income, business assets, occupational group, household size and earner:dependency ratio.

Statistical comparisons were made across the clusters in terms of reported, socio-economic, demographic variables, as well as cost of illness. Parametric one-way analysis of variance (ANOVA) was used to test for between-group differences in mean values and categorical variables were tested by chi square tests. Where the expected cell size was under five, Fisher's Exact Test was used. In order to test the stability of the solution obtained, we randomly split samples and performed cluster analysis on each subset. We compared the split two samples with the original. Statistical analyses were performed using SPSS for windows statistical packages.

**Identification of Clusters**

Four clusters were identified comprising 90 percent of the cross-sectional sample in round 4. The level of agreement between split samples were the same. In conclusion the cluster solution was robust.

Table 8.1  Socio-economic variables by cluster

| Variables | C1 (n=178) self-employed | C2 (n=190) casual unskilled | C3 (n=124) Female headed households | C4 (n=67) Casual skilled | P |
|---|---|---|---|---|---|
| Land (mean and se) bhighas | 0.27 (0.011) | 0.15 (0.05) | 0.201 (0.05) | 0.23 (0.03) | <0.036 |
| Animals (mean and se) | 0.315 (0.03) | 0.019 (0.01) | 0.12 (0.03) | 0.11 (0.019) | <0.0001 |
| Household business assets (mean and se) Taka | 4549.42 (756.14) | 89.32 (33.24) | 344.04 (103.13) | 176.42 (95.65) | <0.0001 |
| Household savings (mean and se) Taka | 688.46 (172.83) | 353.33 (80.52) | 367.87 (134.48) | 416.43 (92.24) | <0.0001 |
| Household loans (mean and se) Taka | 368.02 (72.24) | 250.70 (28.90) | 248.25 (43.94) | 325.82 (66.55) | <0.0001 |
| Household income per cu (mean and se) Taka | 868.71 (39.88) | 657.64 (45.93) | 585.35 (68.26) | 853.97 (81.18) | <0.0001 |
| Total expenditure per cu (mean and se) Taka | §578.35 (37.33) | 572.70 (14.10) | 509.98 (20.90) | 567.74 (23.09) | <0.0001 |
| Food expenditure per cu (mean and se) Taka | 466.31 (12.46) | 498.68 (12.55) | 435.95 (16.72) | 535.87 (32.88) | <0.0001 |

**Table 8.2 Demographic characteristics by cluster**

| Variables | C1 (n=178) self-employed | C2 (n=190) casual unskilled | C3 (n=124) Female headed households | C4 (n=67) Casual skilled | P |
|---|---|---|---|---|---|
| Household size (mean and se) | 5.26 (0.15) | 4.34 (0.12) | 4.63 (0.18) | 4.47 (0.17) | <0.0001 |
| Household type: | | | | | |
| Female headed | 2 | 0 | 49 | 0 | |
| Male headed | 176 | 190 | 75 | 67 | <0.0001 |
| Earner: dependency ratio (mean and se) | 2.202 (0.13) | 1.989 (0.098) | 1.579 (0.13) | 2.226 (0.15) | <0.004 |

*The clusters*

Cluster 1 (n=178) was the richest group in the Dhaka slums. This group owned more land and animals than other groups and by far the most business assets. The group was mainly self-employed (70 percent). Eighteen percent were in permanent work and 9 percent were dependent self-employed. Savings were highest in this group compared to other groups. Total income and total expenditure was higher in this group. Food expenditure as a percent of income was lower compared to the other groups. Household loans were higher showing that this group was credit worthy. The household size was also higher, compared to the other groups and household structure was mainly male headed. The earner:dependency ratio was second highest after cluster 4. This group worked 25 days/month, the highest among the groups (Table 8.1; Table 8.2).

Cluster 2 (n=190) had the least land, animals and the least business assets. Ninety-nine percent were dependent self-employed. Total expenditure was second highest and food expenditure was the second highest after cluster 1. Food expenditure as a percent of income was second lowest. The household size was smaller than other groups, and household structure was male headed. The earner:dependency ratio was lower than cluster 1 and cluster 4. Loans were the lowest of any group. Household savings were lower than other groups. This group worked 21 days/month, the second highest days work/month after cluster 1 (Table 8.1 and Table 8.2).

Cluster 3 (n=124) This cluster owned land and animals but less than cluster 1 and cluster 4. Business assets were second highest after cluster 1. Total and food expenditure was lower among the clusters, and food expenditure as a percentage of income was second highest (113 percent). The loans were least among the clusters. Household savings were third highest after cluster 1 and cluster 4. The group was mainly casual unskilled (83 percent), and 11 percent were dependent self employed. The household size was second largest after cluster 1. The household type was 40 percent female headed. The earner:dependency ratio was lowest among the clusters, and the days work was 20 days/month (Table 8.1 and Table 8.2).

Cluster 4 (n=67) had the second largest amount of land and the third largest number of animals. Business assets were the second lowest among the Dhaka clusters, 95 percent were skilled casual workers and 0.7 percent were family workers. Household savings were second highest after cluster 1. Household loans were second highest after cluster 1. Total expenditure and food expenditure was highest among the clusters. Food expenditure as a percentage of income was higher than other clusters (139 percent). The household size was third highest among the clusters, and household type was male headed. The earner:dependency ratio was the highest among the clusters. The group worked 19.5 days/month, the lowest among the clusters (Table 8.1 and Table 8.2).

Table 8.3 The cost of ill health

| Variables | C1 (n=178) self-employed | C2 (n=190) casual unskilled | C3 (n=124) Female headed households | C4 (n=67) Casual skilled | P |
|---|---|---|---|---|---|
| Percent of household with labour days lost due to illness | 20.22 | 31.05 | 44.35 | 20.35 | <0.0001 |
| Total work days off per month due to illness (mean and se) | 2.24 (0.42) | 4.28 (0.59) | 7.58 (1.01) | 2.89 (0.83) | <0.0001 |
| Household work days off/month due to illness (mean and se) | 0.932 (18.23) | 1.15 (0.28) | 4.68 (0.89) | 1.16 (0.42) | <0.0001 |
| Cost of illness health expenditure/month (mean and se) Taka | 68.75 (18.23) | 56.93 (25.66) | 61.61 (19.04) | 54.21 (16.04) | <0.990 |
| Income lost due to illness /month (mean and se) Taka | 28.6 (9.6) | 30.9 (11.75) | 46.2 (15.10) | 15.40 (6.90) | <0.0001 |
| Cost of illness health expenditure/month: total household income (%) (mean and se) | 2.62 (0.56) | 2.12 (0.48) | 2.561 (0.60) | 2.125 (0.50) | <0.988 |
| Income loss due to illness/month: total household income (%) (mean & se) | 18.01 (0.95) | 17.12 (0.46) | 30.30 (2.26) | 11.60 (0.55) | <0.0001 |

## The cost of ill health

The work days lost due to illness was highest in the female headed household cluster (cluster 3) and lowest in the richest cluster (cluster 1) ($p<0.0001$). Similarly, household work days off due to illness was highest among the female headed household cluster (cluster 3) and least in the richer cluster (cluster 1) ($p<0.0001$). Also 20 percent of households in the richest cluster lost labour days due to illness, and in cluster 3, the poorest cluster, 44 percent of households lost labour days due to illness. The highest mean number of workdays lost was in the cluster 3 households, 7.58 days lost compared to cluster 1 where 2.24 workdays were lost.

Household workdays lost due to illness were also higher in the cluster 3 households (4.68 days lost, compared to 0.932 days lost in cluster 1. Income lost due to illness, was higher in cluster 3 (female headed households) and as a percentage of household income was also higher in cluster 3, compared to other clusters.

Expenditure on health care was not significant between clusters in total or as a percentage of household income, only 2 percent of household income was expended on health expenditure. The cost of health expenditure was less than income lost due to workdays forgone due to illness. Only three people gave help with cash or kind.

## Discussion

We used cluster analysis to identify groups within the Dhaka slums who report similar patterns of livelihoods. Cluster analysis has not been used widely in public policy analysis but such analysis is potentially of relevance as results are generated for natural groupings of vulnerable households.

In this study, four groups were identified with different socio-economic and demographic variables. Ninety percent of the cross sectional sample were accounted for by one of the four clusters identified. The first cluster (cluster 1) was the richest and owned most land, animals and business assets. Savings and total income were higher than in other clusters, and household loans were higher, showing that these households were creditworthy. Days worked were higher than other clusters. These compared to the poorest cluster (cluster 3), which included the female headed households. Household income and expenditure were lowest among the clusters and household loans were less than in any other clusters. Household size was second highest after cluster 1. Work done was mainly casual unskilled and household workdays available per month were also lower than other cluster.

Households suffered a high number of days work lost due to illness. Twenty percent of households in the richest cluster (cluster 1) lost labour days due to illness, and 44 percent of the poorest households (cluster 3) lost labour days due to illness. The highest mean number of workdays lost was 7.58 days lost in the poorest households (cluster 3) compared to 2.24 workdays lost in the richest (cluster 1). Illness also resulted in more household workdays lost due to illness in the Cluster 3 households compared to cluster 1 households (4.68 days lost compared to 0.932 days lost). Health expenditure on illness was similar across groups.

Pryer (1993) previously used cluster analysis to identify livelihood groups in the Khulna slums in Bangladesh. In this study, average earnings lost due to illness accounted, on average, for about 10 percent of all monthly income. The poorest group lost the greatest number of labour days due to illness, and average earnings lost amounted to 24 percent of monthly income. In the same households, most family members were malnourished and a higher proportion of women and children worked, despite very limited income earning opportunities (Pryer, 1993). The pattern in Dhaka is similar, but the experience of ill health may be greater, and the differential between the richest and poorest households is greater.

Illness may have serious consequences if it leads to a loss of income. The risk is particularly common for unskilled workers, because he/she is paid on a daily basis and the employer has little to gain by waiting for him/her to return. Instead, the employer offers the job to another individual who is waiting for work. While illness occurs in individuals the costs fall on households. Sickness in one member influences household decisions regarding the allocation of family resources. It is evident from the current study that there are households at risk of serious economic demise following adult illness.

Health policy options are customarily targeted as "risk groups" such as children or older people. It is important that more imaginative policy options are considered to mitigate the adverse effects of adult ill health among the urban poor. Health insurance schemes, for example, offer considerable potential to provide care for the sick on account of their redistributive effects and their capacity to spread the economic burden of disease from the sick to the non sick (Mills, 1983). In Bangladesh there are two well known health insurance schemes: Gonosasthya Kendra (GK) health care systems in Savar, and the Grameen health programme (GB). Enrollment in the GK scheme is voluntary, by household, and fees are dependent on socio-economic position. It covers clinic attendance and after one week extends to hospitalisation. In contrast, the Grameen re-paid health plan evolved as a benefit for groups participating in GB credit programmes. Initially this covered only clinic attendance but was later extended to include hospitalisation and made accessible to households outside the GB credit programmes (Desmet et al., 1999). The urban environment is likely to be a complex one in which to initiate community based health insurance on account of the eclectic mix of provision, populations and wide socio-economic divisions. Progress is now being made in urban areas in other south and south-east Asian countries and should be more available in Bangladesh (Carrin et al., 1999; Normand, 1999; Ron, 1999).

## Conclusions

The prevalence of sickness-induced loss of employment was found to be very high in the Dhaka slums; it represented substantial loss of earnings and was disproportionately borne by the poorest households. More emphasis should be placed upon community health insurance and credit schemes to ease the financial burden and distress incurred following sickness-induced loss of income. Both of the existing community health insurance schemes in Dhaka – the Grameen health programme, and the Gonoshastha Kendra health care system (Desmet et al., 1999) – should be supported and developed to cover all areas.

# References

Aldenderfer, M.S., Blashfield, R.K. (1984), *Cluster analysis series: Quantitative Applications in Social Sciences*, Sage Publications, London.
Blashfield, R.K. (1976), 'Mixture models tests of cluster analysis: accuracy of four agglomerative hierarchical methods', *Psychological Bulletin*, 83 (3), pp. 377–388.
Carrin, G., De Graeve, D., Deville, L. (1999), 'Introduction to the special issue on the economics of health insurance in low and middle-income countries', *Social Science and Medicine*, 44, pp. 859–864.
Desmet, M., Chowdhury, A.Q. and Islam, Md K. (1999), 'The potential for social mobilisation in Bangladesh: The organisation and functioning of two health insurance schemes', *Social Science and Medicine*, 48, pp. 925–938.
Everitt, B. (1980), *Cluster Analysis*, Heinemann Educational Books, London.
Feachem, R.G.A., Kjellstrom, T., Murray, C.J.L., Over, M. and Phillips, M.A. (eds) (1992), *The Health of Adults in the Developing World*, Oxford University Press, Oxford.
Mills, A. (1983), 'Economic aspects of health insurance', in Lee, K., Mills, A. (eds), *The Economics of Health in Developing Countries*, Oxford University Press. Oxford.
Normand, C. (1999), 'Using social health insurance to meet policy goals', *Social Science and Medicine*, 48, pp. 865–869.
Over, M., Randall, O.E., Huber, J.H. and Solon, O. (1992), 'The consequences of adult ill health', in Feachem, R.G.A., Kjellstrom, T., Murray, C.J.L., Over, M. and Phillips, M., *The Health of Adults in the Developing World*, Oxford University Press, Oxford.
Pryer, J.A. (1993), 'The impact of adult ill health on household income and nutrition in Khulna, Bangladesh', *Environment and Urbanization*, 5(?), pp 35–49
Ron, A. (1999), 'NGOs in community health insurance schemes: examples from Guatemala and Philippines', *Social Science and Medicine*, 48, pp. 939–950.

Chapter 9

# Strategies for Coping with Costs of Work Disabling Ill Health among Household Heads

*We examine the coping strategies followed by slum dwellers when household members are struck with illness. Strategies include borrowing money, diversifying income sources, women going to work, reducing expenditure, use of savings, sale of assets, merging households, movement of family members, movement to rural areas, use of gifts and other help. A particular purpose of this chapter is to illustrate the range of strategies taken and their possible effects, positive and negative.*

## Introduction

Ill health is frequently considered to be a characteristic of poverty. In the urban settings of developing countries, the combined effect of old pathogens and the new health risks, including environmental pollution and stress, means that disease burdens are particularly high among the poor. The very poor conditions and high levels of morbidity have been particularly highlighted in the case of large and rapidly growing cities (Brockerhoff and Brennan, 1997). But until recently little attention has been paid to the role of ill health in causing and perpetuating poverty. This probably reflects the general neglect of adult ill health in developing countries (Feachem et al., 1992).

Early investigations into the impact of ill health on the economic circumstances of households and populations tended to show little impact. But recently it has been recognised that these studies had methodological limitations. In particular they failed to adequately examine the direct and indirect effects of illness (Over et al., 1992). Pryer (1993) examines the cost of illness (direct and indirect) in the slums of Khulna. The results show that the poorest households lost more income than the richest households, as a percentage of income earned. Wratten (1995) identifies increased health risks as a special character of urban poverty and draws attention to the spatial of industrial and residential functions, crowded living conditions, inadequate provision of basic amenities, and ineffective pollution control and accident prevention.

**Table 9.1** Self reported illness and injury (14 day period prevalence) among male and female adults (16–64 years old)

| Illness | Adult female (15–64) | Adult Male (15–64) | All (15–64) |
|---|---|---|---|
| Diarrhoea | 3.4 | 3.6 | 3.5 |
| Cough/cold | 18.9 | 18.9 | 18.8 |
| Fever | 27.3 | 20.7 | 24.2 |
| Headache | 27.1 | 17.4 | 22.6 |
| Abdominal pain | 9.7 | 7.1 | 8.5 |
| Injury | 2.0 | 2.6 | 2.3 |
| Other illness | 23.3 | 12.8 | 18.4 |
| Any illness | 65.9 | 52.4 | 59.7 |
| N | 833 | 720 | 1553 |

Tables 9.1 and 9.2 illustrate the period prevalence of illness in the study population. When an adult is ill, then effects may follow with respect to employment, intra-household and extra-household relationships.

**Table 9.2** Self reported illness (14 day period prevalence) among adults (15–64 years) by relation to household head

|  | Fever | Headache | Abdominal pain | Any illness | N |
|---|---|---|---|---|---|
| Male head | 21.6 | 18.0 | 7.4 | 54.6 | 584 |
| Female head | 44.9 | 29.2 | 4.5 | 79.8 | 89 |
| Wife of male head | 27.3 | 27.8 | 11.7 | 67.6 | 616 |

## Employment Insecurity

Illness may have serious consequences if it leads to a loss of income. As previously stated, the risk is particularly common for unskilled workers, because he/she is paid on a daily basis and the employer has little to gain for waiting for him/her to return, instead the employer offers the job to an other individual who is waiting for work.

Individuals who are involved in skilled work tend to have a stronger network of support than those engaged in unskilled work. The strength of the network reduces the threat of job loss while he/she is ill. However if he/she is ill for a long time the employers often opt to recruit a new person when there has been a long period of absence from the job.

> Hakim, a trader, has been suffering from rheumatic fever for a long time. Due to this illness he was not doing well in his business. As a result, he consumed a large part of his working capital and finally lost credit-worthiness. This means it is now difficult for him to restart his business and he plans to become involved in unskilled work.

Fear of loss of employment often pushes sick individuals to resume work before their complete recovery from illness. Employment insecurity forces these workers into a cycle of repeated illness and low productivity which results in the continual degradation of their human and material capital.

## Effects of illness on intra-household relations

The impact of illness on the household economy may have effects on household relations. Loss of income, rising expenditure and the need for adjustments for household maintenance may produce internal tension and conflict.

> Hossain, a rickshaw puller, was living with his fourth wife. After having three children (one died) within three years, his wife became too weak to do her household work. Then he got a fifth wife on the plea that he needed a woman to maintain his family.

Husbands leave their wives when they become pregnant or after the birth of the baby, as the wives become more of a liability in terms of ill health and less able to contribute economically to the household.

> Monowara was living with her current husband, Tomsher, and her son, Sumon (nine), the result from a previous marriage. When Sumon was suffering from fever, Tomsher refused to provide him with proper treatment. Monowara tried her best to cure him but finally he died. This unfortunate event resulted in a clash between Monowara and Tomsher. "From this shock, I have learnt a lot about my husband. I exhausted all my savings for him to take training as a driver. Now he is not taking care of my child and me. He is forcing me to go back to work although I am not totally well. In future I will save only for my child and for myself", she said.

Step-children have a weak claim to care and treatment when ill, and their illness can be an important source of conflict between adult members.

## Effects of illness on social networks

In the slum context the most accepted strategy by households was to seek help from a social network during the illness of a family member. The people who are strong can bear the cost of maintaining a strong network which can provide support in different forms during an illness. Within the context, people who have a strong patron–client relationship with owners enjoy different types of support during the illness period, especially if the ill person is an earner.

Harun, a painter, had an accident during work. He was employed by a contractor who was his uncle. The contractor paid all the expenditure (twenty thousand Taka) for his treatment, including two major operations on his eyes.

Sufia, a maidservant, received Taka 100 from her employer when her six-year-old daughter became seriously ill due to fever. She was allowed to take leave for three days and her employer paid her for those days.

These examples illustrated that people received help from different persons rather than any form of institution.

Households, nevertheless are active in seeking ways of mitigating the adverse effects of adult illness. A typical sequence of responses reported by slum household illness in this study was as follows:

1  Borrowing money without interest.
2  Diversifying income sources.
3  Sending women to work.
4  Expenditure reduction.
5  Use of savings.
6  Sell assets.
7  Merge households.
8  Move to kin's family in urban areas.
9  Move to rural areas.
10 Gifts and help.

## Strategies to cope with illness

*Taking loans*

Taking loans is the first response when faced with illness-induced economic difficulty.

Sobuz and his wife are both involved in income generating activities. When his wife suffered from chicken pox, he borrowed money from his co-workers for his wife's treatment. There was not enough for both the treatment and to maintain the household costs, as he had lost the wife's income. He then borrowed more money from other colleagues – without interest.

Delwar, during the period of his son's illness, was unable to pull a rickshaw. He borrowed money from the rickshaw owner after the death of his son. He spent money for rituals. The owner allowed him to pay the loan in daily instalments with the rent of the rickshaw at the end of the day.

*Reducing expenditure*

To cope with illness of an earner, people try to reduce their household expenditure, particularly food expenditure. Women often play a crucial role in managing the household finances during times of crisis. They may adopt diverse strategies to reduce household food expenditure, including gathering wild and discarded food, buying low quality items, and shopping at times and locations where prices are lower.

> Sufia, wife of Jainal, decided not to spend more than 30 Taka per day, while her son, Al-amin, was suffering from diarrhoea. She omitted fish and meat from their meals for some days to reduce food costs. She used rice and lentils and pasted potatoes for preparing breakfast, lunch and dinner, and sometimes fried egg for her husband. She also cooked all the meals at the same time to reduce fuel costs.

The above examples illustrate two ways to reduce household expenditure: from food expenditure (the most common one), and from fuel costs.

### *Diversifying income sources*

People will try to diversify their income sources in face of illness in an earner in order to maintain their necessary consumption levels. The fact that the household is affected by illness can create barriers to options. Three main options could be exploited: current workers can work longer hours; new individuals can enter the workforce; non-workers related income generating strategies can be used, for example taking in a paying guest or lodger.

> Akkas Mia, a petty trader, is also a rickshaw puller in order to generate cash for treatment of his son who was suffering from jaundice. Due to his son's illness, his wife Rohima was not able to go out to work as a maidservant. To maintain their household expenditure and to manage the extra expense for treatment, he started to pull a rickshaw during his leisure time.

### *Women to work*

As households become poorer, and particularly face a crisis such as an earner becoming ill, the households involve their female members in the labour market.

> Razzaq, a fish trader, is suffering from eczema and is not able to continue his work regularly. Previously he was employed as a manager of one part of the slum. He was getting Taka 750 per month and the room was rent free. Now, due to his illness, he has lost part of his income and has to pay for his room. He involved his daughter in garment factory work to increase the family's income.

> Hasem Mollah, a vegetable seller, was unable to walk to sell his items due to old age. On the other hand, it was not possible for his wife to go out for work as there are no members to do the household work. Then she found work which can be done at home. She started to cook for some boarding house members, from where she is able to supplement the household expenditure.

These examples illustrate how women's contributions are dynamic during crisis.

### *Use of savings*

In the slum context, households rarely have savings, but some of the working and non-working women have some form of secret savings. Non-working women save money from household expenditure, and working women save money from their income.

Rani, mother of Pipasa, managed money for the treatment of her daughter when she was suffering from fever. Her husband gave money every day to buy rice and other food items. She managed to save Taka 225 from this money after nine months. After three days, when her husband was in his rural district, she used these savings for the treatment of her daughter.

Sufia works as a maidservant. Since she is responsible for purchasing the items for family consumption, she created savings of Taka 350 by reducing food expenditure with the intention to buy furniture. When her grandchild became ill she spent that money on her treatment.

These examples represent patterns of use of women's savings. It is interesting that these savings have been spent in the same way. For many households it seems that the savings are small and often adequate to cope with the high cost of treatment. Where adequate savings exist, the use of savings was a highly preferred strategy.

We save money for times of crisis, and illness, particularly of earners, is a severe crisis for our livelihoods.

## *Selling assets*

Selling assets is found to be a less common practice of managing the treatment costs of ill members. There are two reasons for this. One may be that they do not have enough assets to sell. Another may be that they do not want to sell their productive assets which they have accumulated after a long struggle.

Jainal firstly took a loan to treat his wife who was suffering from rheumatic fever. When he failed to repay the loan of Taka 2000 by pulling his rickshaw, he sold his rickshaw.

This shows how people can lose their assets as a result of illness.

## **Socio-cultural strategies**

### *Merging households*

It was observed that during the illness of family members people merge their households with kinsmen as a coping strategy with the intention of reducing the expenditure and also reducing the work load of the household.

Gani and his younger brother were living in neighbouring slums of Pulpar slum. While the wife of Gani's younger brother was suffering from jaundice the doctor prescribed her to take rest. Then the two families started to live in the same slum while Gani's wife and daughter helped the household with an ill member through cooking and taking care of the child.

### *Move to the rural home*

A further strategy which may be employed in the face of illness is to send some household members back to the rural home. This is more common among those who have a good economic base in their rural area. Poorer households who have few assets in their rural area appear to adopt this strategy only when they run out of options within the city.

> Abul, a rickshaw puller, sent his family to the rural area while his wife and one of his daughters became ill. Initially, when his wife fell ill, he tried to manage on the income of his daughter and himself. But when his daughter also became ill, he decided to send the rest of the family to the rural area.

*Gifts and help*

Taking help and receiving gifts from others may also be a strategy for some households. This appears to be more common for the worst-off households. Assistance may be received from relatives, friends and employers. Such assistance can take different forms, in cash or in kind.

> Harun, a painter, had an accident during work. He was employed by a contractor who was his uncle. The contractor paid all the expenditure (approximately 20,000 Taka) for his treatment which included the cost of two major eye operations.

> Sufia, a maidservant, received 100 Taka from her employer when her daughter of six years fell seriously ill due to fever. She was allowed to take leave for three days and her employer paid her for those days.

The above examples are cited as to where the sources of remittances came from. Two are from his/her employers.

## Discussion

This chapter explores coping strategies when a household member fell ill. While illness occurs in individuals, the costs fall on the household. Sickness in one member influences household decisions regarding the allocation of financial resources. Both the costs of illness and strategies to cope with them can only be understood in a household framework of sequence of coping strategies as listed earlier.

The findings of this study indicate that coping with the costs of illness largely occurred at the level of the household itself, and that inter-household transfers of financial or time resources played a smaller role (Sauerborn et al., 1996). Chen's study (1991) of rural Indian farmers coping with drought, and Adams' work (1992) on household coping with food insecurity, also emphasised the central role of the household coping. However, evidence suggests that inter-household transfers are more acceptable in the context of food shortage than in the context of health care (Adams, 1992). In the present study, both kin and community support were generally available to the poorest households. This is in agreement with other authors in India, including Agarwal's observation (1992) of strong community support for poor households in India. Not surprisingly, other household characteristics such as economic dependency ratio and wealth had a strong influence on coping strategies. In spite of the importance of the household in coping with illness, policy has customarily been targeted at individuals at risk by characteristics such as age and gender. One lesson from the current study is that there are households at risk of being pushed into poverty and calamity as a result of catastrophic illness. Most households did lose income due to illness. However, even when coping was successful in the short run, it is likely to increase vulnerability in the long run by reducing the household's ability to cope with future adverse events. While selling assets enabled the household to cover health expenditure, it also made them poorer and less prepared to cope with future economic and social crises.

In the last chapter we described health insurance schemes as a possible vehicle for helping to offset the adverse effects of adult ill health. The coping strategies adopted indicate that there are other policy options which might also be required to strengthen the capability of urban households by lending money in times of crisis. A second way to diversity income sources, by promoting business acumen and by increasing income earning opportunities. Thirdly, an option is to develop credit schemes for poor households and to enhance access to credit for poor households (Desmet et al., 1999).

## References

Adams, A.M. (1992), 'Seasonal food insecurity in the Sahel: nutritional, social and economic risk among Bamana agriculturalists in Mali', Doctoral thesis, University of London.

Agarwal, B. (1992), 'Social security and the family: Coping with seasonality and calamity in rural India', in Ahmad, E., Dreze, J., Hills, J. and Sen, A. (eds), *Social Security in Developing Countries*, Oxford University Press, Oxford.

Brockerhoff, M., Brennan, E. (1997), 'The poverty of cities in the developing world', Population Council Research Division Working Paper No 96, Population Council, New York.

Chen, M.A. (1991), *Coping with Seasonality and Drought*, Sage, New Delhi.

Desmet, M., Chowdhury, A.Q. and Islam, Md K. (1999), 'The potential for social mobilisation in Bangladesh: The organisation and functioning of two health insurance schemes', *Social Science and Medicine*, 48, pp. 925–938.

Feachem, R.G.A., Kjellstrom, T., Murray, C.J.L., Over, M. and Phillips, M.A. (eds) (1992), *The Health of Adults in the Developing World*, Oxford University Press, Oxford.

Over, M., Randall, O.E., Huber, J.H. and Solon, O. (1992), 'The consequences of adult ill health', in Feachem, R., Kjellstrom, T., Murray, C.J.L., Over, M. and Phillips, M. (eds), *The Health of Adults in the Developing World*, Oxford University Press, Oxford.

Pryer, J.A. (1993), 'The impact of adult ill health on household income and nutrition in Khulna, Bangladesh', *Environment and Urbanization*, 5(2), pp. 35–49.

Sauerborn, R., Adams, A. and Hien, M. (1996), 'Household strategies to cope with the economic costs of illness', *Social Science and Medicine*, 43(3), pp. 291–301.

Wratten, E. (1995), 'Conceptualising urban poverty', *Environment and Urbanization*, 7, pp. 11–36.

Chapter 10

# Women's Negotiation Control and Well-being within the Households

*The overall management of material resources has been traditionally the responsibility of the head of household. However, a close examination of the data suggests that women are often playing a significant role in the management of material resources within the household. In households where the head of household manages the budget, the spouse earns more, but has less assets and savings compared to female controlled households, where women work more days and have a common fund. Violence against women within marriage is frequent, but tolerated in order to gain some protection from other men. Women's health and children's nutritional status was better in female controlled households compared to male controlled households. In Sen's terminology, though working for an income enables women to secure a better fall-back position, their rights still remain weak, and the broader social, economic, and political structures continue to weigh against women. With support from the policy community, it seems likely that working women could lead to favourable changes in gender inequalities, with greater options for control of their own lives.*

**Introduction**

Sen's model of the household is a site of co-operative conflict (Sen, 1990). Sen assumes that co-operation between household members will take place as long as it leads to outcomes that are preferable to those that prevail in the absence of co-operation. Bargaining arises over the choice between alternative co-operative outcomes on the one hand, and whether to co-operate at all, on the other. Differences in bargaining power between household members arise because of the range of options facing members, should household co-operation break down (the fall-back position). Factors include the perceived significance of their contributions to household prosperity; the degree to which members identify their self-interests; and finally the ability of some members to exercise coercion, threat, and violence over others. Women's perceived contribution is an important factor affecting women's bargaining power within the household. This is likely to be related to the visibility and extent of productive work. The greater visibility of remunerated outside work is seen as a crucial factor in determining women's fall-back position. Research shows that earnings appear to strengthen their role in the household decision making and claims on household resources, greater mobility and independence (Acharya and Bennet, 1983; Creevy, 1996; Sood, 1991).

In contrast, much recent work has argued that earning an income through work is not sufficient to fundamentally alter women's position, and far from leading to empowerment, women's work may represent a further dimension of exploitation by families and employers (Lessinger, 1990; Greenhalgh, 1991; Desai and Jain, 1992; Shami, 1990). Attention is drawn to the resilience of cultural norms and social structures which act to constrain women's options and reinforce their subordination, regardless of their work status. Kabeer (1995) suggests that these divergent conclusions in part reflect the fact that women's experience of work varies between settings. The nature of work performed, the reasons for entering work, the type and size of remuneration, and the contribution to overall household income, are all likely to have important implications for the degree to which such work affects women's position. Also, importantly, the extent of the pre-existing gender inequalities and the rigidity of prescribed norms of behaviour will affect the effects of women's employment on household power relationships. In Bangladesh, with its strong patriarchal tradition and sharp gender segregation of work and space, we might expect to find waged employment having a relative impact on household decision making. But in urban areas, opportunities to participate in paid employment are far greater and a number of studies have explored the implications of these activities for household power relations. Amin et al. (1997) studied the garment factory workers, and argue that women have gained a new role and life stage when they participate in this type of employment prior to marriage. They find evidence of increased independence and access to important networks of information and support among these workers. Haque (1998) also carried out a detailed case study on women's work in non governmental organisation (Gonoshathaya Kendra) and concluded that many workers made significant changes to their identities.

**Method**

Much of the data in this chapter is derived from a special survey designed to explore intra-household decision making. A series of analyses are presented. Initially we examine decision making in purchase of food, education and health care along three dimensions: source of money, management of money and purchase of goods. We then go on to classify households as 'male controlled' or 'female controlled' on the basis of money management. In subsequent analyses we have contrasted the characteristics of 'male controlled' and 'female controlled' households. We looked at a range of associations including relationships with socio-economic variables, women's visiting rights, violence and divorce and the health and nutritional status of women and children.

**Table 10.1 Intra-household negotiations around food, medical treatment, education and clothes**

| Variables | Source of money | | Manager | Purchaser |
|---|---|---|---|---|
| | Main (Head) | Second (Joint) | Relationship to head | Relationship to head |
| Rice | 48% | 47% | Spouse 55%<br>Head 42% | Spouse 34%<br>Head 60% |
| Vegetables | 47% | 47% | Spouse 62%<br>Head 35% | Spouse 50%<br>Head 43% |
| Fish/meat | 48% | 46% | Spouse 59%<br>Head 38% | Spouse 42%<br>Head 51% |
| Snacks for children | 40% | 43% | Spouse 65%<br>Head 31% | Spouse 53%<br>Head 35% |
| House rent | 33% | 29% | Spouse 58%<br>Head 39% | Spouse 28%<br>Head 69% |
| Cooking utensils | 44% | 49% | Spouse 61%<br>Head 36% | Spouse 49%<br>Head 44% |
| Male clothes | 47% | 43% | Spouse 46%<br>Head 50% | Spouse 6%<br>Head 88% |
| Spouse's clothes | 47% | 47% | Spouse 61%<br>Head 35% | Spouse 33%<br>Head 63% |
| Children's clothes | 42% | 43% | Spouse 58%<br>Head 38% | Spouse 25%<br>Head 69% |
| Children's education | 21% | 27% | Spouse 60%<br>Head 37% | Spouse 41%<br>Head 56% |
| Adult male medical treatment | 47% | 44% | Spouse 41%<br>Head 56% | Spouse 10%<br>Head 85% |
| Spouse's medical treatment | 46% | 46% | Spouse 55%<br>Head 43% | Spouse 30%<br>Head 65% |
| Children's medical treatment | 42% | 43% | Spouse 57%<br>Head 40% | Spouse 34%<br>Head 61% |

## Results

Table 10.1 shows that most money is from the head of household, although joint money was particularly important for snacks for children, cooking utensils, children's clothes and children's medical treatment. The manager of purchases is almost always the spouse, apart from male clothes, which the head of the household manages. The purchaser is always the head of the household, but the spouse purchases vegetables, snacks for children, and cooking utensils.

**Table 10.2  Women's socio-economic variables among female controlled households and male controlled households**

| Variables | Control of the budget | | P |
|---|---|---|---|
| | Female controlled households (n=342) | Male controlled households (n=225) | |
| Women's work last 30 days<br>(yes)<br>(no) | 204<br>46 | 138<br>179 | <0.0001 |
| Women's income in last 30 days<br>mean and (se)<br>Taka | 645.49<br>(46.00) | 993.69<br>(175.97) | <0.007 |
| Own money kept from earnings<br>(yes)<br>(no) | 75<br>126 | 10<br>37 | <0.025 |
| Know husband's earnings:<br>Exact<br>Approximately<br>No idea | 133<br>151<br>27 | 50<br>108<br>42 | <0.0001 |
| Common fund<br>(yes)<br>(no) | 251<br>11 | 69<br>16 | <0.0001 |
| Women's productive assets<br>mean and (se)<br>Taka | 507<br>(143.50) | 207.46<br>(98.06) | 0.300 |
| Women's animals<br>mean and (se)<br>Taka | 2783.33<br>(795.90) | 1141.25<br>(642.25) | <0.01 |
| Women's own savings<br>(yes)<br>(no) | 112<br>230 | 58<br>167 | <0.056 |

**Table 10.2** (continued)

| Variables | Control of the budget | | P |
|---|---|---|---|
| | Female controlled households (n=342) | Male controlled households (n=225) | |
| Women's own: save from household budget (yes) (no) | 141 201 | 59 166 | <0.0001 |
| Women's own: save from rice (yes) (no) | 117 225 | 91 134 | <0.078 |
| Women's best saris mean and (se) | 2.091 (0.1030) | 2.387 (0.1523) | <0.095 |
| Work location Home Slum Mohammadpur Dhaka | 36 20 122 25 | 3 1 29 13 | <0.002 |
| Husband would allow work Any type of work To work at home Respect her for working Salary is good Forbidden working Other Husband does not know | 18 15 19 13 61 4 2 | 12 20 20 15 101 5 2 | <0.026 |
| Household members working mean and (se) | 2.24 (0.0048) | 1.20 (0.00312) | <0.0001 |

Table 10.2 shows that more women in female controlled households worked in the last 30 days compared to male controlled households, but women in female controlled households earn less compared to male controlled households. More women in female controlled households kept money from their earnings, and have a common fund, and owned more productive assets, and animals. And more family members were working compared to male controlled households. More women save, save from the budget and from rice purchases, and more women work in Mohammadpur, and more husbands allow women to work if the salary is good in female controlled households than in male controlled households.

**Table 10.3   Women's visiting rights among female controlled households and male controlled households**

| | Control of the budget | | |
|---|---|---|---|
| Variables | Female controlled households (n=342) | Male controlled households (n=225) | P |
| Visit friends: need permission | | | <0.0001 |
| (yes) | 199 | 165 | |
| (no) | 143 | 60 | |
| Married daughter: contact last year: | | | <0.056 |
| Weekly | 15 | 5 | |
| Monthly | 10 | 3 | |
| 2/3 months | 5 | 5 | |
| 2/3 yearly | 0 | 3 | |
| yearly | 3 | 1 | |
| Brother contact last year: | | | <0.012 |
| Weekly | 43 | 37 | |
| Monthly | 30 | 24 | |
| 2/3 monthly | 30 | 20 | |
| 2/3 yearly | 31 | 29 | |
| yearly | 112 | 56 | |
| indirect | 32 | 14 | |
| no contact | 11 | 4 | |
| Medical centre: need permission | | | <0.002 |
| (yes) | 118 | 106 | |
| (no) | 198 | 99 | |
| Shopping: need permission | | | <0.001 |
| (yes) | 141 | 198 | |
| (no) | 125 | 99 | |

Table 10.3 shows that more women in female controlled households need permission to visit their friends and medical centre, but less women need permission for shopping compared to male controlled households. More women visited their married daughter and brother in female controlled households compared to male controlled households.

**Table 10.4 Men's violence and divorce threats among female and male controlled households**

| Variables | Control of the budget | | P |
|---|---|---|---|
| | Female controlled households (n=342) | Male controlled households (n=225) | |
| Marriage legally registered | | | <0.019 |
| (yes) | 199 | 150 | |
| (no) | 118 | 57 | |
| Have marriage documents | | | <0.002 |
| (yes) | 131 | 113 | |
| (no) | 187 | 94 | |
| Husband's verbal abuse to wife: | | | <0.068 |
| Often | 39 | 39 | |
| Sometimes | 182 | 112 | |
| Never | 94 | 53 | |
| Husband's beaten wife: | | | <0.014 |
| Often | 16 | 19 | |
| Sometimes | 84 | 65 | |
| Never | 215 | 120 | |
| Husband's divorce threat: | | | <0.003 |
| Often | 6 | 13 | |
| Sometimes | 36 | 32 | |
| Never | 273 | 159 | |
| Husband's new wife threat: | | | <0.006 |
| Often | 5 | 13 | |
| Sometimes | 27 | 21 | |
| Never | 283 | 170 | |

Table 10.4 shows that in female controlled households, more women have marriage legally registered, and marriage documents, compared to male controlled households. In female controlled households there is the same verbal abuse which happens often, but more verbal abuse which happens sometimes, compared to male controlled households.

There was a pattern for husbands beating their wives, divorce threat and threat of a new wife. In female controlled households, this was less often for the three types of violence when compared to male controlled households.

**Table 10.5 Women's health and children's nutritional status among female and male controlled households**

| Variables | Control of the budget | | P |
|---|---|---|---|
| | Female controlled households (n=342) | Male controlled households (n=225) | |
| Women's cough/cold suffered (yes) (no) | 33 280 | 46 158 | <0.0001 |
| Women's other illness suffered (yes) (no) | 19 293 | 56 248 | <0.004 |
| Women's old injury suffered (yes) (no) | 0 313 | 5 201 | <0.079 |
| Weight for age (Z-Score) mean and (se) | -0.995 (0.125) | -1.3027 (0.465) | <0.081 |

Table 10.5 shows that in female controlled households, there was less women's cough or cold, and less of other illnesses, and less of old injuries compared to male controlled households. Weight for age in children was better on average in female controlled households, compared to male controlled households.

## Discussion

Though frugality and prudent use of resources are regarded as positive traits in Bangladeshi women, the control and overall management of material resources has been traditionally the responsibility of the male head of household. However, a close examination of the study data suggests that women are often playing a significant and overt role in the management of material resources within households. In households where the head of the household manages the budget, the spouse earns more money, but has less assets and savings compared to female managed households where women work more days, have a common fund, own more assets and save more but earn less.

Kabeer (1995) found that in the garment workers households there was a predominance of pooling. She argues that women were the managers only where their holding this role did not threaten the established gender hierarchies. Thus only older women or non-working women would be assigned this responsibility. In this study we found that working women were more likely than non-working women to play a management role. Nevertheless, we can conclude that reports of money management imply a fundamental shift in gender relations. It is important to recognise the potentially important distinction between money management and control (Pahl, 1989). The management of income reported may amount to little more than carrying out someone's else's decision. However, being in control of the finances does not offer the possibility of exerting much influence over allocation of resources if income is low and insecure.

Despite that, it is clear that women are in control of the household budgets. To this extent women are stepping into the traditionally male sphere. It also appears that working women are assuming these new roles and increase the chances of women exerting influence over expenditures and therefore their own access to resources. In many cases the influence of women may be covert in nature as women do not want to rock the boat too much. It is also clear that in some cases more overt actions are possible.

An important finding in this study was that children's nutritional status was better in female controlled households compared to male controlled households. Similar findings have emerged in a couple of other studies.

Castle (1992) sought to compare whether women with low or high autonomy significantly differed in their health seeking behaviour and the consequent affect on their children's nutritional status. Women's position was assessed according to their intra-household support and/or autonomy ranging from lone daughter in-law to female head. Data was derived from a household census for each member of 180 villages between 1989 and 1991 in Mali. The findings showed that women's status and decision making power did affect their children's nutritional status; mothers occupying the position of the lone daughter-in-law had the highest proportion of malnourished children. In contrast, under half of the daughters-in-law who had peers with whom they could share household responsibilities showed fewer malnourished children.

In Mali the household shows a bargaining position whereby decisions relating to children's health and care reflect the household's own political and social economy. The data here indicates that relatively autonomous women (those living with their sisters-in-law in laterally extended households were more likely to consult their husbands. Where women are the sole daughter-in-law and if the mother-in-law lives in the same household, the mother must consult the mother-in-law about major decisions affecting the children. The mother-in-law in this case is the "resource keeper" controlling information, cash, and often diagnosis. In this way the mother had little say how her child was diagnosed or treated.

Doan and Bisharat (1990) did a study in Jordan and analysed whether or not low levels of mother's autonomy had a detrimental effect on the children's nutritional status, or whether the availability of additional earners and domestic helpers in the extended families was important. Data was collected for 1341 households in 1985 for urban settlements in Amman. Nutritional status was measured by weight-for age. Using women's position in the household and taking into account income, the mother's education, place of residence, and the child's sex, the results of this study again suggested that low autonomy led to low child nutritional status. The authors describe the Arab households as typically stratified by gender and age. A very common arrangement is for young mothers to be living with her husband's parents and, just as in Mali, they are subjected to the dual authority of the husband and the mother-in-law. The latter extending her control to include decisions concerning her grandchildren. Indeed she runs the household, decides on what the children will be fed, controls the financial resources and decides how to treat a child for illness. Inevitably the mother-in-law's decision will clash with the mother's and the study showed that the mother's action was detrimental to the child's health due to lack of knowledge. Availability of potential helpers and earners within the household was associated with better child nutritional status after controlling for other factors. However, the extended set-up was also thought to contribute to crowding and less privacy, therefore less communication between husband and wife and general undermining of a young mother with an overbearing mother-in-law.

The effect of secondary level of schooling had a positive effect on the child's nutritional status, whether in nuclear or extended family. Low women's maternal autonomy, irrespective of her education, age, and household size had a strong negative influence on child's nutritional status. On the contrary, high women's maternal autonomy had a positive effect on children's nutritional status. Once again it seems that maternal bargaining power in the household decision making system makes a difference in the well-being of her children (Doan and Bisharat, 1990).

Our data suggests that slum women are acting in a number of ways to try to secure their own and their children's well-being. Women siphon off money in various ways for their own personal expenditure, and seek to accumulate savings and assets. These behaviours appear to be due to a heightened sense of vulnerability and need to protect personal interests in the uncertain climate of the slum. Working for money appears to increase a woman's room for manoeuvre.

Although there are signs of change is important to emphasise the resilience of traditional gender ideologies and structural constraints on women's options. In Sen's (1990) terminology, though working for an income enables women to secure a somewhat better fall-back position, their rights still remain weak. The broader social, economic and political structures continue to be heavily weighed against women and thus limit their access to resources of various types. This reinforces the dominance of men within the family despite changes in the balance of financial contributions.

Though discrimination against women is multifaceted, physical insecurity stands out as a particularly severe constraint on women's options. In common with recent studies (Kabeer, 1995; Martin, 1998, Naved, 1997) fear of robbery and rape was a common theme in women's lives. Violence against women remains endemic and marriage is seen as the only means of obtaining protection. This means that women remain socially dependent upon men despite the potential of some economic independence. Moreover, women are frequently having to tolerate abuse within marriage in order to gain some protection from other men.

In the study of population the findings from this study and other recent studies suggest that gender identities are in flux within the poor urban setting in Bangladesh, and therefore the opportunities exist for re-negotiation for better terms for women. With support from policy and programme intervention, it seems likely that the increasing involvement of women in income earning work could lead to favourable changes in gender inequalities, bringing women greater options for control of their lives.

## References

Acharya, M. and Bennet, L. (1983), 'Women in the subsistence sector: economic participation and household decision making in Nepal', World Bank Staff Working Paper No. 256, World Bank, New York.

Amin, S., Diamond, I., Naved, R., Newby, M. (1997), 'Transition to adulthood of female factory workers: some evidence from Bangladesh', Working Paper No. 102, Population Council Research Division, New York.

Castle, S.E. (1992), 'Intra-household differentials in women's status: household function and focus as determinants of children's illness management in rural Mali', *Health Transition Review*, 3(2), pp. 137–157.

Creevy, I. (1996), *Changing women's lives and work*, UNIFEM, Intermediate Technology, London.

Daon, R.M. and Bisharat, L. (1990), 'Female autonomy and child nutritional status in the extended family, Amman, Jordan', *Social Science and Medicine*, 31(7), pp. 783–789.

Desai, S. and Jain, D. (1992), 'Maternal employment and changes in family dynamics: the social context of women's work in rural South India', Working Paper No. 39, Population Council Research Division, New York.

Greenhalgh, S. (1991), 'Women in the informal enterprise: empowerment or exploitation?', Working Paper No. 33, Population Council Research Division, New York.

Haque, T. (1998), 'Redefining gender roles in urbanizing Bangladesh', Paper presented at the European Network of Bangladesh Studies Workshop, University of Bath, UK.

Kabeer, N. (1995), 'Necessary, sufficient or irrelevant? Women's wages and intra-household power relations in urban Bangladesh', Institute of Development Studies Working Paper No. 25, Sussex.

Lessinger, J. (1990), 'Work and modesty: the dilemma of women market traders in Madras', Dube, L. and Palriwala, R. (eds), *Structures and Strategies: women, work and family*, Sage, New Delhi.

Martin, N. (1998), 'Vulnerability, marriage and violence: restructuring of intra-household relationship in a resource poor urban community in Bangladesh', Paper presented at the European Network of Bangladesh Studies Workshop, 16–18 April, University of Bath, UK.

Naved, R. (1997), 'Female labour migration and its implication for marriage and child bearing in Bangladesh', paper presented at the Population Council Workshop on adolescence and marriage among female garment workers of Dhaka, Bangladesh Institute of Development Studies, Dhaka.

Pahl, J. (1989), *Money and Marriage*, Macmillan Press, London.

Sen, A. (1990), 'Gender and co-operative conflicts', in Tinker, I. (ed.) *Persistent Inequalities: Women and World Development*, Oxford University Press, Oxford.

Shami, S. (1990), *Women in Arab Society: work patterns and gender relations in Egypt, Jordan and Sudan*, BERG/UNESCO, France.

Sood, R. (1991), *Changing status and adjustment of women*, Manak Publications, New Delhi and Jaipur, India.

Chapter 11

# Factors Affecting Adult Body Mass Index

*Anthropometric data of adults aged 20–59 was analysed to assess their nutritional status. Body mass index (BMI) was the measure used. Undernutrition was related to demographic, economic, social and environmental factors. More females were undernourished than males. Female headed households had worse nutritional status than male headed households. Logistic regression results show that 50–59 year olds were the most undernourished. Beri Badh was the most undernourished area. Families with deficit financial situation, casual wage workers, unskilled and dependent self employed were the most likely to suffer low BMIs. Families without involvement with credit organisations and those with poor environmental facilities were more likely to have a poor BMI.*

**Introduction**

It is well established that there are relationships between socio-economic factors and body mass index (BMI), and that low BMI is a dimension of poverty. Social, cultural and economic factors are difficult to assess and most work, however, uses proxy measures such as income or occupation of the head of the household. Earlier work by Pryer (1993) indicates that BMI was associated with livelihood groups, where the poorest group (female headed households and casual unskilled group) had the lowest BMI, in men and women, compared to the richest group (traders and landlords) who had the highest BMI. Several studies have demonstrated that BMI is associated with low income (Nube et al., 1998; Hakeem, 2001; Sarlio-Lahteenkorva and Lahelma, 1999; Delpeuch et al., 2000; Pryer, 1990), low assets (Pryer, 1990), expenditure (Nube et al., 1998), quality of housing and access to services (Nube et al., 1998), occupational groups (Pryer, 1993) and loans (Pryer, 1990). Most surveys provide measures of income or assets and divide these by the number of household members to estimate individual shares. Disentangling what happens within the household, such as who has access to what assets or resources is difficult (Sen, 1991). In this study, we did collect information on assets from every member and also conducted a special survey on control of resources, which will allow more sophisticated subsequent analyses. In this chapter we describe the relationships between body mass index, socio-economic, demographic and environmental factors within the study population.

## Methods

BMI has been calculated by dividing the subject's bodyweight (kilograms) by square of height (metres). The nutritional status has been categorised as severe chronic undernutition, mild to moderate chronic undernutrition and normal nutritional status respectively following the cutoff levels of <16, 16–18.5 and >18.5 respectively (Beaton et al., 1990; Gibson, 1990).

*Statistical analysis*

BMI values for each male and female adult were calculated using Microsoft® Excel 97. Data so obtained was processed under Stata 6.0 (Stata, 1999) to identify, group and compare undernourished adults. Simple percentages were derived from cross-tabulations. The outcome measures were taken in two groups: (a) Individual adult-specific nutritional status based on body mass index classified as severe (BMI<16) mild to moderate (BMI 16–18.5) and overall (BMI≤18.5) chronic undernutrition and (b) Family-specific adult nutritional status, with families classified as "with at least one malnourished adult" based on body mass index categorised as severe (BMI <16), mild to moderate (BMI 16–18.5) and overall (BMI≤18.5) chronic undernutrition. The risk factors that showed associations with the various outcomes that were statistically significant or close to significant, were assessed for their joint inference on the outcomes by logistic regression. The regression model incorporates adults' sex, age group, area of residence, self reported financial situation, occupation of household head, organisational affiliation and source of drinking water as independent variables. These have been tested to see their effects on each of the outcome variables of chronic undernutrition (BMI≤18.5).

Table 11.1 describes the percentage of malnourished adults by sex and age group. There were more malnourished females than malnourished males in all age groups. The difference in proportions between males and females was significant for severe malnutrition and for overall nutritional status.

## Results

Table 11.2 shows the influence of family structure on the prevalence of malnutrition. The percentage of adults with low BMI was not significant by family structure for severe, mild to moderate or overall. But the percentage of households with at least one malnourished adult was worse in joint–extended for severe, mild to moderate and overall malnutrition compared to other family structures.

**Table 11.1** Percentage of malnourished adults (BMI <18.5) by sex and age group

| Age in years | Sex | Adults (N) | Severe | Mild to moderate | Overall |
|---|---|---|---|---|---|
| All ages | Males | 521 | 8.5 | 40.5 | 51.3 |
|  | Females | 576 | 10.8 | 49.3 | 57.8 |
|  |  |  | p=0.2 | p<0.003 | p<0.03 |
| 20–29 | Males | 168 | 7.1 | 38.1 | 45.9 |
|  | Females | 294 | 7.8 | 53.6 | 60.7 |
|  |  |  | p=0.8 | p<0.001 | p<0.002 |
| 30–39 | Males | 186 | 7.0 | 44.4 | 53.8 |
|  | Females | 180 | 9.4 | 45.0 | 57.0 |
|  |  |  | p=0.4 | p=0.3 | p=0.5 |
| 40–49 | Males | 125 | 11.2 | 43.2 | 54.4 |
|  | Females | 72 | 18.1 | 41.7 | 59.8 |
|  |  |  | p=0.2 | p=0.8 | p=0.5 |
| 50–59 | Males | 42 | 11.9 | 47.6 | 59.5 |
|  | Females | 30 | 30.0 | 36.7 | 66.7 |
|  |  |  | p<0.05 | p=0.4 | p=0.5 |
| P value for males of different age groups |  |  | P=0.43 | P=0.37 | P=0.73 |
| P value for females of different age groups |  |  | P<0.0003 | P=0.55 | P<0.03 |

**Table 11.2** Influence of family structure on the prevalence of adult malnutrition

|  | Type | Head & spouse | | Head, spouse & children | | Head & children | | P |
|---|---|---|---|---|---|---|---|---|
|  |  | N | % | N | % | N | % |  |
| % of adults with low BMI | Severe | 53 | 9.4 | 757 | 8.5 | 50 | 12.3 | 0.15 |
|  | Mild to Moderate | 53 | 39.6 | 39.6 | 757 | 50 | 46.4 | 0.36 |
|  | Overall | 53 | 49.0 | 757 | 53.7 | 50 | 58.7 | 0.42 |
| % of households having at least one malnourished adult | Severe | 47 | 10.6 | 512 | 11.1 | 47 | 22.3 | <0.01 |
|  | Mild to Moderate | 47 | 38.3 | 512 | 53.3 | 47 | 62.0 | <0.002 |
|  | Overall | 47 | 44.7 | 512 | 60.0 | 47 | 70.3 | <0.004 |

**Table 11.3 Influence of area of residence on the prevalence of malnutrition among adults**

|  | Type of Malnutrition | Agargoan | | Central Mohammadpur | | Beri Badh | | P |
|---|---|---|---|---|---|---|---|---|
|  |  | N | % | N | % | N | % |  |
| % of adult population with low BMI | Severe | 504 | 8.7 | 429 | 9.6 | 155 | 13.6 | 0.21 |
|  | Mild to Moderate | 504 | 45.8 | 429 | 39.6 | 155 | 54.8 | <0.004 |
|  | Overall | 504 | 54.5 | 429 | 49.2 | 155 | 68.4 | <0.0002 |
| % of households having at least one malnourished adult | Severe | 337 | 11.3 | 279 | 13.6 | 105 | 19.1 | 0.12 |
|  | Mild to Moderate | 337 | 53.7 | 279 | 47.7 | 105 | 61.0 | <0.05 |
|  | Overall | 337 | 60.2 | 279 | 54.5 | 105 | 72.4 | <0.006 |

Table 11.3 compares areas of residence on the prevalence of adult malnutrition. Percentage of adults with low BMI, as well as households with at least one malnourished adult showed that Beri Badh had the worst prevalence of malnutrition among adults and households, compared to the other two areas.

**Table 11.4 Influence of loan membership involvement of family members on the prevalence of malnutrition in adults**

|  | Type of Malnutrition | No family members involved | | At least one family member is involved | | P |
|---|---|---|---|---|---|---|
|  |  | N | % | N | % |  |
| % of adult population with low BMI | Severe | 634 | 10.6 | 463 | 8.4 | 0.24 |
|  | Mild to Moderate | 634 | 47.3 | 463 | 41.4 | <0.05 |
|  | Overall | 634 | 57.9 | 463 | 49.8 | <0.01 |
| % of households having at least one malnourished adult | Severe | 440 | 13.9 | 287 | 12.2 | 0.52 |
|  | Mild to Moderate | 440 | 52.1 | 287 | 53.3 | <0.74 |
|  | Overall | 440 | 59.1 | 287 | 61.0 | <0.61 |

Table 11.4 shows the influence of loan membership of family members on the prevalence of malnutrition in adults. No family involvement has the most prevalence of mild to moderate and overall malnutrition in adults, compared to at least one member involved. There was no difference by type of malnutrition in households having at least one malnourished adult.

**Table 11.5  Influence of self-perceived financial situation in households in the last 30 days on the prevalence of adult malnutrition**

|  | Type of malnutrition | Deficit | | Break even/ surplus | | P |
|---|---|---|---|---|---|---|
|  |  | N | % |  |  |  |
| % of adults with low BMI | Severe | 668 | 10.0 | 429 | 9.1 | 0.61 |
|  | Mild to Moderate | 668 | 46.9 | 429 | 41.3 | <0.05 |
|  | Overall | 668 | 56.9 | 429 | 50.4 | <0.03 |
| % of households having at least one malnourished adult (low BMI) | Severe | 447 | 13.9 | 280 | 12.1 | 0.50 |
|  | Mild to Moderate | 447 | 54.1 | 280 | 50.0 | 0.28 |
|  | Overall | 447 | 61.7 | 280 | 56.8 | 0.18 |

Table 11.5 compares the influence of self-perceived financial status in households over the last month on the prevalence of malnutrition in adults. Deficit situation has the worst prevalence of mild to moderate and overall malnutrition in adults compared to break even or surplus financial situation. There was no difference by type of malnutrition in households having at least one malnourished adult by self-perceived financial situation.

**Table 11.6  Influence of monthly income on the prevalence of malnutrition in adults**

|  | Type | <2,000 Tk | | 2,000–2,499Tk | | 2,500–3,499Tk | | 3,500–4,499Tk | | 4,500+ Tk | | P |
|---|---|---|---|---|---|---|---|---|---|---|---|---|
|  |  | N | % | N | % | N | % | N | % | N | % |  |
| % of adults with low BMI | Severe | 301 | 9.6 | 150 | 11.3 | 326 | 8.3 | 153 | 11.1 | 156 | 10.3 | 0.81 |
|  | Mild to Moderate | 301 | 45.5 | 150 | 50.0 | 326 | 49.7 | 153 | 37.9 | 156 | 35.3 | <0.01 |
|  | Overall | 301 | 55.2 | 150 | 61.3 | 326 | 58.0 | 153 | 59.0 | 156 | 45.5 | <0.04 |

*Note:* Tk = Taka (Bangladesh currency); US$1 = 48 Taka.

Table 11.6 compares income groups on the prevalence of malnutrition in adults. The percentage of adults with low BMI had the least prevalence of mild to moderate and overall malnutrition in adults in income groups over 4,500 Taka.

**Table 11.7  Influence of household head's occupation on the prevalence of malnutrition in adults**

|  | Type of malnutrition | Regular salaried worker | | Casual wage workers skilled | | Casual wage workers unskilled | | Dependent self-employed | | Self employed | | P |
|---|---|---|---|---|---|---|---|---|---|---|---|---|
|  |  | N | % | N | % | N | % | N | % | N | % |  |
| % of adults with low BMI | Severe | 80 | 8.8 | 55 | 7.3 | 270 | 13.0 | 204 | 6.9 | 179 | 6.7 | 0.11 |
|  | Mild to Moderate | 80 | 32.5 | 55 | 36.4 | 270 | 46.3 | 204 | 53.9 | 179 | 49.7 | <0.01 |
|  | Overall | 80 | 41.3 | 55 | 43.6 | 270 | 59.3 | 204 | 60.8 | 179 | 56.4 | <0.01 |
| % of households having at least one malnourished adult | Severe | 58 | 17.2 | 52 | 7.7 | 129 | 11.6 | 227 | 9.3 | 190 | 13.1 | 0.39 |
|  | Mild to Moderate | 58 | 36.2 | 52 | 42.3 | 129 | 45.7 | 227 | 48.0 | 190 | 48.2 | 0.51 |
|  | Overall | 58 | 50 | 52 | 48.1 | 129 | 54.3 | 227 | 52.0 | 190 | 56.0 | 0.71 |

Table 11.7 compares the household head's occupation on the prevalence of malnutrition in adults. Dependent self-employed had the worst prevalence of mild to moderate and overall malnutrition compared to the other occupational groups. There was no difference in the type of malnutrition among households who had at least one malnourished adult by type of occupation.

**Table 11.8** Comparison of per capita floor space in square metres between households having at least one malnourished adult and households with no malnourished adult

| Type of malnutrition | Households having at least one malnourished adult | | | Households having no malnourished adult | | | P |
|---|---|---|---|---|---|---|---|
| | N | Mean | sd | N | Mean | sd | |
| Severe | 89 | 2.21 | 0.12 | 575 | 2.36 | 0.07 | 0.39 |
| Mild to Moderate | 354 | 2.21 | 0.06 | 310 | 2.49 | 0.11 | <0.01 |
| Overall | 404 | 2.21 | 0.06 | 260 | 2.53 | 0.12 | <0.01 |

Table 11.8 compares per capita floor space between households having at least one malnourished adult and households with no malnourished adults. There was a significant difference in per capita floor space among mild to moderate and overall malnourished adults in households with at least one malnourished adult, compared to households with no malnourished adult.

**Table 11.9** Influence of drinking water on the prevalence of malnutrition in adults

| | Type of malnutrition | Tube well | | Tap | | P |
|---|---|---|---|---|---|---|
| | | N | % | N | % | |
| % of adults with low BMI | Severe | 435 | 9.2 | 579 | 9.8 | 0.72 |
| | Mild to Moderate | 435 | 51.0 | 579 | 33.9 | <0.001 |
| | Overall | 435 | 60.0 | 579 | 49.7 | <0.0001 |

Table 11.9 compares adults with low BMI who drink either tap water or tube well water. Tap water has the least prevalence of mild to moderate and overall adult malnutrition compared to tube well water.

**Table 11.10  Influence of sex of household head on the prevalence of malnutrition in adults**

|  | Type of malnutrition | Female head N | % | Male head N | % | P |
|---|---|---|---|---|---|---|
| % of adults with low BMI | Severe | 109 | 13.2 | 988 | 9.2 | 0.13 |
|  | Mild to Moderate | 109 | 45.5 | 988 | 37.6 | 0.11 |
|  | Overall | 109 | 54.7 | 988 | 51.4 | 0.51 |
| % of households having at least one malnourished adult | Severe | 83 | 15.7 | 644 | 12.9 | 0.48 |
|  | Mild to Moderate | 83 | 54.4 | 644 | 38.6 | <0.007 |
|  | Overall | 83 | 61.4 | 644 | 49.4 | <0.04 |

Table 11.10 describes the influence of household head on the prevalence of adult malnutrition. There was no difference between female and male headed households in terms of the type of malnutrition in adults. But percentage of households with at least one malnourished adult in terms of mild to moderate and overall malnutrition was significant with female heads having the worst prevalence of malnutrition.

**Table 11.11  Influence of electricity in the household on the prevalence of adult malnutrition**

|  | Type of malnutrition | No electricity N | % | Electricity N | % | P |
|---|---|---|---|---|---|---|
| % of adults with low BMI | Severe | 475 | 11.4 | 539 | 8.0 | <0.07 |
|  | Mild to Moderate | 475 | 47.6 | 539 | 42.1 | <0.07 |
|  | Overall | 475 | 59.0 | 539 | 50.1 | <0.004 |
| % of households having at least one malnourished adult | Severe | 314 | 15.3 | 350 | 11.7 | 0.18 |
|  | Mild to Moderate | 314 | 55.3 | 350 | 51.4 | 0.30 |
|  | Overall | 314 | 64.0 | 350 | 58.0 | 0.11 |

Table 11.11 describes the influence of electricity in households on the prevalence of malnutrition in adults. The percentage of adults with low BMI was more prevalent in households with no electricity for severe, mild to moderate and overall malnutrition in adults compared to households with electricity.

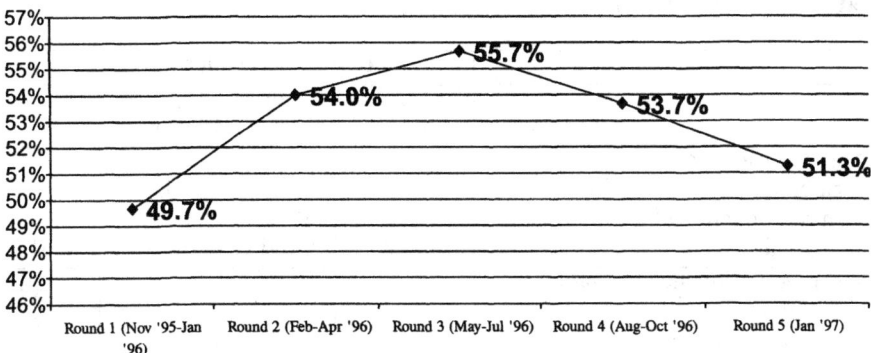

**Figure 11.1** Seasonal variations in the percentage distribution of low BMI in adults (BMI≤18.5)

Figure 11.1 shows the seasonal variation in the percentage distribution of low BMI. The highest prevalence of low BMI was in May to July, 1996, and the lowest prevalence of low BMI was in November to January, 1995.

**Table 11.12** Logistic regression (unadjusted and adjusted) of malnutrition among adults in relation to different socio-demographic, economic and environmental factors

|  | Body Mass Index (≤18.5) | | | |
|---|---|---|---|---|
|  | Unadjusted Odds ratio | P value | Adjusted Odds ratio | P value |
| Sex |  |  |  |  |
| Male | 1 |  | 1 |  |
| Female | 0.77 | 0.03 | 0.43[1] | 0.004 |
| Age group (years) |  |  |  |  |
| Among males |  |  |  |  |
| 20–29 | 1 |  | 1 |  |
| 30–39 | 0.86 | 0.48 | 0.78 | 0.30 |
| 40–49 | 0.77 | 0.27 | 0.67 | 0.14 |
| 50–59 | 0.95 | 0.89 | 0.85 | 0.67 |
| Among females |  |  |  |  |
| 20–29 | 1 |  | 1 |  |
| 30–39 | 1.38 | 0.09 | 1.77 | 0.05 |
| 40–49 | 1.75 | 0.04 | 2.57 | 0.02 |
| 50–59 | 2.36 | 0.04 | 1.53 | 0.56 |

**Table 11.12 (continued)**

|  | Body Mass Index (≤18.5) | | | |
|---|---|---|---|---|
|  | Unadjusted Odds ratio | P value | Adjusted Odds ratio | P value |
| Area of residence | | | | |
| Agargoan | 1 | | 1 | |
| Central Mohammadpur | 0.81 | 0.13 | 0.64 | 0.05 |
| Beri Badh | 1.80 | 0.001 | 1.53 | 0.01 |
| Self-reported financial situation last 30 days | | | | |
| Surplus/Break even | 1 | | 1 | |
| Deficit situation | 1.30 | 0.03 | 0.03 | 0.04 |
| Occupation of principal earner | | | | |
| Regular salaried worker | 1 | | 1 | |
| Casual wage worker (skilled) | 1.10 | 0.78 | 1.07 | 0.85 |
| Casual wage worker (unskilled) | 2.07 | 0.005 | 1.44 | 0.08 |
| Dependent self-employed | 2.21 | 0.003 | 1.65 | 0.03 |
| Unpaid family worker | 1.00 | 0.03 | 1.57 | 0.13 |
| Self-employed | 1.84 | 0.21 | 1.54 | 0.14 |
| Credit organisation involvement | | | | |
| Involved with any credit organisation | 1 | | 1 | |
| Not involved | 1.40 | 0.008 | 1.23 | 0.02 |
| NGO credit involvement | | | (2) | |
| Involved | 1 | | | |
| Not involved | 1.38 | 0.03 | | |
| Last month household income (Tk) | | | | |
| <2000 | 1 | | 1 | |
| 2000–2499 | 1.46 | 0.07 | 1.46 | 0.05 |
| 2500–3499 | 1.20 | 0.28 | 1.04 | 0.85 |
| 3500–4499 | 0.84 | 0.39 | 0.88 | 0.64 |
| 4500+ | 0.71 | 0.08 | 0.79 | 0.37 |
| Floor area per consumption unit | | | | |
| less than 2.5 m$^2$ | 1 | | 1 | |
| 2.5 to less than 5 m$^2$ | 0.97 | 0.80 | 0.87 | 0.39 |
| 5 m$^2$ or more | 0.48 | 0.01 | 0.42 | 0.006 |
| Electricity Supply | | | | |
| With supply | 1 | | 1 | |
| Without supply | 1.43 | 0.007 | 1.10 | 0.64 |
| Source of drinking water | | | | |
| Tap | 1 | | 1 | |
| Tube well | 1.43 | 0.001 | 0.88 | 0.05 |

*Notes*:
(1) Age effect in youngest age group, 20–29.
(2) Omitted because strongly related to previous factor.

Table 11.12 presents logistic regression analysis for the prevalence of malnutrition in adults in relation to socio-demographic, economic and environmental factors. There was a sex difference, with females having a significant odds ratio for low BMI compared to males, which means that women were more malnourished compared to men. There was no difference in age for males, but there was a difference in age for females, with 30–39 and 40–49 years having the worst BMI compared to younger and older age groups. Beri Badh area of residence had the worst BMI compared to other areas. Deficit situations in self reported financial situation had the worst BMI compared to surplus or break even. Casual wage workers unskilled and dependent self-employed had the worst BMI. Households not being involved in credit organisations and NGO credit organisations had the worst BMI compared to those involved in credit organisations and NGO credit organisations. Those households which had income 2,000–2,499 Taka had worse BMIs than those with higher incomes. Floor areas per consumption unit 5m$^2$ or more predicted better BMIs than less floor area per consumption unit. Those households without electricity had worse BMIs than those with electricity supply. Finally tube well water supply predicted worse BMI than tap water.

## Discussion

The nutritional situation of adults was distinctly adverse, with as many as 54 percent showing a BMI of 18.5 km/m$^2$ or less, and almost one tenth (9.7 percent) showing a BMI less than 16. Although comparative figures for the general population are not available, this shows a strong degree of need.

Among younger adults, there was more BMI deficit in females than in males. The interpretation of this must be undertaken with care. Some of the difference may be attributable to the different body constitutions of males and females. There is evidence that in many geographical regions the prevalence of fatness is higher among women than among men (Shetty and James, 1990). In a large survey in Brazil of 16,641 females and 17,135 males, the BMIs in females were greater after 12 years of age and also showed more variability (Branca and Abdulle, 1993). In a study among Tanzanian adult tuberculosis patients more males were found malnourished than females (77 percent vs 58 percent) on admission, with respect to body mass index (BMI) (Kennedy et al., 1996). Despite these indications that females show greater BMI values compared to their male counterparts of the same age group, no separate cut-off points for BMI in females have been set. However, the differences between younger females and males here are considerable. As well as the sheer magnitude of the problem of adult malnutrition, the finding that is still more disturbing is the rapid rise in severe malnutrition among females with age. This is not mirrored among the men, and although the relative numbers of older women is quite small, they are clearly a potentially very vulnerable group and merit particular attention of policy and of targeted interventions.

Adult nutritional status varied between the three slum locations, with Beri Badh faring the worst. That there should be area variation is not surprising, though its magnitude should be noted. Identification of Beri Badh as an area of higher vulnerability and higher risk of adverse outcomes such as poor nutritional status was clear in the qualitative work and underlines the need to identify area of particular need in targeted interventions.

BMI in households where self-perceived financial status and income were worse (in financial deficit households compared to break even or surplus households), and households with income less than 2,500 Taka had the worst BMI, compared with those households who had higher incomes. Other studies have found that BMI was worst in low income households (Nube et al., 1998; Hakeem, 2001; Sarlio-Lahteenkorva and Lahelma, 1999; Delpeuch et al., 2000; Pryer, 1990). Households where the head of household's occupational group was in occupations such as casual wage worker (unskilled) and dependent self-employed had the worst BMI compared to other occupational groups. Pryer (1990; 1993) also found that unskilled labour and dependent self-employed labour had the worst BMI for women and men in Khulna Bangladesh.

BMI was worse in the monsoon season (May to July) where monsoon season appears to be a time of increased hardship, and also shows increased frequencies of work loss by the income generating population, especially affecting those engaged in the construction industry during the rainy season. Morbidity from water borne diseases increases during the rainy season also affecting work loss. Impact of the usual price hike during the monsoon period cannot be ruled out as contributing to poor BMI.

## Conclusions

Fifty-four percent of the adult population had BMI less than 18.5, and almost 10 percent had BMI less than 16. It is unfortunate that although one third of the population of Dhaka consists of slum people, the National Food and Nutrition Policy 1997, published by the Ministry of Health and Family Welfare of the Government of Bangladesh (Bangladesh National Food Policy, 1997), has no mention of improving the nutritional status of this particularly vulnerable section of the population. It is equally unfortunate that the country's biggest nutrition intervention programme "The Bangladesh Integrated Nutrition Project (BINP)", currently operating in 60 thanas in collaboration with partner NGOs, has no plan to work in urban slums (Bangladesh National Food Policy, 1997). This neglect of slum people amounts to non-adherence to the World Declaration on Nutrition (1992) Food and Agriculture Organisation, (1992), which affirms countries' determination to implement the Plan of Action for Nutrition and strongly urges priority to protect and promote the nutritional well-being of the most vulnerable households. Nutritional well-being should be adopted as a key objective in human development to enable all people to lead fully productive lives and contribute to the development of the community and the nation with dignity. Poor slum dwellers are now an integral part of city life, and the smooth running of the city is impossible without them. Yet they are the most deprived community of the city living in inhuman conditions and suffering from chronic hunger and with exceptional levels of malnutrition, especially affecting young children.

This study has shown the magnitude of the nutritional problem and identified some key factors of malnutrition among slum adults. It is hoped that concerned authorities and others will extend their whole-hearted efforts and commitments to these problems affecting the most vulnerable population groups.

**References**

Bangladesh Integrated Nutrition Project (1996), *Project Implementation Volume* (PIV), Ministry of Health and Welfare, Government of Bangladesh, May, pp. 1–94.

Bangladesh National Food and Nutrition Policy (1997), Ministry of Health and Family Welfare, Government of Bangladesh, pp. 1–25.

Beaton, G., Kelly, J., Kevany, R., Martorell, R. and Mason, J. (1990), 'Appropriate use of anthropometric indices in children', December, ACC/SCN State of the Art series on Nutrition Policy, Discussion Paper No. 7, United Nations Administrative Committee on coordination: subcommittee on nutrition, pp. 1–51.

Branca, F., Abdulle, A. (1993), 'Famine in Somalia', letter to the *Lancet*, 5 June, 341(8853), p. 1478.

Delpeuch, F., Traissac, P., Martin-Prevel, Y., Massamba, J.P. and Maire, B. (2000), 'Economic crisis and malnutrition: socio-economic determinants of anthrometric status of pre-school children and their mothers in an African urban area', *Public Health Nutrition*, 3(1), pp. 39–47.

Food and Agriculture Organization and World Health Organization (1992), *International Conference on Nutrition Final Report*, Rome, Italy, December 1992, pp. 9–55.

Gibson, R.S. (1990), 'Anthropometric Assessment', in Gibson, R.S. (ed.), *Principles of Nutritional Assessment*, Oxford University Press, Oxford, pp. 155–208.

Hakeem, R. (2001), 'Socio-economic differences in height and body mass index of children and adults living in urban areas of Karachi, Pakistan', *European Journal of Clinical Nutrition*, 55(5), pp. 400–406.

Kennedy, N., Ramsay, A., Uiso, L., Guttman, J., Ngowi, F.I. and Gillespie, S.H. (1996), 'Nutritional status and weight gain in patients with pulmonary tuberculosis in Tanzania', *Transactions of the Royal Society of Tropical Medicine and Hygiene*, Mar-April, 90(2), pp. 162–6.

Nube, M., Aseno-Okyere, W.R. and van den Boom, G.J. (1998), 'Body Mass Index as indicator of living in developing countries', *European Journal of Clinical Nutrition*, 52(2), pp. 136–44.

Pryer, J.A. (1990), 'Socio-economic and environmental aspects of undernutrition and ill health in an urban slum in Bangladesh', unpublished PhD thesis, London School of Hygiene and Tropical Medicine.

Pryer, J.A. (1993), 'Nutritionally vulnerable households in the urban slum economy: a case study from Khulna, Bangladesh', in Schell, L.M., Smith, M.T. and Bilsborough, A., *Urban Ecology and Health in the Third World*, Cambridge University Press, Cambridge, pp. 61–74.

Sarlio-Lahteenkorva, S. and Lahelma, E. (1999), 'The association of body mass index with social and economic disadvantage in women and men', *International Journal of Epidemiology*, 28(3), pp. 445–9.

Sen, A.K. (1990), 'Gender and cooperative conflicts', in Tinker, I. (ed), *Persistent Inequalities: women and world development*, Oxford University Press, Oxford.

Shetty, P. and James, W.P.T. (1990), 'Body Mass Index. A measure of chronic energy deficiency in adults', FAO Food and Nutrition Paper No. 56, FAO, Rome.

Stata Statistical Software (1999), Release 6, StrataCorp, Strata Press, 702, University Drive East, College Station, Texas 77840.

Chapter 12

# Investing in Children's Nutritional Status

*Wasting was more prevalent among older girls compared to older boys. Logistic regression results show that females are better nourished compared to boys. Female headed households have less stunted children, but more wasting compared to male headed households. Children in the age group 24–59 months are more likely to be stunted, but show less wasting and more underweight children compared to the younger age group (3–23 months). Beri Badh had the worst stunting and underweight children of areas covered. Financial deficit households are more likely to be stunted, more likely to be wasted and more likely to be underweight. In conclusion, undernourished children were related to demographic, economic, social and environmental factors.*

**Introduction**

It is well established that undernutrition is not randomly distributed within a given population, but is a dimension of poverty. In urban areas, the ability of a household to command sufficient food resources is primarily dependent upon social and economic variables, such as social networks, employment, income and assets. Households are often characterised by a dependence upon the market, not only for employment, but also for food and other basic needs.

Earlier work by Pryer (1990) indicates that urban slum households are not homogeneous. Particular strategies are adopted to maintain the integrity of the household in the face of adversity. Such livelihood groups may be more appropriate targets for assistance by policy makers than individuals or households identified on account of single characteristics such as poor nutritional status, or lack of material resources.

Several studies conducted in urban areas of developing countries have demonstrated that undernutrition in children is associated with low income (Pryer, 1990; Huttly et al., 1991; Jongpiputvanich et al., 1992; Khin-Maung et al., 1992; Engle, 1993), low assets (Pryer, 1990; Rica and Becker, 1996), morbidity (Huttly et al., 1991; Mbago and Namfua, 1992; Defo and Young, 1993; Madzingira, 1995; Ricca and Becker, 1996), employment (Pryer, 1990), total household expenditure (Engle, 1993), low education of the mother (Jogpiputvanich et al., 1992; Ricca and Becker, 1996; Doan and Bishatarat, 1990; Lima et al., 1990; Rao and Balakrishna, 1990; Engle, 1991), social networks (Lima et al., 1990), housing status (Ricca and Becker, 1996; Engle, 1991; Islam et al., 1994; Thaver et al., 1990) and sanitation

(Islam et al., 1994). Demographic variables including household size (Doan and Bisatarat, 1990; Rao and Balakrishna, 1990), birth order (Jongpiputvanich et al., 1992; Engle, 1991) and female gender (Huttly et al., 1991; Mbago and Nufua, 1992; Doan and Bishatarat, 1990; Thraver et al., 1990; Ramphlele et al., 1991) are also associated with undernutrition.

In this chapter we describe nutritional status of children by socio-economic, demographic, health, and environmental factors.

## Statistical analysis

The outcome measures were: (a) individual child specific nutritional status, based on stunting (HAZ<-2SD), wasting (WHZ<-2SD) and underweight (WAZ <-2SD), with measures of <-2SD designated "severe" and measures of <-2SD but >-3SD designated "moderate", and (b) family specific child nutritional status, with families classified as "with at least one malnourished child", for stunting, wasting and underweight separately, each at the "severe" and "moderate" level. Statistical testing of differences between percentages across levels of each risk factor was carried out with allowance for household clustering in using the "svy" command Stata (Stata Corp, 1999). The risk factors that showed associations with outcomes that were statistically significant or close to significant were assessed for their joint inference on the outcomes by logistic regression. The logistic regression model incorporates child's sex, sex of household head, age, living area, self reported financial situation, latrine use by children, and diarrhoeal episodes in the last 14 days, as independent variables. These were tested to see their effects on each of the outcome variables: stunting, wasting and underweight (WAZ <-2SD).

## Results

Table 12.1 presents the percentage distribution of malnourished children. Older children were more likely to be stunted compared to younger children. Younger children were more likely to be wasted, compared to older children. There were no significant differences in the proportion of underweight children by age groups, although young children were more likely to be underweight compared to older children. But older children were moderately underweight, compared to younger children.

Table 12.2 presents influence of mother's and father's literacy on the prevalence of malnutrition in children. Mother's literacy, whatever level of education did not affect children's stunting, wasting and underweight. Father's literacy was related to the prevalence of stunting but not to wasting or underweight.

**Table 12.1** Percentage distribution of malnourished children classified by Z scores and age group

| Category of malnutrition | Age Group | No of Children | Severe | Moderate | Overall |
|---|---|---|---|---|---|
| Stunted | 3–24 months | 163 | 30.7% | 28.2% | 58.9% |
| | 24–59 months | 274 | 42.0% | 32.1% | 74.1% |
| | P value | | <0.01 | 0.40 | <0.001 |
| Wasted | 3–24 months | 163 | 9.8% | 28.8% | 38.6% |
| | 24–59 months | 277 | 3.3% | 23.5% | 26.8% |
| | P value | | <0.004 | 0.21 | <0.01 |
| Underweight | 3–24 months | 178 | 40.5% | 31.5% | 72.0% |
| | 24–59 months | 281 | 38.1% | 36.0% | 74.1% |
| | P Value | | 0.61 | 0.32 | 0.62 |

**Table 12.2** Influence of father's and mother's literacy on the prevalence of malnutrition in children

| | Type of Malnutrition | No Schooling | | 1–5 years Schooling | | 6 years + Schooling | | P Value |
|---|---|---|---|---|---|---|---|---|
| | | N | % | N | % | N | % | |
| Mother's literacy % of children | stunted | 274 | 70 | 107 | 73 | 24 | 71 | 0.86 |
| | wasted | 278 | 32 | 107 | 32 | 24 | 21 | 0.52 |
| | underweight | 289 | 74 | 113 | 77 | 25 | 76 | 0.82 |
| Father's literacy % of children | stunted | 229 | 75 | 114 | 69 | 61 | 30 | <0.0001 |
| | wasted | 233 | 31 | 114 | 32 | 61 | 36 | 0.74 |
| | underweight | 242 | 74 | 118 | 76 | 66 | 69 | 0.64 |

Table 12.3 presents the influence of housing construction on the prevalence of malnutrition in children. As can be seen from the table, wasted and underweight children were highest in complete katcha, compared to other building types. There was no difference in stunting by housing construction. The percentage of households with at least one malnourished child was greatest in households occupying complete katcha for wasted and underweight children.

**Table 12.3  Influence of housing construction on the prevalence of malnutrition in children**

| | Type of malnutrition | Complete katcha | | Katcha wall + tin roof | | Complete tin | | Complete brick or combined | | P value |
|---|---|---|---|---|---|---|---|---|---|---|
| | | N | % | N | % | N | % | N | % | |
| % of children | stunted | 95 | 66.3 | 240 | 70.8 | 25 | 52.0 | 40 | 60 | 0.17 |
| | wasted | 95 | 39.0 | 241 | 31.0 | 25 | 16.0 | 40 | 12.5 | <0.01 |
| | underweight | 98 | 79.6 | 251 | 75.3 | 25 | 64.0 | 43 | 58.0 | <0.03 |
| % of households with at least one malnourished child | stunted | 81 | 67.9 | 204 | 70.6 | 23 | 47.8 | 31 | 61.3 | 0.14 |
| | wasted | 81 | 42.0 | 204 | 35.3 | 23 | 17.4 | 31 | 12.9 | <0.01 |
| | underweight | 81 | 86.4 | 204 | 77.9 | 23 | 60.9 | 31 | 67.7 | <0.03 |

Table 12.4 presents the influence of latrine use by children on the prevalence of malnutrition. Non-sanitary latrine use had the highest prevalence of stunted, wasted and underweight children compared to better latrines.

**Table 12.4  Influence of latrine use by children in households on the prevalence of malnutrition in children**

| | Type of Malnutrition | Non-sanitary | | Better | | P value |
|---|---|---|---|---|---|---|
| | | N | % | N | % | |
| % of children | stunted | 334 | 73 | 65 | 55 | <0.004 |
| | wasted | 334 | 32 | 66 | 18 | <0.02 |
| | underweight | 342 | 78 | 78 | 72 | <0.01 |
| % of households having at least one malnourished child | stunted | 279 | 71 | 64 | 48 | <0.0005 |
| | wasted | 279 | 36 | 64 | 19 | <0.008 |
| | underweight | 279 | 80 | 64 | 63 | <0.002 |

Table 12.5 presents household income among households with no malnourished child and households who have at least one malnourished child. Households with at least one stunted or underweight child had a lower household income than those without. There were no differences in household income between households with at least one wasted child and those without.

**Table 12.5  Comparison of mean gross monthly household income in Taka between households with no malnourished child and households having at least one malnourished child**

| Type of Malnutrition | Households having at least one malnourished child | | | Households having no malnourished child | | | P Value |
|---|---|---|---|---|---|---|---|
| | N | Mean | sd | N | Mean | sd | |
| Stunted | 256 | 2816 | 96 | 120 | 4487 | 1432 | <0.05 |
| Wasted | 128 | 3977 | 1330 | 248 | 3025 | 144 | 0.32 |
| Underweight | 290 | 2747 | 85 | 86 | 5379 | 1994 | <0.003 |

Table 12.6 presents the influence of self-perceived financial situation in the last 30 days on the prevalence of malnutrition in children. The households with a deficit in financial situation had more stunted, wasted and underweight children, than households with break even or surplus income. The same results were found for percentage of households having at least one malnourished child.

**Table 12.6  Influence of self-perceived financial situation in households in the last 30 days on the prevalence of malnutrition in children**

| | Type of Malnutrition | Deficit | | Break even/ surplus | | P value |
|---|---|---|---|---|---|---|
| | | N | % | N | % | |
| % of children | stunted | 257 | 72.8 | 180 | 62.2 | <0.02 |
| | wasted | 258 | 35.3 | 182 | 15.3 | <0.03 |
| | underweight | 268 | 78.7 | 191 | 65.5 | <0.002 |
| % of households having at least one malnourished child | stunted | 224 | 71.9 | 152 | 62.5 | <0.06 |
| | wasted | 224 | 39.3 | 152 | 26.3 | <0.01 |
| | underweight | 224 | 81.7 | 152 | 70.4 | <0.01 |

Figure 12.1 presents the seasonal distribution of stunting, wasting and underweight children. The percentage of stunting, wasting and underweight children was highest in August to October and lowest in November to January.

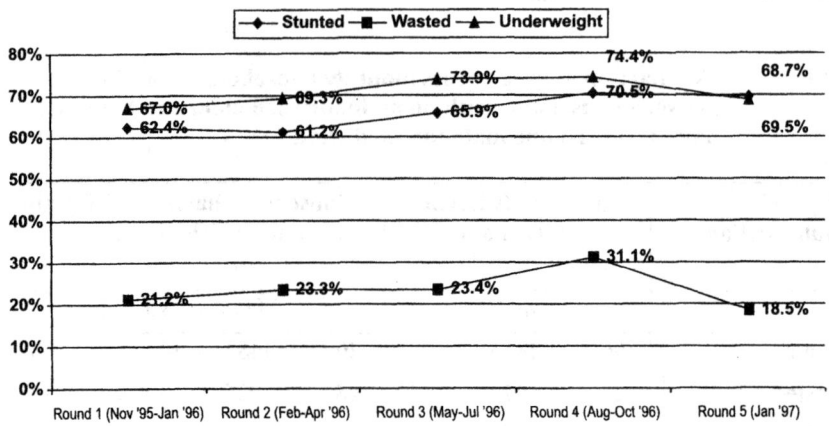

**Figure 12.1** Seasonal variation in the percentage distribution of the stunted, wasted and underweight children

**Table 12.7** Logistic regression (unadjusted and adjusted) of prevalence of malnutrition in children, socio-demographic, economic, health and environmental factors

| | Stunting | | | | Wasting | | | | Underweight | | | |
|---|---|---|---|---|---|---|---|---|---|---|---|---|
| | Unadjusted | | Adjusted | | Unadjusted | | Adjusted | | Unadjusted | | Adjusted | |
| | Odds ratio | P | Odds ratio | P | Odds ratio | P | Odds ratio | P | Odds ratio | P | Odds ratio | P |
| Sex | | | | | | | | | | | | |
| Boy | 1 | | 1 | | 1 | | 1 | | 1 | | 1 | |
| Girl | 0.97 | 0.90 | 0.98 | 0.93 | 0.84 | 0.40 | 1.0 | 1.0 | 0.74 | 0.15 | 0.95 | 0.82 |
| Sex of household head | | | | | | | | | | | | |
| Male headed | 1 | | 1 | | 1 | | 1 | | 1 | | 1 | |
| Female headed | 0.52 | 0.10 | 0.40 | <0.04 | 1.04 | 0.92 | 1.40 | 0.52 | 0.52 | 0.57 | 0.50 | <0.08 |
| Age Group (months) | | | | | | | | | | | | |
| 3–23 | 1 | | 1 | | 1 | | 1 | | 1 | | 1 | |
| 24–59 | 2.0 | <0.001 | 2.2 | <0.001 | 0.58 | <0.009 | 0.57 | <0.02 | 1.11 | 0.62 | 1.18 | 0.50 |

## Table 12.7 (continued)

| | Stunting | | | | Wasting | | | | Underweight | | | |
|---|---|---|---|---|---|---|---|---|---|---|---|---|
| | Unadjusted | | Adjusted | | Unadjusted | | Adjusted | | Unadjusted | | Adjusted | |
| | Odds ratio | P | Odds ratio | P | Odds ratio | P | Odds ratio | P | Odds ratio | P | Odds ratio | P |
| Area of residence | | | | | | | | | | | | |
| Agargoan | 1 | | 1 | | 1 | | 1 | | 1 | | 1 | |
| Central Moh'dpur | 0.87 | 0.52 | 0.91 | 0.75 | 0.93 | 0.74 | 1.34 | 0.28 | 0.55 | <0.008 | 0.67 | 0.15 |
| Beri Badh | 1.80 | <0.08 | 1.84 | <0.09 | 0.91 | 0.75 | 0.79 | 0.47 | 1.28 | 0.48 | 1.07 | 0.86 |
| Self-reported financial situation | | | | | | | | | | | | |
| Surplus/break even | 1 | | 1 | | 1 | | 1 | | 1 | | 1 | |
| Deficit situation | 1.62 | <0.02 | 1.55 | <0.06 | 1,61 | <0.03 | 1.84 | <0.01 | 1.95 | <0.002 | 1.63 | <0.04 |
| Cooking location | | | | | | | | | | | | |
| Outside sleeping room | 1 | | 1 | | 1 | | 1 | | 1 | | 1 | |
| Inside sleeping room | 1.26 | 0.31 | 1.04 | 0.88 | 1.40 | 0.12 | 1.34 | 0.23 | 1.53 | <0.08 | 1.30 | 0.35 |
| Latrine use by children | | | | | | | | | | | | |
| Better | 1 | | 1 | | 1 | | 1 | | 1 | | 1 | |
| Worse | 1.93 | <0.02 | 1.89 | <0.06 | 2.27 | <0.02 | 2.10 | <0.06 | 2.21 | <0.004 | 1.55 | 0.19 |
| Diarrhoea in the last 14 days | | | | | | | | | | | | |
| Suffered | 1 | | 1 | | 1 | | 1 | | 1 | | 1 | |
| Not suffered | 1.07 | 0.78 | 1.25 | 0.40 | 0.94 | 0.80 | 1.30 | 0.32 | 0.72 | 0.18 | 0.91 | 0.73 |

Table 12.7 presents logistic regression analysis for prevalence of malnutrition by socio-demographic, economic, health and environmental factors. There was no sex difference in stunting, wasting or underweight. In this analysis female headed households had less stunted and underweight children than male headed households and older children were more likely to be stunted or wasted but not underweight Beri Badh had the highest odds ratio for stunting, wasting and underweight, compared to Agargoan and Central Mohaddpur. For self reported financial situation, a financial deficit situation had the highest odds ratio for stunting, wasting and underweight compared to a surplus or break even situation. Worse latrine use had a

higher odds ratio for stunting, wasting and underweight children than better latrine use, but there was no association with diarrhoea or cooking location.

## Discussion

This chapter describes children's nutritional status by demographic, economic, social and environmental factors. First we discuss the prevalence of undernourished children. The prevalence of stunting was 58 percent for 3–24 months, and 74 percent among older children (24–59 months), which far exceeds the WHO threshold criteria for high level of stunting (40 percent) (WHO, 1999). The prevalence of wasting among ULS children was 39 percent for younger children and 27 percent for older children, which is double the WHO criteria for wasting (15 percent) (WHO, 1999). The prevalence of underweight children was 72 percent for younger children and 74 percent for older children, which was double the WHO very-high-level criteria for underweight children at 30 percent (WHO, 1999).

As can be seen from Figure 12.2 which graphs the results from three nutritional surveys in Bangladesh – Child Nutrition Study of Bangladesh 1995–96 (CNSB); Nutrition Surveillance Project 1998 (NSP) and Urban Livelihood Project (ULS) – the present study (ULS) has the highest prevalence for stunting, wasting and underweight children, compared to the Child Nutrition Survey of Bangladesh, 1995–1996, and the Nutrition Surveillance Project, 1998.

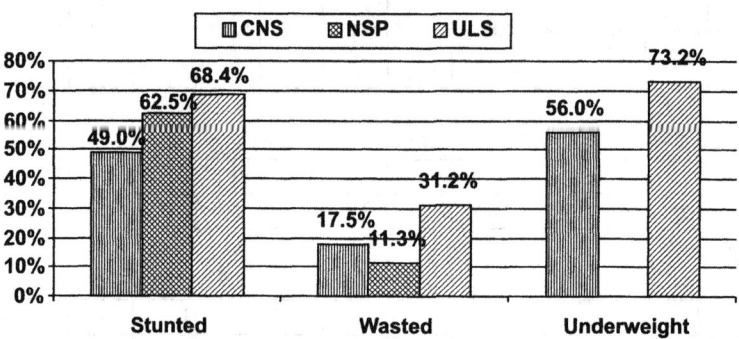

**Figure 12.2** Prevalence of stunted, wasted and underweight children as observed in Bangladesh

In this study, older children were more likely to be stunted and wasted than younger children, which is consistent with findings elsewhere (Victoria, 1992; Keller, 1988; Saxena et al., 1997). However the lower prevalence of stunting and underweight in female headed households is surprising and as yet unexplained (Rogers, 1996; Johnson and Rogers, 1993). The pattern of seasonal malnutrition is nevertheless consistent with other results from Bangladesh, where malnutrition is highest in August–October (the monsoon period) and lowest in November–January (the winter season).

Studies have revealed that malnutrition is associated with low education of the mother (Jongpiputvanich et al., 1992; Ricca and Becker, 1996; Doan and Bishatavat, 1990; Lima et al., 1990; Rao and Balakrishna, 1990; Engle, 1991). In this study mother's literacy was not associated with the prevalence of malnutrition among children. However, father's literacy did demonstrate an association, at least with stunting – the higher the literacy, the better the outcome. This finding may be regarded as important for a male dominated society where women's opinion is often ignored. Literate fathers understand the need of adequate nutrient intake by their children, and as the household decision maker, their knowledge is reflected in procuring foods for the children. On the contrary, women, although being literate, often fail to influence their husbands for such needs. However, the Child Nutrition Survey of Bangladesh (Bangladesh Bureau of Statistics, 1997) shows a declining prevalence of malnutrition among children, irrespective of rural or urban, with increasing levels of literacy of mothers and caretakers.

Housing structures is related to children's malnutrition in many other studies (Ricca and Becker, 1996; Engle, 1991; Islam et al., 1994; Thaver et al., 1990). The katcha (straw) house has the higher prevalence of wasted and underweight children compared to children from tin or brick houses. Similarly, latrine use has been associated with malnutrition in other studies (Islam et al., 1994; Huttly et al., 1991). Non-sanitary latrine use by children was associated with stunting, wasting and underweight children.

Many studies have shown that low income is associated with under-nutrition (Pryer, 1990; Huttly et al., 1991; Jongpiputvanich et al., 1992; Khin-Maung et al., 1992; Engle, 1993). This study compares the income of households with at least one malnourished child, and households with no malnourished child. Households with at least one malnourished child had significantly lower income and a higher prevalence of stunting and underweight children, but not those with wasting, compared to households with no malnourished child. Similarly, the influence of self-perceived financial situation in households showed that households who perceived that they were in deficit, had significantly higher prevalence of stunting, wasting and underweight children, compared to households who perceived that they were break-even or in surplus. Similar results were found when percentage of households having at least one malnourished child was compared to households with no malnourished children.

A number of reports on nutritional status in Bangladesh (Bangladesh Bureau of Statistics, 1997; Nutrition Surveillance Project, 1998), as well as the Urban Livelihoods Study, have shown the poor state of nutrition of children living in urban slums. The slum population is a group, which has been and is still neglected as a target group for nutrition policy. This study tries to find out the magnatude of malnutrition and identifies some key factors that are associated with child malnutrition in the slum population. We hope that it will provide a stimulus to government and non government organisations to seek constructive ways forward which might begin to address the most basic human needs of the urban poor.

Logistic regression showed that female headed households are more likely to be stunted or underweight compared to male headed households in agreement with other studies (Rogers, 1996; Johnson and Rogers, 1993). Older children are more likely to be stunted and wasted than younger children (Victora, 1992; Keller, 1988; Saxena et al., 1997). Households with a deficit financial situation were more likely to be stunted, wasted and underweight, which agrees with many other studies (Pryer, 1993; 1993b; Huttly et al., 1991; Jongpiputvanich et al., 1992; Khin-Maung et al., 1992; Engle, 1993). Lastly, households with poor latrine use by children, were more likely to be stunted or wasted, compared to households who used better latrines for their children (Islam et al., 1994; Huttly et al., 1991).

In conclusion, all reports on children's nutritional status in Bangladesh (Bangladesh Bureau of Statistics, 1997; Nutrition Surveillance Project, 1998) have unanimously shown the highest prevalence of malnutrition in children living in slums. The Government of Bangladesh has no plans to improve the nutritional status of children in this most vulnerable group. This negligence to slum people may be assumed as a symbol of non-adherence to the World Declaration on Nutrition (1992). From the analyses, undernourished children were related to demographic, economic, social and environmental factors.

**References**

Bangladesh Bureau of Statistics (1997), *Child Nutrition Survey of Bangladesh, 1995–96*, Ministry of Planning, Statistics Division, Government of Bangladesh, Dhaka 1997, pp. 1–144.

Defo, B.K. and Young, T.B. (1993), 'Correlates of malnutrition among children under two years of age admitted to hospital in Yaounde, Cameroon', *Journal of Tropical Paediatrics*, 39, pp. 68–75.

Doan, R.M. and Bishatarat, L. (1990), 'Female autonomy and child nutritional status in the extended family, Amman, Jordan', *Social Science and Medicine*, 31(7), pp. 783–789.

Engle, P.L. (1991), 'Maternal work and child care strategies in peri-urban Guatemala: Nutritional effects', *Child Development*, 62(5), pp. 954–965.

Engle, P.L. (1993), 'Influences of mother's and father's income on children's nutritional status in Guatemala', *Social Science and Medicine*, 37(11), pp. 1303–1312.

Epidemiological Information (Epi Info) (1999), Version 6.0, Center for Disease Control, Atlanta, USA, and World Health Organization, Geneva, Switzerland.

Huttly, S.R.A., Victora, C.G., Barros, F.C., Teixeira, A.M.B. and Vaughn, P.J. (1991), 'The timing of nutritional status determination: Implications for interventions and growth monitoring', *European Journal of Clinical Nutrition*, 45, pp. 85–95.

Islam, M.A., Rahman, M.M. and Mahalanabis, D. (1994), 'Maternal and socio-economic factors and the risk of severe malnutrition in a child: a case-control study', *European Journal of Clinical Nutrition*, 48, pp. 416–424.

Johnson, F.C. and Rogers, B.L. (1993), 'Children's nutritional status in female headed households in Dominican Republic', *Social Science and Medicine*, 37(11), pp. 1293–1301.

Jongpiputvanich, S., Poomsuwan, P. and Phittayanon, P. (1992), 'Prevalence and risk factors of protein energy malnutrition (PEM) in pre-school children of

Klong-Toey Slum, Bangkok, Thailand', *Journal of the Medical Association of Thailand*, 75(1), pp. 39–44.

Keller, W. (1988), 'The Epidemiology of Stunting', in Waterlow, J.C. (ed.), *Linear growth retardation in less developing countries*, New York, Raven Press, Nestlé Nutrition workshops series, Vol. 14.

Khin-Maung, U., Khin, M., Wai, N.N., Hman, N.W., Myint, T.T. and Butler, T. (1992), 'Risk factors for the development of persistent diarrhoea and malnutrition in Burmese children', *International Journal of Epidemiology*, 21(5), pp. 1021–1029.

Lima, M., Figuira, M.D. and Ebrahim, G.J. (1990), 'Malnutrition among children of adolescent mothers in a squatter community of Redclife, Brazil', *Journal of Tropical Paediatrics*, 36, pp. 14–19.

Madzingira N. (1995), 'Malnutrition in children under five in Zimbabwe: Effects of social-economic factors and disease', *Social Biology*, 42(3–4), pp. 239–246.

Mbago, M.C.Y. and Namfua, P.P. (1992), 'Some determinants of nutritional status of one-to-four-year-old children in low income areas in Tanzania', *Journal of Tropical Paediatrics*, 38, pp. 299–306.

Nutrition Surveillance Project (1998), 'Report of the 49 round (urban; April, 1998)', Helen Keller International (Bangladesh) and Institute of Public Health Nutrition, Government of Bangladesh, Dhaka.

Pryer, J.A. (1990), 'Socio-economic and environmental aspects of undernutrition and ill health in an urban slum in Bangladesh', unpublished PhD Thesis, London School of Hygiene and Tropical Medicine.

Pryer, J.A. (1993a), 'Nutritionally vulnerable households in the urban slum economy: a case study from Khulna, Bangladesh', in Schell, L.M., Smith, M.T. and Bilsborough, A. (eds), *Urban Ecology and Health in the Third World*, Cambridge University Press, Cambridge, pp. 61–74.

Pryer, J.A. (1993b), 'The impact of adult ill health on household income and nutrition in Khulna, Bangladesh', *Environment and Urbanization*, 5(2), pp. 35–49.

Ramphlele, M.A., Helap, M. and Trollip, D.K. (1991), 'Health status of hostel dwellers, part III, Nutritional status of children 0–5 years', *South African Medical Journal*, 79, pp. 705–709.

Rao, K.V. and Balakrishna, N. (1990), 'Discriminant function analysis: a case study of some socio-economic constraints on child nutrition', *Indian Journal of Medical Research*, 92, pp. 66–71.

Ricca, J.A. and Becker, S. (1996), 'Risk factors for wasting and stunting among children in Metro Cebu, Philippines', *American Journal of Clinical Nutrition*, 63, pp. 966–75.

Rogers, B.L. (1996), 'The implications of female household headship for food consumption and nutritional status in the Dominican Republic', *World Development*, 24(1), pp. 113–28.

Saxena, N., Nayar, D. and Kapil, U. (1997), 'Prevalence of underweight, stunting and wasting', *Indian Pediatrics*, 34(7), pp. 627–31.

Stata Statistical Software (1999), Release 6, StataCorp, Stata Press, 702, University Drive East, College Station, Texas 77840.

Thaver, I.H., Ebrahim, G.J. and Richardson, R. (1990), 'Infant mortality and undernutrition in the squatter settlements of Karachi', *Journal of Tropical Paediatrics*, 36, pp. 135–140.

Victora, C.G. (1992), 'The association between wasting and stunting: an international perspective', *Journal of Nutrition*, 122, pp. 1105–1110.

Chapter 13

# Intra-household Distribution of Nutritional Vulnerability

*Extending the unit of measurement from the individual to the household may enhance the utility of natural indicators. Such a classification may enable patterns of intra-household undernutrition to be identified and to characterise different problems and causes.*

*We also provide two detailed profiles, one featuring a female headed household and how the household became undernourished and a second in which ill health in a main earner caused the household to become malnourished.*

## Introduction

Dugdale (1985) proposed that the utility of nutritional indicators may be enhanced by extending the unit of measurement from the individual to the household. Such a classification may enable patterns of intra-household undernutrition to be identified and to characterise different problems and causes. Household anthropometry has been advanced as being of potential value in increasing the efficiency of targeted interventions (Dugdale, 1985; Payne, 1992). To date the application of household has been limited (Pryer, 1990; Gillespie and McNeill, 1992; Kogi-Makau, 1988).

## Method

The nutritional characteristics of mothers, fathers, adolescents, children 5–10 years and children less than five were examined. For each group, nutrition was classified as (+) if at least 50 percent of individuals in the group had a satisfactory nutritional status, else nutritional status was classified as (–). A nutritional cut-off of WHZ<–25D was used for children up to 10 years and a BMI of <18.5 was used as a cut-off for adults. Households with similar patterns were then grouped and a classification was developed. Finally, the distribution of the intra-household nutritional patterns across the livelihood clusters identified in chapter 3 was investigated.

**Table 13.1  Patterns of intra-household anthropometry**

| Pattern | Mother | Father | >10 years | 5–10 years | <5 years | Study households (%) |
|---|---|---|---|---|---|---|
| A  | + | +/NA | +/NA | + | + | 5.2 |
| B1 | − | −/NA | −/NA | −/NA | − | 15.0 |
| B2 | − | NA   | −/NA | −/NA | − | 3.8 |
| C1 | − | −    | −/NA | −/NA | + | 7.6 |
| C2 | − | −    | −/NA | + | + | 1.4 |
| D1 | − | +    | +/NA | +/NA | − | 7.2 |
| D2 | − | +    | +/NA | − | + | 4.3 |
| D3 | − | +    | +/NA | − | − | 2.9 |
| D4 | − | +/NA | −    | −/+ | − | 3.8 |
| E1 | + | −    | +/NA | +/NA | − | 3.8 |
| E2 | + | −    | −/NA | −/NA | + | 2.4 |
| E3 | + | −    | −/NA | −/NA | − | 6.3 |
| F1 | − | −    | +/NA | +/NA | − | 7.2 |
| G1 | + | +    | +/NA | +/NA | − | 8.1 |
| G2 | + | +    | +/NA | − | − | 2.9 |
| H1 | − | +    | +/−  | +/NA | + | 4.3 |
| H2 | + | −    | −/NA | + | + | 5.2 |
| H3 | − | −    | +/NA | +/NA | + | 1.9 |
| H4 | + | +    | −/NA | −/NA | + | 6.3 |

*Notes*: For each group, nutrition was classified as (+) if at least 50 percent of individuals in the group had satisfactory nutritional status, else nutritional status was classified as (−). A nutritional cut-off of WHZ<−2SD for children up to 10 years old; and BMI of <18.5 was used for the rest. NA indicates there were no household members in the category.

**Results**

Table 13.1 shows the patterns of intra-household nutrition. In total, 19 patterns were identified. The majority of households had at least one member below the weight-for-height BMI cut-off. Only 5.2 percent of households had all members "adequately nourished" (pattern A). In households with pattern A, members may have been small in stature, reflecting chronic growth retardation in childhood, but their present nutritional status was satisfactory.

Nearly 19 percent of households exhibited pattern B, whereby at least 50 percent of members in each age category were below the weight-for-height or BMI cut-off. We interpreted this pattern as being due to inadequate food entitlements. There were two main variants to pattern B. B1 comprised households where mothers and fathers were present, whereas B2 consisted solely of female headed households.

Pattern C, accounted for 9 percent of the study households. Here at least 50 percent of household members in each category, except for children under five years old (and also children aged 5 to 10 years in pattern C2) were below the weight-for-height and BMI cut-off. These patterns seem to run counter to the concept of pre-school children being the most vulnerable of household members. An examination of the households exhibiting these patterns reveals that in 32 percent of cases it was a breast-fed infant who was nutritionally protected (perhaps temporarily). But in the remaining cases, children of weaning age and older were neither wasted or stunted. It is possible that purposive child protection strategies could have been adopted in these households – for example, through a positive allocation of maternal care-time, and through efficient disease and feeding management.

Patterns D1, D2, D3 and D4 together accounted for 18.2 percent of the study households and linked undernutrition in the mother with one or more of her children. These patterns could be interpreted as poor health and nutritional status of the mother having secondary effects on children. Alternatively, pattern D4 could be interpreted as a positive allocation of nutritional resources towards the male household head, with secondary effects on younger children.

Pattern E1, E2 and E3 has exhibited in 12.5 percent of households which linked undernutrition in fathers with children under five and/or five to ten years old. Patterns E1 and E2 may be due to a coincidence of morbidity in both the father and the child. Another possible interpretation could be illness in the father leading to a diversion of maternal care-time, either through increased domestic demands or the necessity of the mother becoming an income earner. Pattern E3, which linked undernutrition in the father with members in all ages, except the mother, was an unexpected finding.

Pattern F1 was exhibited in 7.2 percent of households which linked undernutrition in both parents with under five-year-old children. It may be hypothesised that members above the weight-for-height cut-off in the 5–10 years, or above 10 years of age, were household earners. An examination of the households exhibiting pattern F1 revealed that in 42 percent of cases it was adolescent male earners who were above the cut-off. In these households this pattern could be interpreted as preferential allocation of nutritional resources towards adolescent male earners. In the remaining households, 14 percent had non-working female adolescents above the BMI cut-off, and in 44 percent of households it was non-earning 5–10 year old children of either sex who were above the cut-off. Perhaps in these cases, older children could fend for themselves.

Finally, patterns H1, H2, H3 and H4, which together accounted for 17.7 percent of households, indicate isolated undernutrition amongst mothers, fathers, both fathers and mothers, or amongst other adults or adolescents. In the case of one parent of adolescent only, this could be due to disease; or alternatively, in the case of mothers, could be a result of the effect of income on her nutritional status, or misallocation of household resources. In the case of both parents being undernourished, this could indicate a low household food entitlements being disproportionately borne by parents, or alternatively due to illness.

The household anthropometric patterns identified here indicated a broad nutritional aetiology amongst the slum households. No one household anthropometric pattern predominated. The classification developed indicated that undernutrition at the household level was a considerable problem. Forty-five percent of households exhibited patterns B, C, D4, E3 and F1, which link undernutrition amongst several categories of household members. A further 20.6 percent of households displayed patterns D1, D2, D3 and E1, which link undernutrition in either the mother or father with children under 5 years, and five to ten years old. Twenty-three percent of households exhibiting pattern B contained a severely undernourished child.

Table 13.2 shows the distribution of the household anthropometric patterns across the livelihood clusters identified in chapter 3. There was a marked difference in the proportion of households exhibiting pattern B. Forty-five percent of households in cluster 3 exhibited this pattern, compared to three percent in cluster 1. However cluster 3 also had the highest proportion of households exhibiting pattern C (14 percent compared with 3 percent in cluster 1, 10 percent in cluster 2 and 7 percent in cluster 4). It was hypothesised that this pattern is indicative of purposive child protection strategies. It was interesting that in most cluster 3 households exhibiting this pattern it was little boys who were nutritionally protected, which in the Bangladesh context could be interpreted as gender biased purposive child protective strategy. Satisfactory nutritional status in all household members was most common in cluster 1 (12.5 percent), but was also found in over 5 percent of cluster 3 households, indicated a proportion of these households avoid nutritional vulnerability. Pattern G1, indicating isolated malnutrition amongst pre-school children was concentrated in cluster 1 and cluster 4. It is hypothesised that this distribution might be explained by weaning practices, particularly bottle feeding, as an explanation for poor nutritional status amongst children in relatively richer slum households. Higher proportions of households in the richer livelihood groups also exhibited patterns indicating isolated undernutrition in mothers (H1), fathers (H2) and in adolescents or children aged 5–10 years (H4), possibly the outcome of disease rather than inadequate food supply.

Finally, adequate nutritional status only in fathers (D4), only in mothers (E3) or in adolescents of 5–10 year olds (F1) was distributed across the clusters and might substantiate the hypothesis that such patterns represent the preferential allocation of nutritional resources to earners in these households.

In the analyses we have presented it is clearly those households that exhibit pattern B that are the most vulnerable. Such situations will have arisen, consequent upon impoverishment, for example due to inadequate income, or to illness in an adult earner. The process of impoverishment affects the whole household. We present two examples which graphically illustrate the process and the struggle.

## Table 13.2 Intra-household anthropometric patterns by livelihood groups

| Pattern | Mother | Father | >10 years | 5–10 years | <5 years | C1 Self-employed (n=178) | C2 Dependent self-employed (n=190) | C3 Female headed (n=124) | C4 Casual skilled (n=67) |
|---|---|---|---|---|---|---|---|---|---|
| A  | +  | +/NA | +/NA | +    | +  | 12.5 | 2.0  | 5.6  | 3.5  |
| B1 | -  | -/NA | -/NA | -/NA | -  | 3.1  | 14.1 | 28.5 | 10.7 |
| B2 | -  | NA   | -/NA | -/NA | -  | 0.0  | 0.0  | 16.3 | 0.0  |
| C1 | -  | -    | -/NA | -/NA | +  | 3.1  | 8.4  | 12.2 | 5.3  |
| C2 | -  | -    | -/NA | +    | +  | 0.0  | 1.4  | 2.0  | 1.8  |
| D1 | -  | +    | +/NA | +/NA | -  | 12.5 | 5.6  | 2.0  | 10.8 |
| D2 | -  | +    | +/NA | -    | +  | 3.1  | 5.6  | 2.0  | 5.3  |
| D3 | -  | +    | +/NA | -    | -  | 3.1  | 5.6  | 2.0  | 0.0  |
| D4 | -  | +/NA | -    | -/+  | -  | 3.1  | 2.8  | 4.1  | 5.3  |
| E1 | +  | -    | +/NA | +/NA | -  | 9.3  | 4.2  | 0.0  | 3.5  |
| E2 | +  | -    | -/NA | -/NA | +  | 0.0  | 2.8  | 0.0  | 5.3  |
| E3 | +  | -    | -/NA | -/NA | -  | 0.0  | 7.0  | 6.1  | 8.9  |
| F1 | -  | -    | +/NA | +/NA | -  | 9.3  | 7.0  | 8.1  | 5.3  |
| G1 | +  | +    | +/NA | +/NA | -  | 15.6 | 5.6  | 2.0  | 12.5 |
| G2 | +  | +    | +/NA | -    | -  | 3.1  | 2.8  | 6.1  | 0.0  |
| H1 | -  | +    | +/-  | +/NA | +  | 6.3  | 7.0  | 2.0  | 1.8  |
| H2 | +  | -    | -/NA | +    | +  | 0.0  | 7.0  | 2.0  | 8.9  |
| H3 | -  | -    | +/NA | +/NA | +  | 0.0  | 1.4  | 2.0  | 3.5  |
| H4 | +  | +    | -/NA | -/NA | +  | 15.6 | 5.6  | 0.0  | 7.1  |

*Notes*: For each group, nutrition was classified as (+) if at least 50 percent of individuals in the group had a satisfactory nutritional status, else nutritional status was classified as (-). A nutritional cut-off of WHZ<-2SD was used for children up to 10 years old and a BMI of <18.5 for the rest. NA indicates that there are no household members in the category.

## The process of impoverishment

### Case one: a female headed household

Mina, a Hindu widow, aged 42, lives with her son aged 14 and her three daughters aged 12, 9 and 58 months. Of the seven children to whom she has given birth, two died during the first month of life. In 1995 all household members except the son were undernourished. However, by 1997, all members were below the weight-for-age and BMI cut-off. Mina had a BMI of only 15.8 and suffered "body weakness" and chronic "gastric" for which she was unable to afford medical treatment.

In 1997, all members were contributing to the household budget, even the under-five child. Mina worked over 90 hours a week as a domestic servant and water carrier; her son worked 104 hours a week as an apprentice in a workshop; the 12-year-old daughter gleaned rice and vegetables from the market daily, and the 9-year-old and 58-month-old daughters begged in the market. Household income in cash and kind averaged 61 percent of the slum poverty line. They owned no productive assets and household possessions were minimal.

*Household history* Mina was born in the village of Kamkhola in Khulna district. Her paternal grandfather was a farmer and owned around four bighas of land. Her father, disinherited as a result of protracted family quarrels, migrated to Dhaka when Mina, the youngest of four daughters, was only two years old. In Dhaka her father worked as an unskilled labourer and her mother as a domestic servant. As she grew older, Mina, like her older sisters before her, contributed to the household budget by working as a servant until, at the age of 12 years, her marriage was arranged to a distant cousin, Ashok Lal. On her marriage Mina migrated to her husband's home village where he farmed 12 bighas of land which he jointly owned with his two brothers. He also worked for a potter. But then came the liberation war of Bangladesh in 1971 and the family were Hindu. Mina's husband sold all the family land for far below the market value. They were subsequently threatened and robbed and finally fled to a refugee camp in India. On their return in 1971 the house was occupied by Muslims, and the Hindu potter with whom Ashok had worked had also fled. Without any means of livelihood they migrated to a slum in Dhaka where Mina's parents lived. Ashok Lal worked as a dependent vegetable seller with Mina's father, and Mina once again became a domestic servant in the house of one of the slum landlords.

By 1990, it was apparent that Ashok Lal had contracted TB. They moved to a small plot of land adjacent to Mina's landlord and her husband share-cropped a small plot of land belonging to the landlord. He did this work until 1992 when his illness compelled him to give it up. He suffered for a further two years until his death in 1994, six months before we visited Mina.

Mina told us that her husband refused treatment up until the last six months of his life, when he then received treatment from a variety of homeopaths, spiritual healers and allopaths, including a TB specialist. The Taka 3,000 cost of treatment was met mainly by an award in a court case, lodged by the landlord in their name, over the death of Mina's father in a road accident three years previously.

During the last stages of her husband's illness and in the early months afterwards, Mina was heavily dependent upon the patronage of her employer/landlord. He arranged for her husband's funeral and in 1994 paid for hospital treatment for Mina during a severe attack of dysentery. He also arranged for an interest free loan from an NGO income generating scheme for the marriage of her second daughter just before her husband's death, and occasionally donated food for the family when the children were hungry.

In 1995 when this family was first visited, all household members, apart from the son, were severely malnourished. Mina's BMI at the time was only 12.4; the two daughters were 75 percent weight for height, and the 10 year old was 64 percent of weight for height. Household food consumption as assessed by dietary recall was only 980 kcals daily. Mina, though obviously aware of their food shortage, could not take out loans due to her inability to repay, and she had no assets to sell or pawn. The only loan contracted was from the NGO totalling 259 percent of her household monthly income. Mina's relationship with her patron was differential; without his help she perceived that they might not have survived. Yet he paid her less than 50 percent of the market rate for domestic service.

The repercussions of the household level of stress on Kohinoor, the youngest daughter, were similar to those in cluster 4 livelihood group. Firstly, the mother, grandmother and the Hindu midwife ('dai') stated that Kohinoor had been extremely small at birth. Mina discarded her colostrum and fed Kohinoor sugar water for three days. From three days to five months Kohinoor was exclusively breast-fed: thereafter she was weaned onto rice gruels and then onto family food. Supplementary breast-feeding continued up until 18 months of age when Mina's milk supply dried up. Direct evidence from the growth charts show growth faltering from an early age, indicative of infection and/or inadequate food intake. Kohinoor fluctuated from 49 to 52 percent weight-for-age from 8–27 months. Her mother confirmed that Kohinoor was frequently ill, although there was no evidence of NGO clinic consultation for treatment. Mina told us that treatment was not sought when Kohinoor was ill. Before her husband's death this was due to his religious conviction to which he bound all household members. In 1994 Mina worked around 90 hours a week. In her absence, her 10-year-old daughter assumed responsibility for child care. However, her own critical condition (64 percent weight for height) made her physically incapable of discharging the responsibilities forced upon her. In November 1995, an NGO referred the three daughters to a Nutrition Rehabilitation Unit (NRU) but the mother refused due to her work commitments. By January 1996 the NGO made an exception to the rule that children could be admitted to the NRU only if accompanied by their mother. The three daughters were under the guardianship of the eldest son and stayed at the NRU for 3–4 weeks. Kohinoor's weight-for-height had improved to 80 percent on discharge, although she was still below 60 percent weight-for-age.

Two years later, in 1998, the family were again visited. Mina reported that the support which her patron had originally offered had gradually diminished over time. Mina still worked for her patron, whilst her son had managed through charitable help of a neighbour to get an "apprenticeship" with a Hindu workshop owner. The nutritional condition of the female members of this household was still critically low and Kohinoor was still in the severe malnutrition category. In addition an NGO had diagnosed the three daughters to be suffering from TB. Significantly, Mina did not co-operate with the NGO in their treatment, despite daily visits by NGO workers to their home. It was difficult to obtain a clear explanation from Mina as to her non-co-operation. After lengthy probing, she explained that the fate of her daughters lay in the hands of god. Fieldworkers and neighbours were perceptive in their comments – there was another family crisis at the time. Mina's second daughter had returned home with her infant after having allegedly been assaulted by her husband. Mina had been unable to afford a radio; promised as part of the marriage dowry two to three years previously. It took Mina two months to borrow the money to purchase the radio and send her daughter back to her husband. Field workers and neighbours commented that Mina's physical weakness and ill health, together with the present and future economic pressures of maintaining and marrying these three young daughters, could be an important contributor to benign neglect.

In this household the perpetuation of a condition of severe child malnutrition appears to be due primarily to intense poverty and severe constraints on maternal time. The household was assetless, and financial returns from the 90 hours that Mina worked per week were inadequate to maintain household needs, necessitating all of the children to economically contribute to the household maintenance, even the under-five child. Despite high levels of maternal and child labour participation, household income was still below the poverty line, and all of the household members were undernourished. TB in the daughters, which remained untreated despite intensive efforts by fieldworkers, was also a contributory factor. Although the details of this profile are unique, they typify those seen on other profile households dependent upon female domestic wage labour.

*Case two: sickness in the breadwinner*

Abdullah, aged about 50, lives with his wife Hasna, aged about 35, and their five daughters aged 22, 18, 15, 10 and 55 months. The 18-year-old daughter was married but was separated from her husband. She had borne two children, both female, who a nongovernmental organisation suggested were both severely malnourished and died during the first year of life. Another daughter, aged 22, was also separated from her husband and had given birth to a daughter who also died within the first months of life. She returned to her natal home on the separation from her husband, but had been forced to leave and to support herself as a resident domestic servant. Hasna also gave birth to seven children, two of whom died in the first year of life. She also had two miscarriages, one before and one after the birth of Shahana, the youngest severely undernourished daughter.

In December 1997 at the end of the study period, there were three earners to three dependants. The 15-year-old daughter worked as a domestic servant; the 10-year-old scavenged in the market place for broken rice. Abdullah was chronically ill with chest pain and stomach pains. He was able to work at home for a few hours a day, on five or six days a month, weaving fishing nets. All household members were undernourished and household income was only 30 percent of the poverty line. They owned minimal household and productive assets and were deeply indebted, loans amounting to over nine times their monthly income.

*Household history* Abdullah was born in the village of Pakhimara in Khulna district. His paternal grandfather was originally a large farmer, but the land was gradually washed away by the river Shesbati, and his father worked as a woodcutter. Abdullah was the third of his parents' surviving children. He was sent to his uncle in Khulna to work as an unskilled labourer, remitting his wage to the home village. Six or seven years later his father died from protracted diarrhoea, at a time of crop failure and hardship in the village. Abdullah's mother sold all the possessions to pay for her husband's treatment, and they were also deeply indebted. The family responded by selling their plot of household land and migrated to kin in India, where they remained for four or five years returning when the crisis had ended.

At the age of 27 or 28 Abdullah married Hasna. Two daughters were born. In 1968 Abdullah became partially paralysed. Hasna sold her marriage gold, her husband's tools and other possessions to finance treatment by a series of religious and homeopathic healers. Abdullah's condition did not improve. Unable to survive, they sold the materials of which the house was constructed, and migrated to Dhaka in the hope of survival and treatment. There they lived in a squatter settlement and survived during the first year by Hasna's begging with the youngest daughter who subsequently died. During this time Abdullah was treated by a homeopath and his paralysis was so reduced that he was able to start working again in the wood depot of a Bihari who had given alms regularly to Hasna.

During the liberation war of Bangladesh in 1971, they went to their home village for safety. When they returned to Dhaka, the Bihari for whom Abdullah had worked had been killed and his depot looted. Abdullah did a variety of casual jobs. Then in 1973-77 he starting dealing in the lucrative black market for wheat, and the household entered a phase of accumulation. In three or four years Abdullah told that his capital had grown to 10,000 Taka. But in 1977-78 there was a dramatic decline in the black market supply of wheat and Abdullah was forced to disinvest. He spent 6,000 Taka for consumption and the treatment of Hasna who was severely ill with her seventh pregnancy and later miscarried. In addition, 3,000 Taka was stolen from their home. Abdullah was forced to close his wheat business and did a variety of casual jobs. His worsening health status meant that he could not work regularly. In 1994, Abdullah was totally incapacitated and unable to work for a period of four months. Assets accumulated during the good years of 1974-77 were sold to meet consumption needs and to finance his medical treatment. At the same time Hasna started working as a servant, but later gave this up on the birth of her youngest daughter, and the third daughter (aged 10 years) took her place.

On our first visit in 1995, the household were virtually assetless and under severe economic strain. Abdullah, due to ill health, was only able to work 15 days per month as a fisherman. His 12-year-old daughter worked in the food market as a servant and her eight-year-old sister accompanied her and collected fallen and broken rice. Monthly income amounted to only 40 percent of the poverty line. Abdullah could not afford to consult a medical practitioner. Instead, he regularly visited various drug stores and on the advice of traders purchased paracetamol tablets to ease the stomach, head and chest pains, and also vitamin tablets. He also consulted various homeopaths and spiritual healers. Outstanding credit at three stores totalled 1,000 Taka (twice the household monthly income). They also owed Taka 5,000 to two food shops, Taka 250 to various neighbours and Taka 1,000 to a slum income generating scheme run by an non governmental organisation, which they used for consumption. The family survived by cutting back on food consumption, which included fasting for 2 to 3 days per month. Abdullah, Hasna and the two youngest daughters were undernourished. The youngest was referred to a Nutrition Rehabilitation Unit (NRU), but the mother refused to go due to her domestic responsibilities.

In mid-1994, Hasna responded to the crisis by entering the Indian sari black-market, a trade which, despite its risks, has become increasingly common with slum women. Slum women considered it to be the only economic option available to them (apart from prostitution) where potential earnings could be equivalent to mens'.

Hasna borrowed Taka 1,000 from the richer slum women at an interest of 10 percent monthly, and purchased a small consignment of black market saris 3 to 4 times a week. By December 1994, Abdullah was incapacitated from wage work for 25 days per month. However, Hasna knew the risks of this type of illegal trading; four of her women friends known to us had been detained. Indeed, saris worth 750 Taka had been confiscated from Hasna at the Indian border in October 1994, which represented all her working capital. Group discussions with female black-market Indian sari traders in the slum revealed that sexual harassment and favours were also common. A young girl aged about 13 years who came from one of the poorest families in the slum had "disappeared" at the Indian border during a trip with the women to buy saris. The women were convinced that she had been taken for prostitution in Calcutta.

In the same year, an assessment was made of how such a chronic condition of poverty and stress had affected Shahana, the youngest severely malnourished daughter. Indirect evidence from Hasna and the local "dai" who delivered Shahana suggested that she was small at birth. In the slum 50 percent of infants were born of low birth weight. After birth Shahana was fed sugar water for the first 3 days, colostrum being discarded, as in common in Bangladesh. She was then exclusively breast-fed from three days to two months and thereafter weaned onto a rice gruel, as Hasna's breast milk supply was reported to be inadequate, possibly because of her own poor nutritional status. Weaning gruels in Bangladesh have been reported as low energy, dense, and highly contaminated (Black et al., 1982). At seven months, solid rice was introduced. Supplementary breast feeding continued, but declined when Hasna started to work and finally ceased when Shahana was 23 months old, as Hasna became pregnant again and later miscarried.

Direct evidence from an NGO record reveals that a pattern of growth faltering indicating either infection and/or inadequate food intake from 12 months of age (the first recorded by the NGO). Shahana had been in a severe weight-for-age category ever since this time. Hasna confirmed the regular bouts of illness, although there was no evidence of an NGO clinic consultation for treatment. Hasna said that medical help was not sought during Shahana's illness. The reason, according to Hasna, lay in deeply embedded spiritual beliefs. Hasna believed that she had been attacked by evil spirits ('bhut') during her pregnancy, and that was the cause of her miscarriage. While Shahana was in the womb, Hasna suffered from a difficult pregnancy, and then a difficult delivery. She attributed this, the smallness of Shahana at birth, and her inadequate milk supply to the same evil spirits (Blanchet, 1984). Although these beliefs are held by many slum mothers, and indeed are common throughout the whole of Bangladesh (Blanchet, 1984), it is possible that they may be relied upon or offered as explanations of misfortune amongst those who have little control over their life circumstances.

Hasna traded for between 6 and 15 hours daily. In her absence Abdullah and Runa (the youngest married daughter) were responsible for child care, but Abdullah was too ill and depressed and Runa mostly absent, socialising with adolescents of her own age in the slum. For the greater part Shahana was left unattended.

In September 1996 this family was contacted again and found to be in the midst of another economic crisis. From 1995 onwards, Abdullah had become totally incapacitated from wage work. For six months he was economically inactive and stayed at home. Hasna, meanwhile, had had consignments of saris confiscated at the border ten times and also had been physically assaulted. The regular confiscation of her working capital meant that potential earnings were never realised and the family were constantly struggling to survive. New laws in Bangladesh meant that not only was it illegal to smuggle saris over the border, but also to sell them in Bangladesh. This resulted in tighter controls. In October Hasna was seven months pregnant when her last consignment of saris was again confiscated and she was severely beaten. Since then Hasna has been unable to trade. Monthly income plummeted from 60–70 percent of the slum poverty line to only 30 percent of the slum poverty line. By December, Shahana was ill with diarrhoea and upper respiratory tract infection and had remained within the severe malnutrition category throughout. Furthermore, all household members had become malnourished.

In this profile, ill health was an initiating factor in the further entrenchment of poverty over two generations. When we first saw this family, available assets had been sold to finance medical expenditure and consumption and the household was vulnerable to the costs of further crises. Levels of child labour participation and consumption indebtedness were already high and nutrition needs jeopardised. Subsequently, the household responded to further incapacitation by relatively low health expenditure financed from further loans, by increasing female and child labour participation, and consumption indebtedness. These responses are typical of many incapacitated and unemployed households. But the profile also clearly illustrates the restricted options available to poor illiterate women faced with an incapacitated male head. The low returns of domestic service forced Hasna into illegal trading in an attempt to feed her family. But the promise of income levels equivalent to men's was never realised. A similar strategy and experience was shared with another chronic incapacitated household.

The repercussion of the household stresses was that Shahana, the youngest daughter, was continuously in the severe nutrition category throughout. Medical and nutritional rehabilitation had been avoided. The mother attributed this to her spiritual beliefs and to a heavy domestic and economic work burden. Adequate child care was not available and neglect was the inevitable result. It is difficult to say that any one of these factors was more responsible than others in producing a state of undernutrition in the household. Indeed, most factors were seen to interact and exacerbate the influence of others.

## References

Black, R.E., Brown, K.H., Becker, S., Alim, A.R.M.A. and Merson, M.H. (1982), 'Contamination of weaning foods and transmission of enterotoxigenic escherichia coli diarrhoea in children in rural Bangladesh', *Transactions of the Royal Society of Tropical Medicine and Hygiene*, Vol. 76, pp. 259–264.

Blanchet, T. (1984), *Women, pollution and marginality: meanings and rituals of birth in rural Bangladesh*, University Press, Dhaka, Bangladesh.

Dugdale, A.E. (1985), 'Family anthropometry: a new strategy for determining community nutrition', *The Lancet*, 21 September (letter).

Gillespie, S. and McNeill, G. (1992), *Food, health and survival in India and developing countries*, Oxford University Press, Delhi, Bombay, Calcutta, Madras.

Kogi, Makau W. (1988), 'Nutritional status and socio-economic factors in the population of a semi-arid region in Kenya', unpublished PhD thesis, London School of Hygiene and Tropical Medicine.

Payne, P. (1992), 'Assessing undernutrition: the need for a reconceptualization', in Osmani, S.R. (ed.), *Nutrition and Poverty*, Oxford University Press, Oxford.

Pryer, J.A. (1990), 'Socio-economic and environmental aspects of undernutrition and ill health in an urban slum in Bangladesh', unpublished PhD thesis, London School of Hygiene and Tropical Medicine.

Chapter 14

# Managing Financial Shocks and Stresses

---

*Thirty percent of households suffered a severe deficit, with female headed households and the area of Beri Badh facing the highest percentage of severe deficit. The main reason for deterioration in financial status was income earning member being incapacitated, followed by earning decreased, and unable to work. The coping strategies for the slum households included changed work, reduced expenditure, and taking loans, with few households taking out mortgages, or selling assets, family migrating or begging. There was no evidence of the moral economy in Dhaka slums; hardly any financial exchange relationships were found.*

---

**Introduction**

The term 'livelihoods system' refers to how people maintain their living so that they are able to function in a particular society which contains externalities such as risk, hazard and economic shock. An important part of livelihoods systems is the existence of a complex structure of social groups. Such an element produces constraints for households or individuals and at the same time accommodates human agency i.e. action of the social actors. Such consequences occur because people are not passive victims in the system, rather they take action and develop alternative systems to protect themselves. For example, within the poor in Indonesia a reciprocal relationship functioned under the system of "moral economy" (Scott 1976). This system enhanced mutual support among the victim social group of people and protected the poor from insecurity often arising out of externalities.

From this perspective, livelihoods system is often understood as being complex, diverse, and comprising a portfolio of activities which are both economic and non-economic in nature. It embraces vulnerability and security, both of which may be significant factors in understanding the system.

**Vulnerability**

Vulnerability is a core but complex concept associated with the concept of livelihoods system because it has various interacting elements, and it is also associated with other concepts, like poverty. One important point to make here is that vulnerability has two sides – external and internal. The external side includes risks, shocks or stress to which the households or individuals are subjected. The internal side includes defencelessness – lack of means to cope without damaging loss (Chambers 1989). Shocks and vulnerability have been conceptualised as a combination of risk of shock and the ability to cope with shock when it occurs. It is important to understand which types of event represent the most important shocks for the urban poor, and how individuals and households respond to such events, including the variation in ability to respond and cope between different groups. In this chapter we will explore the financial situation of the vulnerable households and their coping strategies.

## Method

Analyses are presented for self-reported financial situation in the previous 30 days. Associations with the gender of the household head and area of residence were examined. Additional questions were asked in households reporting deterioration or improvement in financial situation. These data are also presented. We then present a series of vignettes to illustrate in greater depth the strategies adopted to cope with deterioration in financial status.

## Results

Around 30 percent of households reported a severe deficit in their financial situation, a further 30 percent reported a slight deficit and approximately 36 percent reported a break even situation (Table 14.1). Female headed households reported a worse situation than male headed households (Table 14.2). Beri Badh had the greatest percentage of households reporting severe deficit, and the lowest for break even or slight excess (Table 14.3).

**Table 14.1 Self reported financial situation in the past 30 days among all households: September to December 1996**

|  | % of all households |
|---|---|
| Severe deficit | 29.33 |
| Slight deficit | 30.29 |
| Break even | 36.30 |
| Slight excess | 3.85 |
| Excess sufficient to save | 0.23 |
| N | 2182 |

**Table 14.2  Self reported financial situation in the past 30 days among male and female headed households: September to December 1996**

|  | Male headed households (%) | Female headed households (%) | P $X^2$ |
|---|---|---|---|
| Severe deficit | 25.7 | 38.9 | |
| Slight deficit | 30.6 | 33.3 | |
| Break even | 39.9 | 20.8 | <0.002 |
| Slight excess | 3.8 | 4.2 | |
| Excess sufficient to save | 0 | 1.4 | |
| N | 649 | 83 | |

**Table 14.3  Self reported financial situation in the past 30 days among households in three locations: September to December 1996**

|  | Agargoan (%) | Beri Badh (%) | Central Mohammadpur (%) | P $X^2$ |
|---|---|---|---|---|
| Severe deficit | 27.8 | 43.2 | 19.0 | |
| Slight deficit | 30.9 | 31.5 | 30.5 | |
| Break even | 37.2 | 24.3 | 44.7 | <0.001 |
| Slight excess | 3.5 | 0.9 | 5.8 | |
| Excess sufficient to save | 0.4 | 0 | 0 | |
| N | 309 | 104 | 250 | |

Table 14.4 shows that the most important reason for a deterioration in financial status was illness or incapacitation in income-earning member of the household. This was so in 22 percent of households reporting a deterioration in financial situation. The next most important was a decrease in wages or earnings, in 19 percent of households, and then the inability to find work in 18 percent of households. This was followed by the inability to work due to strikes which accounted for 9 percent and various other reasons in single percentages.

When comparisons were made between Agargoan, Central Mohammadpur and Beri Badh, illness of an income earning member was consistently found to be a main reason for a deterioration in financial status (accounting for 20 percent of all cases in all three locations). However, being unable to work was the most important reason in Beri Badh (28 percent of all cases), and appeared to be more important than in the other two areas (Agargoan 15 percent, Central Mohammadpur 18 percent). Reports of other reasons were similar in the three locations.

Comparisons between female and male headed households provided no evidence of important differences in the main reasons reported for deterioration in financial situation.

**Table 14.4  Percentage distribution of main reasons reported for deterioration in financial situation among all households: September to December 1996**

| Main reason reported | % of all cases where deterioration in financial situation reported |
|---|---|
| Income-earning member ill/incapacitated | 21.6 |
| Wage/earnings decreased | 19.3 |
| Unable to find work | 18.1 |
| Unable to work due to strikes | 9.2 |
| Expenditure for medicine/treatment | 3.8 |
| Visitors came | 3.2 |
| Repayment of loans | 3.0 |
| Small profit in business | 1.5 |
| Increase in number of non-earning family members | 1.4 |
| Movement out of the household of an income earner | 1.4 |
| Unable to work because of illness of other family member | 1.1 |
| Loss of employment | 1.1 |
| N | 2373 |

**Table 14.5  Percentage of strategies to stop deterioration getting worse**

| Variables | Yes | No |
| --- | --- | --- |
| Changed work (%) | 26.50 | 73.50 |
| Reduced expenditure (%) | 25.73 | 74.27 |
| Took loan (%) | 81.90 | 18.10 |
| One loan | 36.52 | 63.48 |
| More than one loan | 45.38 | 54.62 |
| Took mortgage (%) | 1.54 | 98.46 |
| Sold assets (%) | 2.23 | 97.77 |
| Family members migrated (%) | 0.46 | 99.54 |
| Begged (%) | 1.16 | 98.84 |

Table 14.5 shows strategies taken by households to stop deterioration in financial situation getting worse. Most took a loan (82 percent), changed work (26 percent) or reduced expenditure (26 percent). Strategies such as taking out a mortgage or selling assets, or family members migrating or begging, were much rarer.

**Table 14.6  Percentage distribution of main reasons reported for improvement in financial situation among all households**

| Main reason reported | % of all cases where improvement in financial situation |
| --- | --- |
| Increase in wages/earnings | 42.3 |
| Family members found good/a lot of work | 31.5 |
| Good profits in business | 10.3 |
| Decrease in household expenses | 3.9 |
| New working member joined household | 1.3 |
| Previously ill member restarted work | 1.0 |
| N | 919 |

Table 14.6 shows the percentage of main reasons reported for improvement in financial situation. The main reason was increase in wages/earnings which amounted to 42 percent, followed by family members found good/a lot of work, which accounted for 32 percent. This was followed by good profit from business (10 percent), with other reasons in single percentages.

## Strategies to cope with deterioration in financial status

*Changing work*

Changing work was adopted as a strategy for coping with deterioration in financial status in 26 percent of cases in the study series. The examples show just what this means in human terms.

> Despite physical complications, Titu Mia was forced to do labour intensive work during the early period of migration to Dhaka. Later he managed to start his own business and shifted from labour intensive activities. This did not improve his economic position very much because from the beginning he had little capital for investment. He could not establish any good working relationships with wholesalers in the market who could provide him with different business items on credit. In addition, he failed to obtain the necessary capital to purchase the required production equipment, so in the end he was forced to do labour intensive work again.

> Sharmin Begum, a divorced woman, came with her two sons to Dhaka about five years ago. After they arrived in Dhaka she started doing a housemaid job while Jasmin, her elder son, started pulling a rickshaw. The second son, Kabir, got work in a tailoring shop as an assistant. Within only six months of having migrated to the city, Jasmin started to learn driving with the help of a friend from the same slum. Though learning to drive cost him nothing but time, it reduced his available time in which to earn income. But it did not affect the household which had other sources of income. Once Jasmin finished his driving lessons and got a driving job, Kabir started to learn cutting and sewing work in exchange for his (Kabir's) income which he surrendered in order to learn his trade.

> Monir Bapari, son-in-law of Jabbar Sheikh, was working in an office. His salary was Taka 1,400 per month. This was not enough to feed his family as he had to pay Taka 900 for food to his father-in-law and Taka 400 for room rent. Recently he resigned from his job. Now he pulls a rickshaw for half a day, and during the rest of the day he receives driving lessons. His wife works in a garment factory. Now he pays the rent of the room from his wife's income and the food expenditure from his own income. His father-in-law bears the cost of his training as a skilled worker to ensure a secure future for his daughter.

> Haslem Mollah, a vegetable seller, had initial working capital of Taka 1,000. He was doing well with his business as he was receiving some vegetables in advance from a wholesaler. Unfortunately, due to bad weather, he failed to recover his capital and was unable to repay the money to the wholesaler. He distributed some of the vegetables among his kin as he did not have any system to preserve them. Now the amount of his working capital is very low and the wholesaler does not provide any items in advance, which means in the interim period he has to do labour intensive work to pay the household expenses.

> Abdul Goni had studied up to class VIII in his village before he migrated to Dhaka. He had been engaged in different types of work including rickshaw pulling, hawking, and later a rickshaw renting business in Dhaka. About five years ago, he learnt to drive a car with help from a friend. During the early period of his driving career he was employed by private owners where the salary was comparatively low, the working hours were long and there was a high probability of job loss. As he was literate he managed to shift into the formal labour market and was employed by a company. His current salary is Taka 3,500 per month. The company also allows overtime work, festival bonuses and medical benefits.

## Minimising household expenditure

Minimising household expenditure is a strategy to improve the economic condition of a household. When households spend 70 percent of their total household expenditure on food, cutting down on this expenditure category seems quite a logical thing to do. Members who are involved in income generating work do not eat outside the house. Either they carry food for lunch from home or, if possible, they return home during lunch time.

> Jesmin works in a nearby garments factory. She has to come back home to take her lunch. It is not possible for her to take lunch with her in the morning, because her mother works as a maidservant and she cooks free of cost at her working place.

> Mannan from Manikgonj, which is very close to Dhaka, left his family in the rural area and is living in a boarding house with two other persons. He can earn more money by pulling a rickshaw in Dhaka city than in Manikgonj. At the same time he reduces his living expenses by sharing one room with other boarding house members. He has food arrangements with a nearby family for which he pays Taka 20 per meal, which is cheaper and is better quality compared to eating at a cheap restaurant.

> Sufia, wife of Jainal, decided not to spend more than Taka 30 per day for three meals, while Al-amin, their son was suffering from diarrhoea. She deducted fish and meat from the meals on some days to reduce food cost. She used rice, lentils and pasted potato for preparing breakfast, lunch and dinner, and sometimes fried eggs for her husband. She also cooked breakfast and lunch at the same time to reduce fuel costs.

> During the illness of Harun, his mother, Maya and his sister spent whole days in income generating work in a garment factory. Besides other strategies, Maya cooked once a day to reduce fuel costs. She cooked for all the members in the morning before going to work.

> Three sisters, Runa, Rina and Hena, were living in a room and all of them were engaged in garment work. Unfortunately, the youngest sister, Rina, was injured during her work. Then the other two sisters stopped using a rickshaw to go to work to reduce their transport costs, as they needed money for the treatment of their youngest sister.

The above examples illustrate the cost reducing mechanisms. The examples described three ways in which household's expenditure was reduced; from food expenditure (which is the most common), fuel costs, and transport costs.

## Taking loans

Taking credit is generally related to the failure of the earning capabilities of a household when there is no alternative to mobilising cash. If the income capabilities are jeopardised due to either internal or external causes, then the household may take out a loan to fulfil its immediate consumption requirements. The internal factors include morbidity or mortality of the income earner, which affects the income flow. External factors include lack of employment. The effect of both the factors (internal or external) on a household with a weak economic base is more acute than in coping households as households with a weak economic base usually lack any safeguard to cope with crisis. The absence of alternative income sources and lack of savings compel households to seek credit.

> Sobuz and his wife were both involved in income generating activities. When his wife suffered from chicken pox, he borrowed money from his co-workers for his wife's treatment. That was not enough for treatment and maintenance of the household expenditure as he lost his wife's income. He then borrowed a larger amount of money from other colleagues for household maintenance.

> Aziz, a rickshaw puller, borrowed Taka 100 from his friend when he lost his job because he was lazy. He then borrowed Taka 2,000 with 40 per cent interest for one month for household maintenance. He finally found another rickshaw owner who would let him pull the rickshaw again.

> Gonesh and Prodip spent a total of Taka 30,000 on their sister's marriage. About half of the money, which came from the savings of the household, was spent on food. The rest was taken on credit to buy a plot of land in her name to secure the marriage. The bridegroom's household demanded the money, but they negotiated and succeeded in keeping it under the ownership of the bride by registering the land in her name.

> Milton Mia had to provide Taka 5,000 as alimony to Kushi, the divorced wife of his son. This was determined in a social court. He borrowed the money with high interest.

> Hasan borrowed Taka 200 on credit to entertain his friends celebrating his marriage. This was essential for him. As he had no savings he had to borrow it from someone else. He took the money from Aktari, the woman he was going to marry.

> Ratan Mia, a rickshaw puller, consumed the money that he borrowed which was on credit with interest (18 percent) from an non governmental organisation. He intended to purchase a rickshaw but failed as the money was not enough. As he had no way to invest it in the productive sector, he spent the money on day-to-day consumption purchases.

## Asset selling

Selling assets was the last option. There may be two reasons behind this. One may be that households do not have enough assets to sell. Another may be that they do not want to sell their productive assets which they have accumulated with great difficulty.

> Joinal, a rickshaw puller, first took a loan when he was very ill. He failed to repay the loan and so instead was forced to sell his rickshaw with dire consequences for his household.

> Faruque, a business man, lost all of his capital because the market fell. He then had to sell his house, which he had built 10 years ago with hard earned cash. He is now living in a rented room with all of his family, which makes them feel vulnerable.

## Family migrated to rural areas

Going back to the rural area as a coping mechanism is common among those who have relatives living there with resources. The poorest households do this as the last option after the result of failures – merging households and moving to a kin's house in the slum.

Aziz became very weak after a serious illness and was unable to work, so he decided to live with his in-laws in the same slum, but this did not work out. He then decided to send his family to his own parents home in the rural areas. He is now a little better and can work a couple of hours a day and lives in a boarding house and shares expenses with the two others who share the same room, to reduce expenditure.

Jamal, a rickshaw puller, sent his family to the rural area when his son and daughter fell ill. They were looked after by his wife who also moved to the rural area. In the meantime, he stayed with a friend in the slum and shared expenses to reduce expenditure.

## *Begging*

In Mina's household (poor female headed household) where her husband had died two years ago, the three daughters begged in the market place and brought home broken rice and fallen flour as well as money from begging.

Hasna had a chronically ill husband, and tried to be self-employed for two years, then her business went down and she lost all of her capital, so one of her daughters worked as a maidservant and the other one begged in the street.

## Discussion

In this chapter we explored the financial shocks and stresses in the slum households. Severe deficit in financial status occurred in 30 percent of households, with female headed households and Beri Badh area facing the highest percentage of severe deficit.

The assessment of a household's economic situation provided by the questionnaire is obviously a subjective matter. The answer provided by an individual is likely to depend on her/his access to information as well as access to resources within the household. Moreover, even if an individual had access to the same information and experience within the household, they may take into consideration different pieces of information in making their assessment. In light of this concern, efforts were made to collect information from the same respondent as far as possible. In this way it was felt that changes in financial situation would be more likely to be identified. Comparisons between households will be also be complicated in individual assessments. Individuals from different households may not have the same understanding of what constitute their basic necessities. For example, in a household that is used to eating fish regularly, the respondent may report a "slight deficit" if they were unable to afford fish very often in the previous month. In contrast, another household who rarely eat fish at all might report their situation as "break even". It is clear that an individual's expectation will affect his/her assessment of the household's current situation. The assessment may also be affected by the condition of the household living nearby, since individuals are likely to compare their own situation to those of their neighbours. It therefore seems likely that assessments may differ from context to context. Having said this, respondents in different areas of our sample do share much in common and it may be that, at least in terms of the assessment of "severe deficit", there does seem to be some consistency. Also, 20–30 percent of households reported "severe deficit" which compared well with the percentages of "declining" households identified by the qualitative team in each of their five study locations.

The main reasons for shocks and stresses was incapacitation of an earner, decrease in wages and inability to find work. To cope households changed work, reduced expenditure, took loans, took mortgages, sold assets, family members migrated or begged. Coping refers to people's short term response to an immediate shock or stress. Most studies on managing risk focus on rural context and examine the household response to food insecurity. These studies show that the poor use three major coping strategies: consumption modification, income increase, and exchange.

Consumption modification is a common strategy which is followed by both the urban and rural poor. This strategy favours the future livelihood at the cost of present suffering. De Waal (1989) finds that in Darfur, Sudan, families chose to go hungry in order to preserve their assets and future livelihoods. In Dhaka, qualitative work found the same behaviour in relation to households forced savings approach (through their participation in economic savings organisations in which people make desperate attempts to save in order to tide themselves over in crisis situations). Limited options lead people to choose temporary starvation in order to increase savings and to have access to assets for secure future livelihoods.

"Income increase" is also a common strategy. This refers to people's initiatives to secure both present and future livelihoods. Households maximise their resources in order to increase the level of household income. For example, in the Dhaka slums the main option was to change work to better paid work or get more people involved in income generating work. Young girls become garment workers to increase the household income, and they also try to save money for their dowry in order to secure their marriage to a suitable partner, to ensure their future.

"Exchange" refers to the insurance system developed on the basis of "moral economy". The moral economy refers to a system which is embedded in the social and moral fabric of rural communities, and which ensures the right to claim on others and obliges a transfer of basic necessities (Scott, 1976; 1985). According to Moser (1995) the system is sustained largely by the long-term self-interest of households in search of mutual insurance against livelihood security. There does not seem much evidence of this in Dhaka slums.

Options are gradually limited by the vicious cycle of difficulties. Common strategies include asset preservation at the cost of self-exploitation. In an exhausted option, the priority would be to preserve assets over meeting immediate food needs until the point of destitution (Corbett, 1988). Mitigation of vulnerability is contingent on people's ability to adapt.

In conclusion, 30 percent of households suffered a severe financial deficit, with female headed households and the area of Beri Badh facing the highest percentage of severe deficit. The main reason for deterioration in financial status was an income earning member being incapacitated, followed by decreased earning and inability to work. The coping strategies for the slum households included changing work, reducing expenditure, and taking loans, with little households taking out mortgages, or selling assets, family migrated or begging. There was no evidence of the moral economy in Dhaka slums, for example hardly any financial exchange relationships were found.

## References

Chambers, R. (1989), 'Editorial Introduction: Vulnerability, Coping and Policy', *IDS Bulletin*, 20 (2), pp. 1–7.

Corbett, J.E.M. (1988), 'Famine and Household Coping Strategies', *World Development*, 16(9), pp. 1009–1112.

De Waal, A. (1989), *Famine that Kills: Darfur, Sudan, 1984–1985*, Clarendon Press, Oxford.

Moser, C. (1995), *Confronting Crisis: A comparative study of household responses to poverty and vulnerability in four poor urban communities*, Environmentally Sustainable Development Studies and Monographs No 8, Washington DC, The World Bank.

Scott, J.C. (1976), *The Moral Economy of the Peasant – Rebellion and Subsistence in South-east Asia*, London, Yale University Press.

Scott, J.C. (1985), *Weapons of the Weak*, London, Yale University Press.

Chapter 15
# Policy Implications

*In this chapter we describe the setting of Dhaka, and poverty alleviation in Bangladesh. We then examine the policy implications of our findings for child labour, marital instability, work disabling morbidity and coping strategies, child and adult undernutrition and morbidity, intra-household distribution of nutritional vulnerability, women's negotiation control and well-being within the household, female workforce and family, and lastly, managing shocks and stresses.*

## Setting

Bangladesh has only around 20 percent urbanisation which is lower than in India, Pakistan and Sri Lanka. However, Bangladesh's levels of urbanisation has experienced the most rapid urban growth. The average urban growth in Bangladesh was about 8 percent during 1961–81 and 5.7 percent during 1981–91. At about 20 percent level of urbanisation, the absolute urban population in Bangladesh was over 22 million in 1991. By 2005, this number will rise to over 45 millions (30 percent) and by 2015 to 68 millions (37 percent) (Islam, 1997).

Dhaka, the oldest, largest and only mega-city in Bangladesh, has a dominant role in its urbanisation process. The city contains one-third of the urban population. It is the main centre for administration, trade and commerce. The rapidly expanding garment industry – the fourth largest employer in the country – is heavily concentrated in Dhaka, which accounts for nearly half of Bangladesh's manufacturing employment, including nearly half of the jobs in the textile industries and three-quarters of jobs in footwear, leather goods and electrical machinery.

Table 15.1 shows the poverty levels in Bangladesh (Source: Summary report of the household expenditure survey, 1995–96, Bangladesh Bureau of Statistics, 1997). In 1995–96, 47.5 percent of Bangladesh's population lived in poverty that is below a poverty line equivalent to a daily calorie intake of 2122 calories for rural areas and 2112 calories for urban areas. Urban poverty in Bangladesh has risen by a third between 1988 and 1996, whilst rural poverty has remained stable. Inequality has risen also from a Gini index of 0.36 in 1983–84 to 0.432 in 1996. Urban incomes remain most unequal with the lowest 20 percent of households accounting for 4.2 percent of urban income, whilst the upper 20 percent appropriate 54.6 percent of urban income (CIRDAP, 1997).

**Table 15.1 Poverty statistics in Bangladesh**

|  | 1983–84 | | | 1988–89 | | | 1995–96 | | |
| --- | --- | --- | --- | --- | --- | --- | --- | --- | --- |
|  | rural | urban | all | rural | urban | all | rural | urban | all |
| Head count Measure of poverty (%) of the population | 61.9 | 67.7 | 62.6 | 47.8 | 47.6 | 47.8 | 47.1 | 49.7 | 47.5 |
| Absolute numbers of poor (in millions) | 51.1 | 7.3 | 58.4 | 6.3 | 49.7 | 45.7 | 55.3 | 9.6 | 64.9 |
| Absolute number of extreme/hard core poor (in millions) | 36.7 | 37.4 | 36.7 | 28.6 | 26.4 | 28.4 | 24.6 | 27.3 | 25.1 |
| Gini-coefficient | 0.360 | | | 0.379 | | | 0.432 | | |

The problem is particularly acute in Dhaka, where about 55 percent of the population live below the poverty line, and 32 percent live below the hard core poverty line. It means that with the total population of Dhaka being 9.3 million, at least 5 million are below the poverty line, including 3 million hard core poor (Islam, 1997).

## Poverty alleviation in Bangladesh

Poverty alleviation has been a popular slogan of successive political leaderships in Bangladesh. However, high levels of poverty have persisted in spite of massive aid. Failure of the government in this respect originates in the lack of vision and ownership for guiding the programme. In practice, no government has translated its declaration of the objectives to eliminate poverty into a coherent programme. The resultant ascendancy of Bangladesh's aid donors over the poverty agenda has been characterised by the high costs of aid delivery arising from lack of co-ordination both amongst donors and with the government. The donor driven process has increasingly led to lack of domestic ownership over the policy agenda to alleviate poverty in Bangladesh and the absence of a democratic mandate for such an agenda.

The waste, mis-targeting, corruption, and inefficient delivery of government programmes have contributed to the emergence of non-government organisations (NGOs), as alternative development institutions, designed to deliver aid more purposively and efficiently to the poor. This move by donors to commit more of their aid through NGOs has generated its own problems of ownership and sustainability. An institutional anarchy now prevails in the area of poverty alleviation where a multiplicity of donors interact with a variety of governmental and NGO institutions to alleviate poverty.

Throughout the 1980s, Bangladesh's development agenda remained heavily influenced by the World Bank's structural adjustment reforms. This is not designed to take into account the impact of the reforms on poverty, which has led to micro-project interventions in the donor organisations to build safety nets for the poor who may fall victim to particular reforms and to support projects targeted to groups of the poor. This particular approach to poverty alleviation has served to segment the poverty programme and has tended to discourage the design of a more holistic approach for eliminating poverty.

NGOs have played a high profile role in promoting poverty alleviation. Bangladesh is known as one of the leaders of the developing world in numbers, scope of work and impact of its NGOs. As of 1996, there were 986 NGOs registered with the NGO Bureau, an office attached to the Prime Minister's Secretariat (World Bank, 2000/2001). Such registered NGOs are eligible to receive foreign grants. Foreign grants were approved for 2,598 projects between 1990 and 1996 involving the funding of around $1.1 million. In 1995, disbursements to NGOs of $170 million came to 11 percent of total aid disbursements and 24 percent of all grant aid to Bangladesh. NGOs have tended to focus on poverty alleviation through programmes and projects in the following areas:

1  Group based mobilisation of the poor and beneficiary participation.
2  Micro-credit.
3  Targeting resources to women.
4  Developing access to common property resources.
5  Health-care and Health education.
6  Non-formal primary education.
7  Non-traditional agricultural extension.
8  Promotion of non-crop agriculture through investment in poultry, livestock and fisheries.
9  Promotion of small and rural industries.
10 Social forestry.

In some areas such as non-formal and health education and particularly micro-credit, Bangladesh is a world leader. Visitors come from around the world to study the Grameen Bank and the Bangladesh Rural Advancement Committee (BRAC) programmes which have been replicated in many developing countries. There is no doubt that NGOs are today a major force in the economy in attempting to target the poor and enhance their earning opportunities.

NGOs have been moderately effective in their efforts to empower the poor. They work by reaching out directly to the poor and mobilising them for group action, not only loosening their ties with their vertical dependency on patron–client relationships, but promoting horizon linkages among the poor to develop their sense of self-worth and social solidarity, and ultimately individual empowerment amongst poor women who have been traditionally the most underprivileged members of Bangladeshi society.

The macro picture of trends in Table 15.1 does not suggest that Bangladesh has made noticeable headway in arresting growth of poverty. The available evidence on national trends in poverty, as well as the local level evidence, suggests that NGO micro-credit programmes are quite successful in raising household income levels of credit recipients, but this has failed to generate enough critical mass at the national or even at the local level to make a dent on poverty, or to sufficiently empower the poor to impact on the social balance of power. The main reason why micro-credit enterprises do not have a more widespread impact on poverty alleviation lies in their innocence of market forces. To give micro-credit to 100 women to rear cattle, for example, does little for such households if the milk market in that area is controlled by a few powerful intermediaries. A more meaningful intervention would be to build either a private or co-operative enterprise owned by the poor, which could provide a stable and remunerative market for their produce through value addition. Grameen Bank and BRAC are indeed moving up market to provide scope for value addition to one of their micro-credit programmes.

NGOs are faced with enormous untapped opportunities to serve as institutional conduits linking small producers, services by micro-credit, and training programmes, to national and global markets. NGOs can provide facilities for value enhancement, quality control, marketing facilities, institutional bargaining power and corporate finance to the poor, which could make them into major players in the productive sector and financial markets of Bangladesh. Grameen Bank controls around 4.5 million Taka (US$ 100 million) of small savings from its borrowers which could be used to invest in new corporate ventures for the poor and could make them stakeholders in private corporate share issues or take over disinvested state-owned enterprises. Special mutual funds to handle such investment for the poor could be set up by Grameen Bank or BRAC or even specialised NGOs. The Bangladesh Government could facilitate this process by legislating that 10–20 percent of all initial public offerings in the stock market be reserved for mutual funds of the poor. Ironically, such reserve offerings had been provided to attract foreign investors to Bangladesh. Thus such opportunities could be provided to the poor.

**Child labour**

According to the national census, 12 percent of the Bangladesh labour force is constituted by children aged under 14 years (Bangladesh Bureau of Statistics, 1997). There has been a reluctance to examine critically the multiple causes of child labour. Clearly export industries are not the only ones employing children. Several other industries producing for a national market also employ children. Child labour has been challenged by NGOs and United Nations agencies promoting the rights of the child. It was argued that child labour should be eliminated since it "deprives children of the right to childhood, prevents access to basic needs, undermines development and health and entails exploitative terms of employment".

In our study, nearly half of boys and girls aged 10–14 years were performing income generating work. Only 7 percent of girls and boys aged 5–16 years attended school compared to 52 percent of those children who were not working. The mean total of income contributed by children in households where children work was 49 percent in female headed households, and 30 percent in male headed households. The percentage of households below the poverty line was 30 percent for female headed households, and 17 percent for male headed households. If we consider an artificial scenario where children's contributions were removed from the household income, the percentage below the poverty line of Taka 532 per consumption unit per month increases from 30 percent to almost 50 percent in female headed households, and 19 percent to 25 percent in male headed households, showing that child income was an important part of household income. The implications for children are to develop programmes for education as well as income generating work at the same time, so that they can continue to work and get basic education. Other programmes also offer training programmes as well as education. Both of these are good for children, as they can earn now and equip themselves for a better form of employment in the future.

## Marital instability

In traditional Bangladeshi society marriage is the only legitimate institution for sexual gratification and bearing and rearing of children. Financial transactions associated with marriage seem to have changed in character in recent years. Whereas Bangali Muslims traditionally exchange bride price, since about the 1950s, dowry payments from the bride's family to the groom have been increasingly common and of larger amounts. Marriage arrangements are made by the guardian, with the bride and groom playing a passive role. The key characteristics of post-marital living arrangements are patrilocal residence, and gender based segmentation of marital roles is high. Divorce or separation are low. That means the stability of conjugal life was high.

In our study there are some similarities and a number of key differences between marriage in the traditional and the slum context. In the slum, marriage is near universal and still seen as the most acceptable context for sexual relations and reproduction. In the slum context, the age gap between spouses and grooms has been reduced slightly from the traditional norms, because females tend to marry later. This is because, unlike traditional society, many girls have to work and save money to contribute to their own marriage. Love marriages are increasing. Many couples arrange their own marriages and exclude the parents' traditional participation. Unlike traditional society, levels of polygamy, divorce, separation and desertion are on the increase in the urban slum. Marriage may thus be seen to be far more unstable in the urban context.

The lack of social cohesion in slum society creates a situation where rumours spread. This sometimes put husband–wife relations under strain and causes marital discord and breakdown. Heterogeneity of slum society is a key cause for marital discord and breakdown. Close familial ties and social control mechanisms no longer operate in many cases. Unlike traditional society, immovable property is absent in the slum context. This means that household members do not have confirmed future economic support. Individuals also participate in the labour market. Thus individuals are becoming self-dependent and familial ties are getting looser. Alienation and social segment are increasing deviant behaviour. For this, husbands are more likely to invest in their own individual self-interest than for household maintenance. This often causes household hardship and discord. Non-payment of dowry is another key cause of marital discord, insecurity, and breakdown. Despite continuing female subordination, the option to join the labour market has a positive effect on women. As they are economically independent, they are sometimes able to reject unhappy marriages. However, the stigma and insecurity continues to be attached to separated women. Thus women face the dilemma of accepting unhappy marriages and gaining social acceptance and security, or rejecting such marriages and facing hardship and rejection by members of the community.

Although the changing nature of slum society provides greater options for urban women, slum women are nevertheless still severely disadvantaged compared to men. The relaxation in pressure against divorce, the weakening of the lineage, and the increased options for female labour can be seen as a positive force for some women, allowing them greater freedom. However, on the whole men appear to be benefiting most from the prevailing climate of marital uncertainty. Women's options for re-partnering following marital breakdown are severely limited, while living alone is not a viable alternative. Children, too, are suffering the effects of marital discord and breakdown. Male irresponsibility towards the family is increasing. Men are failing to perform the traditional responsibilities as providers, and a significant proportion are taking another wife, either through desertion or polygyny. This leads to the creation of female headed households and the entrenchment of female poverty. Children are also abused in step-family settings, being deprived of emotional and material support. In this way the effects of marital instability and family breakdown can be seen to have serious implications for the long-term well-being of slum dwellers.

Policy implications are as follows:

1 The marriage registration system must be changed and made more systematic. The verbal system of marriage and unilateral divorce must be declared illegal and punishable, and photos of the bride and groom must be enclosed in the registration form.
2 Women mostly avoid taking legal action because of the biased judgement of male-dominated local judicial committees. Threats from their husbands or in-laws also lead to discouragement. Shelters for women should be increased to protect them during the period of litigation. At the same time, representation of women in the local political structures must be ensured.
3 Stepchildren are victimised by their step-parents. This has serious implications for the long-term well-being of slum dwellers. The child's rights at the household level, specially those of stepchildren, must be ensured. During the remarriage of parents an agreement must be signed to the effect that their stepchildren get shelter in their new homes, with social and legal and other support.
4 NGOs can take up effective programmes to help women to cope with the trauma and distress following a marital breakdown. For example, single women should be provided with credit, health and income generating programmes.
5 NGOs are imparting training in some selected group members in their legal awareness development programme with the aim that these trained members will share their knowledge with neighbours and the community.
6 Women can form a peer group to help a victim to cope or reduce the marital discord and also get legal help or act as a shelter. This can create pressure on the husband to accept responsibility for his wife and children.

## Work disabling morbidity and coping strategies

Amongst the poor in developing countries, health is often not considered a priority need by many households with income barely enough to meet needs of daily food, shelter and clothing. Illness may have serious consequences if it leads to a loss of income. The risk is particularly common for unskilled workers, because he/she is paid on a daily basis and the employer offers the job to any individual who is waiting for work. Individuals who are involved in skilled work tend to have a stronger network of support, compared to those who work in unskilled work. The strength of the network reduces the threat of job loss during illness, though of course if illness is prolonged, then employers often opt to recruit a new person in their place.

We identified relatively homogeneous groups within Dhaka slum households, who report similar patterns of livelihood. Four groups emerged which may be summarised as "self-employment", "casual unskilled", "female headed" households, and "casual skilled" households on the basis of their socio-economic, demographic, and occupational characteristics. The "self-employed" and "casual skilled" groups were better off in terms of income, assets and creditworthiness. The great burden of adult illness fell in the "casual unskilled" and "female headed" households. In any single month, 30 to 40 percent of these households reported loss of labour days due to illness. On average, about four days per month were lost in casual unskilled households, and over seven days per month were lost in female headed households. The income lost due to illness far exceeded household expenditure to treat illness. A typical sequence of responses to household illnesses included:

1 Borrowing money without interest.
2 Diversification of income sources.
3 Women going out to work.
4 Expenditure reduction.
5 Use of savings.
6 Selling assets.
7 Merging households.
8 Move kin's family in urban areas.
9 Move to rural areas.
10 Gifts and help.

When illness occurs in individuals, the costs fall on the household. Sickness in one member influences household decision making regarding the allocation of financial resources. This study found that coping with the costs of illness largely occurred at the level of the household itself, and that inter-household transfers of financial resources played a minor part. In spite of the importance of the household coping with illness, policy has customarily been targeted at individuals at risk by characteristics such as age and gender. One lesson from the current study is that there are households at risk of being pushed into poverty and calamity as a result of catastrophic illness. Most households did lose income due to illness. However, even when coping was successful in the short term, it is likely to increase vulnerability in the long term by reducing the household's ability to cope with future adverse events. When selling assets enabled the household to cover health expenditure, it also made them poorer and less prepared to cope with future economic and social crises.

What policy options might strengthen the capacity of urban households to cope with financial costs of illness? One suggestion is to develop programmes to increase the asset buffer of households, by lending money to cover the assets to be sold in a crisis. A second way is to diversify income sources, by promoting business acumen and by increasing income earning opportunities. Third is to develop credit schemes for poor households and enhance access to credit for them. And lastly, to develop community health insurance schemes in Dhaka. There are at least two community health insurance schemes: Gonoshashthya Kenra (GK) Health Care System in Savar and Grameen Health Programme (GB). Enrolment in the GK scheme was voluntary per household and based upon a contract between GK and the household. Fees are dependent upon socio-economic position. Coverage starts immediately for clinic attendance, but only after a week for hospitalisation. Before its implementation, the Grameen pre-paid health plan was discussed with members of the GB credit programmes. The groups had to reach a consensus and then all the groups agreed to subscribe and can use the clinics and costs of referral. Hospitalisation was not added until later. The fee structure was less for GB households and more for non-GB households (Desmet et al., 1999). These programmes need to be developed and supported.

## Child and adult undernutrition and morbidity

It is well established that undernutrition and morbidity are not randomly distributed within a given population, but are a dimension of poverty. In urban areas, the ability of a household to command sufficient food resources is primarily dependent upon social and economic variables, such as social networks, employment, income and assets. Households are often characterised by a dependence upon the market, not only for employment, but also for food and other basic needs.

Among children, stunting and underweight was more prevalent in older children; 74 percent of boys and girls were stunted among those aged 24–59 months, compared to 59 percent of children aged 2–24 months. But 74 percent were underweight in the older group, and 72 percent in the younger group. Analyses showed that female headed households had less stunting but more wasting compared to male headed households. Households with a self reported financial situation of severe deficit had more stunting, underweight and wasted children, compared to those with a break even financial situation. Households with worse latrine use by children showed more stunting, underweight and wasting compared to households with better latrine use by children.

Among adults, more females were severely undernourished compared to males. Female headed households had a worse nutritional situation than male headed households. Being in Beri Badh and in a deficit financial situation were associated with poor BMI. Casual workers unskilled and dependent self-employed were the most vulnerable occupations for BMI. In conclusion, undernutrition in adults was related to demographic, economic, social and environmental factors.

Children under five years had the highest period prevalence of illness, followed by female adults. Beri Badh had the highest period prevalence compared to other areas. Female adults had the highest period prevalence compared to male adults, and female heads had the highest period prevalence for fever, pain in the abdomen and any illness compared to male headed households. Female earners also had the highest period prevalence of illness compared to male earners.

The policy implications are poorly focused health services, with out-of-hours working women unable to bring their children for care. If nutritional rehabilitation centres are to be part of the health services, consideration must be given to time constraints faced by women workers, so child carers should be allowed to go instead. Most health care has been directed towards children and mothers, but this study has shown that adult illnesses has the worst effect on household vulnerability indicating that adult focused health care should be available as well as child and maternal health services. For workers, there should be an expansion of work-based health facilities, and policies to ensure health provision in larger enterprises. Underpinning the children's and adult's nutritional status and ill health is poverty. So it is imperative that poverty alleviation policies are implemented, as well as programmes to support female independence.

## Intra-household distribution of nutritional vulnerability

The utility of nutritional indicators may be enhanced by extending the unit of measurement from the individual to the household. Such classification may enable patterns of intra-household undernutrition to be identified and to characterise different problems and causes. Nearly 45 percent of women's households were totally undernourished, compared to other groups. The female headed households were therefore more vulnerable. The policy implications include increasing female earnings. The barriers include limited opportunities for female employment, low rates of return to women's work, poor conditions of employment, inflexible working hours, competing demands for women's time, persistent cultural restrictions and low levels of education and skills. Possible interventions should include encouraging more flexible working arrangements, sharing arrangements among slum women, investment in facilitating structures (for example, transport, child care provision, cooking rotas), promotion and support of home-based activities, creation of a more enabling environment, for example, by challenging continued restrictions. Also improving terms and conditions of existing work, for example, enforcement of labour standards, lobbying of employers, creation of alternative sources of income for women in particular, increase bargaining power and options. Then upgrading skills and education through appropriate adult education schemes. Finally increasing savings through non governmental organisations and linkages to formal financial systems, and put this to work – for example, investment of savings in production sector.

## Women's negotiation control and well-being within the household

The overall management of material resources has traditionally been the responsibility of the head of household. However, a close examination of the data suggests that women are playing a significant role in the management of material resources within the household. In households where the head of household manages the budget, the spouse earns more, but owns less assets and savings compared to female controlled households, where women work more days and have a common fund. Violence against women within marriage is frequent and is tolerated in order to gain some protection from other men. Women's health and children's nutritional status was better in female controlled households, compared to male controlled households. In Sen's terminology, though working for an income enables women to secure a better fall-back position (Sen, 1990), their rights in Bangladesh remain weak, and the broader social, economic and political structures continue to weigh against women. The findings from this study and other recent research suggest that gender identities are in a state of flux within the slum setting in Bangladesh. Therefore the opportunities exist for re-negotiation on better terms for women. With support from appropriate policy and programme interventions, it seems likely that increasing involvement of women in income-earning work could, in the long term, lead to favourable changes in gender inequalities, bringing women greater options and control over their lives.

## Female workforce and family

In Bangladesh, with strong patriarchal tradition and sharp gender segregation of work and space, we might expect to find women's waged work employment having a relatively limited impact on prevailing gender norms. Some changes have occurred in women's roles and their degree of subordination, and the expansion of economic opportunities is largely behind the changes. Factors affecting women working include age, marital status, household head, and income status. Persistent inequalities prevail in women's wages, which are invariably lower than men's for similar types of occupation. Among households with female earners, women contributed 34 percent of total income and 58 percent of total work days by women. Fifty three percent of husbands do not allow women to work at all, which supports male control over female labour. This reinforces women's subordination within and outside the household. For example, as well as working full time, women have responsibility for domestic work and child care work.

*The implications for government are:*

1 Greater investment in labour-intensive industries to absorb female labour, particularly those which can be dominated by female labour, such as industrial sewing, tailoring, textiles and food processing.
2 The government should take responsibility to prevent wage exploitation and discrimination against female workers. The government should ensure implementation of the current law for equal wage.

3   The government should be strict in ensuring observance of the law relating to maternity and maternity leave. The formal sector should provide funds for maternity leave. No women should be sacked for this reason.
4   Reduced and more flexible working hours for married women which will facilitate the combination of their household work and income generating work.
5   Identification of skilled work opportunities for women and arrangement of training to enhance earning potential and security.
6   The government should ensure child care facilities in every factory and industry for breast feeding babies.

*Implications for NGOs are:*

1   Advocacy, training and work opportunity provision to reduce the sex segregation in work.
2   Creative training initiatives to expand appropriate work opportunities for women, including self-employment, home-based activities, part-time and new initiatives to enable women to break into new markets.
3   Awareness-raising programmes on female worker's rights.
4   Organisations of women's unions to increase bargaining power for fair wages, and programmes to change traditional values which inhibit women's participation in work.
5   Community-based networks for job finding, skill-sharing activities, and child care facilities.

## Livelihood groups

To date, policy focused research on the livelihood and survival strategies of poor people has largely concentrated on rural areas (Beck, 1994). However, data from a detailed ethnographic study of an inner city slum in Khula not only provides important information on the considerable heterogeneity of economic activities of the poor, but also demonstrates the possibility that there are broadly homogeneous groups in terms of the level and form of livelihood (Pryer, 1993). This study also illustrates the complex factors that differentiates the urban poor from the better off, and those who are more vulnerable with female headed households being the most vulnerable. In this study, four livelihood groups were identified. The richest group was self-employed, with higher income, land and animals, more business assets and savings. Loans were high, showing that this group was creditworthy. The second richest group was skilled workers who had some land and animals, but less than those in group 1. Business assets were the second lowest. The vulnerable group was female headed households. This group was mainly casual unskilled. Total expenditure, income and savings were the lowest among the groups, while loans were the second highest. The last group was poor and was mainly dependent self-employed; savings, income and expenditure were the second lowest. In conclusion, cluster analysis has identified four groups which differed in terms of socio-economic and demographic variables. The technique could be a useful practical tool of relevance to the development, monitoring and targeting of vulnerable households by public policy in Bangladesh.

## Managing financial shocks and stresses

As explained earlier, the term "livelihood system" refers to how people maintain their living so that they are able to function in a particular society which contains harmful externalities such as risk, hazard and economic shock. Vulnerability is a core but complex concept associated with the concept of livelihood system because it has various interacting elements and it is associated with other concepts such as poverty. The important point to reiterate here is that vulnerability has two sides – external and internal. The external side includes risk, shocks or stress to which the household or individual is subjected. The internal side includes defencelessness, i.e. the lack of means to cope without damaging loss. Shocks and vulnerability have been conceptualised as a combination of shock and the ability to cope when shock occurs. It important to understand which types of event represent the most important shocks for the urban poor and how individuals and households respond and cope. In this study 30 percent of households reported a severe deficit in financial status with female headed households and the area of Beri Badh facing the highest percentages of severe deficit. The main reason for deterioration in financial status was an income earning member being incapacitated due to ill health, followed by earnings decrease and unable to work. The coping strategies for slum households were changed work, reduced expenditure and taking loans, with few households taking out mortgages, or selling assets, and few households migrating or begging. There was no evidence of the moral economy in Dhaka slums. For example, hardly any financial exchange relationships were found.

The implications for income earning members being incapacitated due to illness has already shown that community health insurance schemes are appropriate, as well as credit schemes to mitigate the losses. Regarding decreasing earnings and difficulty finding work, households adopt strategies of seeking alternative employment and increasing the number of workers. At policy level opportunities for diversification with credit for self emloyed workers or enforcement of minimum wages might be considered. Also there are indications that joining a local union can help an individual negotiate for better terms and conditions and presents an option to simply working more days.

## References

Bangladesh Bureau of Statistics (1997), *Statistical Yearbook of Bangladesh*, Government of Bangladesh, Dhaka, Bangladesh.
Bangladesh Bureau of Statistics (1999), *Statistical Yearbook of Bangladesh*, Government of Bangladesh, Dhaka, Bangladesh.
Beck, T. (1994), *The Experience of Poverty: Fighting for respect and resources in village India*, Intermediate Technology Publications, London.
CIRDAP (1997), 'Poverty profile and poverty alleviation effects in Bangladesh, A SAM based analysis', MAP Technical Paper Series No. 1.
Desmet, M., Chowdhury, A.Q. and Islam, Md K. (1999), 'The potential for social mobilisation in Bangladesh: The organisation and functioning of two health insurance schemes', *Social Science and Medicine*, 48, pp. 925–938.

Islam, N. (1997), *Addressing the urban poverty agenda in Bangladesh*, Asian Development Bank University Press, Dhaka.
Pryer, J.A. (1993), 'The impact of adult ill health on household income and nutrition in Khulna, Bangladesh', *Environment and Urbanization*, 5(2), pp. 35–49.
Sen, A. (1990), 'Gender and co-operative conflicts', in Tinker, I. (ed.), *Persistent Inequalities: Women and World Development*, Oxford University Press, Oxford and New York.
World Development Report (2000/2001), *Attacking Poverty*, Oxford University Press, New York.

# Bibliography

Acharya, M. and Bennet, L. (1983), 'Women in the subsistence sector: economic participation and household decision making in Nepal', World Bank Staff Working Paper 256, World Bank, New York.

Adams, A.M. (1992), 'Seasonal food insecurity in the Sahel: nutritional, social and economic risk among Bamana agriculturalists in Mali', Doctoral thesis, University of London.

Agarwal, B. (1992), 'Social security and the family: Coping with seasonality and calamity in Rural India: 171–244', in Ahmad E., Dreze, J., Hills, J. and Sen, A. (eds), *Social Security in Developing Countries*, Oxford University Press, Oxford.

Aldenderfer, M.S. and Blashfield, R.K. (1984), *Cluster Analysis*, Series: Quantitative applications in social sciences, Sage Publications, London.

Aldenderfer, M.S. and Blashfield, R.K. (1994), *Cluster Analysis*, Series: Quantitative applications in social sciences, Sage Publications, London.

Alderman, H. and Gertler, P. (1997), 'Family resources and gender differences in human capital investments', in Haddad, L., Hoddinott, J. and Alderman, H. (eds), *Intra-household Resource Allocation in Developing Countries*, The Johns Hopkins University Press, Baltimore.

Alston, P. (1994), *The Best Interest of the Child: Reconciling culture and human rights*, UNICEF, International Child Development Centre, Florence and Clarendon Press, Oxford.

Amin, S. (1995), 'The poverty–purdah trap in rural Bangladesh: implications for women's roles in the family', Working Papers No. 75, Population Council Research Division, New York.

Amin, S., Diamond, I., Naved, R. and Newby, M. (1997), 'Transition to adulthood of female factory workers: some evidence from Bangladesh', Working Paper No. 102, Population Council Research Division, New York.

Anker, R. (1983), 'Female labour force participation in developing countries: a critique of current definitions and data collection methods', *International Labour Review*, 122 (6), pp. 709–723.

Bangladesh Bureau of Statistics (1996), *Statistical Yearbook of Bangladesh*, Government of Bangladesh, Dhaka, Bangladesh.

Bangladesh Bureau of Statistics (1997), *Child Nutrition Survey of Bangladesh 1995–96*, Ministry of Planning, Statistics Division, Government of Bangladesh, Dhaka, pp. 1–144.

Bangladesh Bureau of Statistics (1999), *Statistical Yearbook of Bangladesh*, Government of Bangladesh, Dhaka, Bangladesh.

Bangladesh Integrated Nutrition Project (1996), *Project Implementation Volume* (PIV), Ministry of Health and Family Welfare, Government of Bangladesh, pp. 1–94.

Bangladesh National Food and Nutrition Policy (1997), Ministry of Health and Family Welfare, Government of Bangladesh, pp. 1–25.
Barret, C. and Carter, M. (1999), *Can't get ahead for falling behind: new directions for development policy to escape poverty and relief traps*, US Agency for International Development, Washington DC.
Beaton, G., Kelly, J., Kevany, R., Martorell, R. and Mason, J. (1990), 'Appropriate uses of anthropometric indices in children', ACC/SCN State of the Art series on Nutrition Policy, Discussion Paper No. 7, United Nations Administrative Committee on coordination: subcommittee on nutrition, pp. 1–51.
Beck, T. (1994), *The Experience of Poverty: Fighting for respect and resources in village India*, Intermediate Technology Publications, London.
Behrman, J.R. and Deolikar, A. (1990), 'The intra-household demand for nutrients in rural south Asia: Individual estimates, fixed effects and permanent income', *Journal of Human Resources*, 24(4), pp. 655–96.
Black, R.E., Brown, K.H., Becker, S., Alim, A.R.M.A. and Merson, M.H. (1982), 'Contamination of weaning foods and transmission of enterotoxigenic escherichia coli diarrhoea in children in rural Bangladesh', *Transactions of the Royal Society of Tropical Medicine and Hygiene*, Vol. 76, pp. 259–264.
Blanchet, T. (1984), *Women, pollution and marginality: meanings and rituals of birth in rural Bangladesh*, University Press, Dhaka, Bangladesh.
Blanchet, T. (1996), *Lost Innocence; Stolen Childhoods*, University Press, Dhaka, Bangladesh.
Blashfield, R.K. (1979), 'Mixture models tests of cluster analysis: accuracy of four agglomerative hierarchical methods', *Psychological Bulletin*, 83 (3), pp. 377–388.
Boydon, J. (1990), 'Child Work and Policy Makers: A comparative perspective on the globalisation of childhood', in James, A. and Prout, A. (eds), *Constructing and Reconstructing Childhood*, The Falmer Press, London, New York and Philadelphia.
Branca, F. and Abdulle, A. (1993), 'Famine in Somalia', letter to the *Lancet*, 5 June, 341 (8853), p. 1478.
Brockerhoff, M. and Brennan, E. (1997), 'The poverty of cities in the developing world', Population Council Research Division Working Paper No. 96, Population Council, New York.
Cain, M. (1977), 'The economic activities of children in a village in Bangladesh', *Population and Development Studies*, September, pp. 20–28.
Caldwell, J. and Caldwell, P. (1992), 'Family systems: their viability and vulnerability', in Berquo, E. and Xenos, P. (eds), *Family Structures and Cultural Change*, Clarendon Press, Oxford.
Carrin, G., De Graeve, D. and Deville, L. (1999), 'Introduction to the special issue on the economics of health insurance in low and middle-income countries', *Social Science and Medicine*, 44, pp. 859–864.
Castle, S.E. (1992), 'Intra-household differentials in women's status: household function and focus as determinants of children's illness management in rural Mali', *Health Transition Review*, 3(2), pp. 137–157.
Centre for Urban Studies (1989), *The Urban Poor in Bangladesh: Volume 1 comprehensive summary report*, Department of Geography, University of Dhaka.

Chambers, R. (1989a), 'Vulnerability, coping and policy', *IDS Bulletin*, 20 (2), pp. 1–8.
Chambers, R. (1989b), 'Editorial Introduction: Vulnerability, Coping and Policy', *IDS Bulletin*, 20 (2), pp. 1–7.
Chen, M.A. (1991), *Coping with Seasonality and Drought*, Sage, New Delhi.
Chippori, P.A. (1997), '"Collective" models of household behaviour: The haring rule approach', in Haddad, L., Hoddinott, J. and Alderman, H. (eds), *Intrahousehold resource allocation in developing countries*, The Johns Hopkins University Press, Baltimore.
CIRDAP (1997), 'Poverty profile and poverty alleviation effects in Bangladesh, A SAM based analysis', MAP Technical Paper Series No. 1.
Corbett, J.E.M. (1988), 'Famine and Household Coping Strategies', *World Development*, 16(9), pp. 1009–1112.
Creevy, I. (1996), *Changing women's lives and work*, UNIFEM, Intermediate Technology, London.
Daon, R.M. and Bisharat, L. (1990), 'Female autonomy and child nutritional status in the extended family, Amman, Jordan', *Social Science and Medicine*, 31(7), pp. 783–789.
Das Gupta, M. (1995), 'Lifecourse perspectives on women's autonomy and health outcomes', *American Anthropologist*, 97(3), pp. 481–91.
De Waal, A. (1989), *Famine that Kills: Darfur, Sudan, 1984–1985*, Clarendon Press, Oxford.
Defo, B.K. and Young, T.B. (1993), 'Correlates of malnutrition among children under two years of age admitted to hospital in Yaounde, Cameroon', *Journal of Tropical Paediatrics*, 39, pp. 68–75.
Delpeuch, F., Traissac, P., Martin-Prevel, Y., Massamba, J.P. and Maire, B. (2000), 'Economic crisis and malnutrition: socio-economic determinants of anthrometric status of pre-school children and their mothers in an African urban area', *Public Health Nutrition*, 3(1), pp. 39–47.
Dercon, S. (1999), 'Income risk, coping strategies and safety nets', Katholike Universiteit, Leuven, Oxford University, Centre for the study of African Economics and World Bank, in *World Development Report 2000/2001: Attacking Poverty*, Oxford University Press, Washington DC and London.
Dercon, S., Gertler, P. (1996), 'Income portfolios in rural Ethiopia and Tanzania: Choices and constraints', *Journal of Development Studies*, 32(6), pp. 850–75.
Dercon, S. and Krishnan, P. (2000), 'In Sickness and in Health: Risk sharing within households in rural Ethiopia', *Journal of Political Economy*, 108(4), pp. 58–75.
Desai, S. and Jain, D. (1992), 'Maternal employment and changes in family dynamics: the social context of women's work in rural South India', Working Paper No. 39, Population Council Research Division, NewYork.
Desmet, M., Chowdhury, A.Q. and Islam, Md K. (1999), 'The potential for social mobilisation in Bangladesh: The organisation and functioning of two health insurance schemes', *Social Science and Medicine*, 48, pp. 925–938.
Dugdale, A.E. (1985), 'Family anthropometry: a new strategy for determining community nutrition', *The Lancet*, 21 September (letter).
Emach, M. (1999), 'Diarrhoeal disease risk in Matlab, Bangladesh', *Social Science and Medicine*, 49, pp. 519–530.

Engle, P.L. (1991), 'Maternal work and child care strategies in peri-urban Guatemala: Nutritional effects', *Child Development*, 62(5), pp. 954–965.

Engle, P.L. (1993), 'Influences of mother's and father's income on children's nutritional status in Guatemala', *Social Science and Medicine*, 37(11), pp. 1303–1312.

Epidemiological Information (Epi Info) (1999), Version 6.0, Center for Disease Control, Atlanta, USA and World Health Organization, Geneva, Switzerland.

Everitt, B. (1980), *Cluster Analysis*, Heinemann Educational Books, London.

Feachem, R.G.A., Kjellstrom, T., Murray, C.J.L., Over, M. and Phillips, M.A. (1992), *The Health of Adults in the Developing World*, Oxford University Press, Oxford.

Food and Agriculture Organization and World Health Organization (1992), *International Conference on Nutrition Final Report*, Rome, Italy, pp. 9–55.

Foster, A. (1995), 'Prices, credit markets and child growth in low income rural areas', *Economic Journal*, 105, pp. 551–70.

Gibson, R.S. (1990), 'Anthropometric assessment', in Gibson R.S. (ed.), *Principles of Nutritional Assessment*, Oxford University Press, Oxford, pp. 155–208.

Gillespie, S. and McNeill, G. (1992), *Food, Health and Survival in India and Developing Countries*, Oxford University Press, Delhi, Bombay, Calcutta, Madras.

Goode, J.W. (1994), *The Family*, Prentice-Hall of India (Private) Limited, New Delhi.

Greenhalgh, S. (1991), 'Women in the informal enterprise: empowerment or exploitation?', Working Paper No. 33, Population Council Research Division, New York.

Haan, de A. (1998), 'Social exclusion: an alternative concept for the study of Deprivation?', *IDS Bulletin*, 29(1), pp. 10–19.

Haddad, L., Hoddinott, J. and Alderman, H. (1997), 'Policy issues and intra-household allocation: Conclusions', in Haddad, L., Hoddinott, J., Alderman, H. (eds), *Intra-household Resource Allocation in Developing Countries*, The Johns Hopkins University Press, Baltimore.

Haddad, L. and Kanbur, R. (1990), 'Are better-off households more equal or less equal?', Policy Research and External Affairs Working Paper 373, World Bank, Washington, DC.

Hakeem, R. (2001), 'Socio-economic differences in height and body mass index of children and adults living in urban areas of Karachi, Pakistan', *European Journal of Clinical Nutrition*, 55(5), pp. 400–406.

Haque, T. (1998), 'Redefining gender roles in urbanizing Bangladesh', paper presented at the European Network of Bangladesh Studies Workshop, University of Bath, UK.

Harpham, T. and Tanner, M. (1995), *Urban Health in Developing Countries: Progress and Prospects*, Earthscan Publications, London.

Harris, J. (1986), 'Vulnerable workers in the urban labour markets of south and south-east Asia: A report to the International Labour Organisation', *Reports in Development*, No. 32, School of Development Studies, University of East Anglia, Norwich.

Hibbard, J.H., Pope, C.R. (1986), 'Gender roles and illness orientation and use of medical services', *Social Science and Medicine*, 17, pp. 129–137.

Hoddinott, J., Alderman, H. and Haddad, L. (1997), 'Introduction: the scope of intrahoushold resource allocation issues', in Haddad, L., Hoddinott, J. and Alderman, H. (eds), *Intra-household Resource Allocation in Developing Countries*, The Johns Hopkins University Press, Baltimore.

Holzmann, R. and Jorgensen, S.L. (2000), 'Social risk management: a new conceptual framework for social protection and beyond', *Social Protection*, Discussion Paper 0006, World Bank, Human Development Network. Washington DC.

Hoque, B.A. and Hoque, M.M. (1994), 'Environment and health', in Rahman, A.A., Huq, S., Haider, R. and Jansen, E.G. (eds), *Environment and Development in Bangladesh*, University Press, Dhaka, Bangladesh.

Hossain, H., Johan, R. and Sobhan, S. (1990), *No better option? Industrial women workers in Bangladesh*, University Press, Dhaka, Bangladesh.

Huttly, S.R.A., Victora, C.G., Barros, F.C., Teixeira, A.M.B. and Vaughn, P.J. (1991), 'The timing of nutritional status determination: Implications for interventions and growth monitoring', *European Journal of Clinical Nutrition*, 45, pp. 85–95.

Islam, M.A., Rahman, M.M. and Mahalanabis, D. (1994), 'Maternal and socio-economic factors and the risk of a severe malnutrition in a child: a case-control study', *European Journal of Clinical Nutrition*, 48, pp. 416–424.

Islam, N. (1996), *Dhaka city to megacity: perspectives on people, places, planning and development issues*, University of Dhaka, Bangladesh.

Islam, N. (1997), *Addressing the urban poverty agenda in Bangladesh*, Asian Development Bank, University Press, Dhaka, Bangladesh.

Jacoby, H. and Skoufias, E. (1997), 'Risk, financial markets and human capital in a developing country', *Review of Economic Studies*, 64(3), pp. 311–35.

Jesmin, S. (1998), *Marital Instability and its Effects on Bustee Women and Children*, Urban Livelihoods Study Monographs 3, Institute for Development Policy Analysis and Advocacy (IDPAA) PROSHIKA, Dhaka, Bangladesh.

Johnson, F.C. and Rogers, B.L. (1992), 'Children's nutritional status in female headed households in Dominican Republic', *Social Science and Medicine*, 37(11), pp. 1293–1301.

Jongpiputvanich, S., Poomsuwan, P. and Phittayanon, P. (1992), 'Prevalence and risk factors of protein energy malnutrition (PEM) in pre-school children of Klong-Toey Slum, Bangkok, Thailand', *Journal of the Medical Association of Thailand*, 75(1), pp. 39–44.

Kabeer, N. (1995a), *Reversed Realities: Gender Hierarchies in Development Thought*, Verso, London and New York.

Kabeer, N. (1995b), 'Necessary, sufficient or irrelevant? Women, wages and intra-household power relations in urban Bangladesh', Institute of Development Studies Working Paper, 25, Sussex.

Kabir, Md A., Rahman, A., Salway, S. and Pryer, J. (2000), 'Sickness among the urban poor: a barrier to livelihood security', *Journal of International Development* (12), pp. 707–772.

Keller, W. (1988), 'The Epidemiology of Stunting', in Waterlow, J.C. (ed.), *Linear growth retardation in less developing countries*, New York: Raven Press, Nestlé Nutrition workshops series, Vol. 14.

Kennedy, N., Ramsay, A., Uiso, L., Gutmann, J., Ngowi, F.I. and Gillespie, S.H. (1996), 'Nutritional status and weight gain in patients with pulmonary tuberculosis in Tanzania', *Transactions of the Royal Society of Tropical Medicine and Hygiene*, Mar–Apr; 90(2), pp. 162–6.

Kesserler, R.C., Brown, R.L. and Browan, C.L. (1981), 'Sex differences in psychiatric help-seeking: evidence from four large-scale surveys', *Journal of Health and Social Behaviour*, 22, pp. 49–64.

Khandker, S.R. (1998), *Fighting Poverty with Microcredit: Experience in Bangladesh*, Oxford University Press, New York.

Khin-Maung, U., Khin, M., Wai, N.N., Hman, N.W., Myint, T.T. and Butler, T. (1992), 'Risk factors for the development of persistent diarrhoea and malnutrition in Burmese children', *International Journal of Epidemiology*, 21(5), pp. 1021–1029.

Kibria, N. (1996), 'Culture, social class and income control in the lives of women garment factory workers in Bangladesh', *Gender and Society*, 9(3), pp. 289–309.

Klasen, S. (1994), '"Missing women" reconsidered', *World Development*, 22(7), pp. 1061–71.

Kogi, Makau W. (1988), 'Nutritional status and socio-economic factors in the population of a semi-arid region in Kenya', unpublished PhD thesis, London School of Hygiene and Tropical Medicine.

Kroeger, A. (1983), 'Health interview surveys in developing countries: a review of methods and results', *International Journal of Epidemiology*, 12(4), pp. 465–81.

Lanjouw, P. and Stern, N. (1999), 'Poverty in Palanpur', *World Bank Review*, 5(1), pp. 23–56

Lessinger, J. (1990), 'Work and modesty: the dilemma of women market traders in Madras', in Dube, L. and Palriwala, R. (eds), *Structures and Strategies: women, work and family*, Sage, New Delhi.

Lima, M., Figuira, M.D. and Ebrahim, G.J. (1990), 'Malnutrition among children or adolescent mothers in a squatter community of Redclife, Brazil', *Journal of Tropical Paediatrics*, 36, pp. 14–19.

Macintyre, S., Ford, G. and Hunt, K. (1999), 'Do women over-report morbidity? Men's and women's responses to structured prompting on a standard question on long standing illness', *Social Science and Medicine*, 48, pp. 89–98.

Madjumder, P.P. (1992), *Marriage, employment and marital adjustment, a case study of educated urban women*, Research Report 132, Bangladesh Institute of Development Studies, Dhaka, Bangladesh.

Madjumder, P.P., Mamud, S. and Asfar, R. (1989), *Squatter life in the Agargoan area*, Dhaka: Bangladesh Institute of Development Studies, Dhaka, Bangladesh.

Madzingira, N. (1995), 'Malnutrition in children under five in Zimbabwe: Effects of social-economic factors and disease', *Social Biology*, 42(3–4), pp. 239–246.

Maloney, C., Aziz, K.M.A. and Sarker, P.C. (1981), *Beliefs and fertility in Bangladesh*, International Centre for Diarrhoeal Disease Research, Bangladesh, Dhaka.

Manning, D.S. (1999), *The role of legal services organisations in attacking poverty*, in World Development Report, 2000/2001, Oxford University Press, Oxford.

Martin, N. (1998), 'Vulnerability, marriage and violence: restructuring of intra-household relationship in a resource poor urban community in Bangladesh', Paper presented at the European Network of Bangladesh Studies Workshop, 16–18 April, University of Bath, UK.

Mbago, M.C.Y. and Namfua, P.P. (1992), 'Some determinants of nutritional status of one-to-four-year-old children in low income areas in Tanzania', *Journal of Tropical Paediatrics*, 38, pp. 299–306.

Miah, M.A.Q., Weber, K.E. and Islam, N. (1988), *Upgrading a Bustee settlement in Dhaka*, Bangkok, Thailand, Division of Human Settlements, Asian Institute of Technology.

Mills, A. (1983), 'Economic aspects of health insurance', in Lee, K. and Mills, A. (eds), *The Economics of Health in Developing Countries*, Oxford University Press, Oxford.

Moser, C. (1995), *Confronting Crisis: A comparative study of household responses to poverty and vulnerability in four poor urban communities*, Environmentally Sustainable Development Studies and Monographs No 8. Washington DC, The World Bank.

Narayan, D., Chambers, R., Shah, M.K. and Petesch, P. (2000), *Voices of the Poor: crying out for change*, Oxford University Press, New York.

Naved, T.R. (1997), 'Female labour migration and its implications for marriage and child bearing in Bangladesh', paper presented at the Population Council Workshop on adolescence and marriage among female garment workers in Dhaka, Bangladesh Institute of Development Studies, Dhaka, Bangladesh.

Normand, C. (1999), 'Using social health insurance to meet policy goals', *Social Science and Medicine*, 48, pp. 865–869.

Nube, M., Aseno-Okyere, W.R. and van den Boom, G.J. (1998), 'Body Mass Index as indicator of living in developing countries', *European Journal of Clinical Nutrition*, 52(2), pp. 136–44.

Nutrition Surveillance Project, Report of the 49 round (urban April, 1998), Helen Keller International (Bangladesh) and Institute of Public Health Nutrition, Government of Bangladesh, Dhaka.

Opel, A.E.A. (1998), 'The labour market: where social resources matter', *Discourse*, 2(1), pp. 49–74.

Osmani, S.R. (1990), *Nutrition and Poverty*, Oxford University Press, Oxford.

Osmani, S.R. (1993), 'On some controversies in the measurement of undernutrition', in Osmani, S.R. (ed.) *Nutrition and Poverty*, Clarendon Press, Oxford.

Over, M., Randall, O.E., Huber, J.H. and Solon, O. (1992), 'The consequences of adult ill health', in Feachem, R., Kjellstrom, T., Murray, C.J.L., Over, M. and Phillips, M. (eds), *The Health of Adults in the Developing World*, Oxford University Press, Oxford.

Pahl, J. (1989), *Money and Marriage*, Macmillan Press, London.

Paul-Majamber, P. and S. Chaudhuri Zohir (1994), 'Dynamics of wage employment: a case of employment in the garment industry', *The Bangladesh Development Studies*, 22(2&3), pp. 197–216.

Payne, P. (1992), 'Assessing undernutrition: the need for a reconceptualization', in Osmani, S.R. (ed.) *Nutrition and Poverty*, Oxford University Press, Oxford.

Pryer, J.A. (1990), 'Socio-economic and environmental aspects of undernutrition and ill health in an urban slum in Bangladesh', unpublished PhD thesis, London School of Hygiene and Tropical Medicine.

Pryer, J.A. (1993a), 'Nutritionally vulnerable households in the urban slum economy: a case study from Khulna, Bangladesh', in Schell, L.M., Smith, M. and Bilsborogh, A. (eds), *Urban Ecology and Health in the Third World*, Cambridge University Press, Cambridge.

Pryer, J.A. (1993b), 'The impact of adult ill health on household income and nutrition in Khulna, Bangladesh', *Environment and Urbanization*, 5(2), pp. 35–49.

Pryer, J.A., Rogers, S., Normand, C. and Rahman, A. (2002), 'Livelihoods, nutrition and health in Dhaka slums', *Public Health Nutrition*, 5(5), pp. 613–618.

Rahman, A. (1998), 'Adult Morbidity and its impact on livelihoods of the urban poor in Bangladesh', Urban Livelihoods Study Working Paper 2, Institute for Development Policy Analysis and Advocacy, Proshika, Dhaka, Bangladesh.

Rahman, H.Z. (1998), 'Poverty issues in Bangladesh: a strategic review', Report commissioned by Department for International Development, UK.

Rahman, S. (1998), 'Levels and characteristics of female participation in work, among the urban poor in Dhaka', Urban Livelihoods Study Working Paper 1, Institute for Development Policy Analysis and Advocacy, Proshika, Dhaka, Bangladesh.

Ramphlele, M.A., Helap, M., Trollip, D.K. (1991), 'Health status of hostel dwellers, Part III, Nutritional status of children 0–5 years', *South African Medical Journal*, 79, pp. 705–709.

Rao, K.V. and Balakrishna, N. (1990), 'Discriminant function analysis: a case study of some socio-economic constraints on child nutrition', *Indian Journal of Medical Research*, 92, pp. 66–71.

Ricca, J.A. and Becker, S. (1996), 'Risk factors for wasting and stunting among children in Metro Cebu, Philippines', *American Journal of Clinical Nutrition*, 63, pp. 966–75.

Rogers, B.L. (1996), 'The implications of female household headship for food consumption and nutritional status in the Dominican Republic', *World Development*, 24(1), pp. 113–28.

Ron, A. (1999), 'NGOs in community health insurance schemes: examples from Guatemala and Philippines', *Social Science and Medicine*, 48, pp. 939–950.

Ross, D.A. and Vaughan, J.P. (1986), 'Health interview surveys in developing countries: a methodological review', *Studies of Family Planning*, 17(2), pp. 78–94.

Rowntree, B.S. (1901), *Poverty: A Study of Town Life*, Macmillan, London.

Sarlio-Lahteenkorva, S. and Lahelma, E. (1999), 'The association of body mass index with social and economic disadvantage in women and men', *International Journal of Epidemiology*, 28(3), pp. 445–9.

Sauerborn, R., Adams, A. and Hien, M. (1996), 'Household strategies to cope with the economic costs of illness', *Social Science and Medicine*, 43(3), pp. 291–301.

Saxena, N., Nayar, D. and Kapil, U. (1997), 'Prevalence of underweight, stunting and wasting', *Indian Pediatrics*, 34(7), pp. 627–31.

Scott, J.C. (1976), *The Moral Economy of the Peasant – Rebellion and Subsistence in South-east Asia*, Yale University Press, London.

Scott, J.C. (1985), *Weapons of the Weak*, Yale University Press, London.
Sen, A.K. (1981), *Poverty and Famines: an essay on entitlement and deprivation*, Clarendon Press, London.
Sen, A.K. (1987), *Resources, Values and Development*, Blackwell, Oxford.
Sen, A.K. (1990), 'Gender and cooperative conflicts', in Tinker, I. (ed.), *Persistent Inequalities: Women and World Development*, Oxford University Press, Oxford and New York.
Sen, A.K. (1997), *Inequality Re-examined*, Harvard University Press, Cambridge, Massachusets.
Shaik, K. (1998), 'The social and demographic correlates of divorce in rural Bangladesh, *Asia Pacific Population Journal*, September.
Shami, S. (1990), *Women in Arab Society: work patterns and gender relations in Egypt, Jordan and Sudan*, BERG/UNESCO, France.
Sharma, U. (1986), *Women's work, class and the urban household*, Tavistock Publications, London.
Shetty, P., James, W.P.T. (1990), 'Body Mass Index. A measure of chronic energy deficiency in adults', FAO Food and Nutrition Paper No. 56, FAO, Rome.
Siddiqui, K., Qudir, S.R., Alamgir, S. and Huq, S. (1990), *Social Formation in Dhaka City*, University Press, Dhaka, Bangladesh.
Sood, R. (1991), *Changing Status and Adjustment of Women*, Manak Publications, New Delhi and Jaipur, India.
Standing, H. (1991), *Dependence and Autonomy*, Routledge, London.
Stata Statistical Software (1999), Release 6, Stata Corp, Stata Press, 702, University Drive East, College Station, Texas 77840.
Stichter, S. (1990), 'Women, employment and the family: current debates', in Stichter, S. and Parpart, J.L. (eds), *Women, Employment and the Family in the International Division of Labour*, Macmillan, London.
Swift, J. (1989), 'Why are the rural people vulnerable to famine?', *IDS Bulletin*, 20(2), pp. 8–15.
Task Force (1992), 'Report of the task forces on Bangladesh development strategies for the 90's Volume III: Developing the Infrastructure', Government of Bangladesh: Dhaka, Bangladesh.
Thaver, I.H., Ebrahim, G.J. and Richardson, R. (1990), 'Infant mortality and undernutrition in the squatter settlements of Karachi', *Journal of Tropical Paediatrics*, 36, pp. 135–140.
Udry, C. (1999), 'Poverty, risk and households', paper presented to World Bank Workshop, July 2000, Washington DC.
Victora, C.G. (1992), 'The association between wasting and stunting: an international perspective', *Journal of Nutrition*, 122, pp. 1105–1110.
White, S. (1992), *Arguing with the Crocodile: gender and class in Bangladesh*, University Press, Dhaka, Bangladesh.
Wingard, D.L., Cohn, B.A., Kaplan, G.A., Cirillo, P.M. and Cohen, R.D. (1989), 'Sex differentials in morbidity and mortality risks examined by age and cause in the same cohort', *American Journal of Epidemiology*, 130(3), pp. 601–610.
World Development Report (1994), *Infrastructure for Development*, Oxford University Press, New York.

World Development Report (1999/2000), *Entering the 21st Century*, Oxford University Press, New York.
World Development Report (2000/2001), *Attacking Poverty*, Oxford University Press, New York.
Wratten, E. (1995), 'Conceptualizing urban poverty', *Environment and Urbanization*, 7, pp. 11–36.
Zaman, K., Baqui, A.H., Yunus, M., Sack, R.B., Bateman, O.M., Chowdhury, H.R. and Black, R.E. (1997), 'Acute respiratory infections in children: a community-based longitudinal study in rural Bangladesh', *Journal of Tropical Pediatrics*, 43(3), pp. 133–7.

# Index

absolute poverty 1, 7
Adams, A.M. 109
Agarwal, B. 109
Ain-O-Salish Kenra (ASK) 21
alliances *see* networking strategies
Amin, S. 71, 72, 112
animal ownership 2, 35, 38, 98–9, 183
asset buffers 106, 120, 170
asset leasing 13
asset ownership 2, 35, 38, 41, 98–9, 120
   importance of 47
asset selling 13, 95, 108, 156, 157, 165, 168, 179–80

babies *see* children
Bangladesh 17–18
   Dhaka 18–19
Bangladesh Integrated Nutrition Project (BINP) 134
Bangladesh Rural Advancement Committee (BRAC) 175, 176
begging 13, 157, 165, 169
Bisharat, L. 119
black market activities 157, 158, 159
Blanchet, T. 56
body mass index (BMI) 150, 151
   adult 4, 123–36, 180
   calculation of 124
   factors affecting 123, 125–33
   family structure and 125, 130
   female 124, 125, 130, 131, 133
   geographical location and 126, 133–4
   income levels and 123, 126, 127–8, 134
   male 124, 125, 130, 131, 133
   occupational status and 128–9
   seasonal variations in 131, 134
borrowing *see* loans/lending
boys *see* children
Brazil 133
breast fed children 151, 155, 158
business assets *see* asset ownership

Cain, M. 59
Caldwell, J. and P. 47
capability theory 2, 9, 14

case studies
   on loans/lending 168
   on nutritional status 153–9
   on work disabling illness 156–9
Castle, S.E. 119
casual workers
   ill health 179
   skilled 2, 3, 35, 41, 99, 104–105, 179, 183
   unskilled 2, 3, 34, 35, 41, 98–9, 101, 179, 183
Chen, M.A.
   *Coping with Seasonality and Drought* 109
child abuse 178
child care 78–9, 80, 81, 183
child education 2, 3, 59, 60–63
child labour 2–3, 59–69
   definition 68
   female 2, 3, 35, 38, 60, 68, 176–7
   importance of 34
   income from 35, 38, 59, 66–7
   level of 64–6, 72
   male 2–3, 35, 38, 59, 60, 176–7
   policy issues 176–7
   reasons for 13, 56
   reduction in 176–7
   regulation of 59
Child Nutrition Study of Bangladesh (CNSB) 144, 145
child poverty 2, 3, 8–9, 56
children
   abandoned 57
   adopted 56–7
   birth weight 158
   breast feeding 151, 155, 158
   club activities 66
   female 4, 9, 59, 180
   fostered 56–7
   health care 90–91
   ill health 3, 9, 85, 90–91, 92–3, 181
   male 4, 9, 180
   malnourished *see* nutritional status
   marital instability, effect on 55–7, 178
   mortality rates 79, 81, 83, 84, 90

nutritional status 4, 9, 118, 119–20, 137–48, 151–9, 180, 181
parental control 47
in poor households 8–9, 47, 52
as step-children 55–6, 105, 178
wasting in *see* nutritional status
children's rights 60, 68, 178
cluster analysis 34–5, 41, 96
*see also* livelihood clusters
community health insurance *see* health insurance schemes
consumption measurement 7–8
coping strategies 12
for financial shocks 5, 165–71
for ill health 3–4, 103–10, 179–80
for marital instability 47, 49–51, 178
socio-cultural 108–109
tolerance/compromise 49–50
credit *see* micro-credit programmes
creditworthiness *see* loans/lending

Daon, R.M. 119
De Waal, A.
*Famine that Kills* 170
debt 156, 157
*see also* income levels; poverty
decision making *see* household management
defencelessness 162, 184
*see also* vulnerability
deserted wives 25, 26, 27–8, 105
*see also* marital instability
divorce 2, 25, 26, 27–8, 30
effects of 9, 43, 47
increase in 43, 178
initiators of 44
threat of 117
unilateral 178
*see also* marriage
domestic violence 2, 46, 49, 117, 120
domestic work 72, 77–9, 80, 81
*see also* female workforce
dowries 59, 177
non-payment of 45, 155, 177–8
payments in lieu of 52
drinking water 129
Dugdale, A.E. 149

education
of children 2, 3, 59, 60–63
effects of 120, 145
literacy levels 60, 138, 139, 145

nutritional status and 138, 139, 145
of women 9, 181
electricity supplies 130
employment *see* labour market
employment insecurity 39, 104–105, 164
entitlement theory 2, 9–10, 14, 19
endowment 9–10, 19–22
exchange 10, 20, 21
environmental issues 103
environmental resources 19–20
ethnographic mapping 31–2, 33–4, 183
Everitt, B.
*Cluster Analysis* 34
expectation levels 45
expenditure levels 35, 38, 113–14, 183
on food 35, 38, 98–9, 107
on health care 95
reductions in 106–107, 165, 167

factions/rival groups 46, 177
family groups 2, 3, 28, 30, 71–82
conformity in 49–50
health care and 119–20
households/household members 4–5, 23–31, 105, 108–109, 111–21, 137, 149–60, 169
lineage groups (*goshti*) 46–7, 177
male irresponsibility towards 54–5
mothers-in-law 119–20
nutritional status and 125, 130
patriarchal tradition 177
size of 98–9
as supportive 51, 52
family planning 79
female controlled households 112, 114–20
female headed households 2, 24, 30, 31, 34, 38, 41, 182, 183
child labour in 176–7
financial management 5, 162, 163, 166, 167
financial shocks 162, 163, 166, 167, 184
formation of 52–3, 178
ill health in 3, 98–100, 153–6, 179
income levels 3, 35, 184
nutritional status 5, 130, 144, 145, 151, 153–6, 180, 181
well-being in 53
work participation 74
*see also* family groups; households/household members
female ill health 3, 87, 88, 90, 91, 92, 93, 118

female independence 111–12, 118–20
female literacy 138, 139, 145
female supported households 34
female workforce 2, 3, 34, 71–82, 112, 178
    attitudes to 80, 181
    domestic work 72, 77–9, 80, 81
    exploitation of 112
    graduation in employment 39–40
    ill health 3, 88
    income levels 71, 75–6, 80, 111–12, 115, 181, 182
    increase in 71
    insecurity of 80
    male control over 3, 77
    marital status 74, 80–81
    numbers of 72–4
    policy issues 182–3
    reasons for working 107
    significance of working 111–12
    status 71–2
    *see also* women ...
financial management 5, 119, 165–71, 179
    female headed households 5, 162, 163, 166, 167
    male headed households 162, 163, 166
    policy issues 184
financial shocks 5, 8, 11–13
    case studies in 166, 167
    cause of 163–4, 170–71
    coping strategies 165–71
    female headed households 162, 163, 166, 167
    male headed households 162, 163, 166, 168
    policy issues 184
food consumption/supply 154–5, 169, 180
    reduction in 170
food expenditure 35, 38, 98–9, 107
foreign aid 174, 175

garment industry 79, 170, 173
gender bias
    in employment 71, 79
    in health care 9
gender inequalities 112, 182
gender relations 118–19, 120
    *see also* marriage
gift giving 109
girls *see* children
Gonosasthya Kendra (GK) health care system 101, 180

Grameen Bank (GB) health programme 101, 175, 176, 180
Gross Domestic Product (GDP) 17
Gross National Product (GNP) 17

Haddad, L. 8
Haque, T. 112
health care 95, 101, 119, 154, 157, 181
    alternative medicine 154, 157
    for children 90–91
    family groups and 119–20
    gender bias in 9
    policy issues 101, 110, 181
    work based 181
    *see also* ill health
health care expenditure 95, 100
health education 175
health insurance schemes 101, 110, 180, 184
household anthropometry 149–50, 152
household expenditure *see* expenditure levels
household management 4, 111–12, 182
household work *see* domestic work
households/household members 23–31, 137
    conflict in 111
    female controlled 112, 114–20
    female headed *see* female headed households
    intra-household negotiations 4, 111–21
    intra-household relations 105, 111
    male controlled 112, 114–20, 130, 156–9, 162, 163, 166, 168, 176, 177, 182
    male headed 30, 31, 34, 35, 38, 53, 76–7, 98, 99
    merging of households 108, 169
    nutritional status 4–5, 149–60
    rural areas, moving back to 108–9, 168–9
    *see also* family groups
housing conditions 139–40, 145
    floor space 132
    latrines 140, 143–4, 145, 146, 180

ill health 3, 20, 83–94
    adult 84–93, 103, 181; *see also* work disabling
    causes of 83, 103
    in children 3, 9, 85, 90–91, 92–3, 181
    coping strategies 3–4, 103–10, 179–80

cost of 99–100, 103
effects of 34, 95–102, 103–106
female 3, 87, 88, 90, 91, 92, 93, 111, 153–6
in female workforce 3, 88
income levels, effect on 100–101; *see also* work disabling
male 3, 87, 88, 91, 92
measurement of 84–5
poverty and 1, 3, 83, 88, 92, 103
prevalence of 85, 90, 92, 103, 104
types of 85–93, 104
as work disabling 3, 34, 95–102, 103–10, 156–9, 163–4, 170, 179–80, 184
*see also* health care; nutritional status; vulnerability
income increase concept 170
income levels 2, 35, 38, 183
child labour and 35, 38, 59, 66–7
in female headed households 3, 35, 184
of female workforce 71, 75–6, 80, 111–12, 115, 181, 182
financial shocks 5, 8, 11–13, 161–71, 184
ill health, effect of 100–101
inequalities in 3, 75–6, 80, 182
minimum wage 184
nutritional status and 123, 126, 127–8, 134, 137, 141, 143, 145–6, 153–9
reduction in 13
significance of 111–12
in urban areas 173
*see also* poverty
income measurement 7–8, 10
income sources 107, 180, 181, 184
institutional structure
as inefficient 174–5
for poverty alleviation 13–14, 22, 174–6
non-governmental organisations (NGOs) 71, 112, 134, 155, 158, 174–6, 178, 183
insurance schemes 13, 170
health insurance 101, 110, 180, 184

Jordan 119–20
judicial system *see* legal system

Kabeer, N. 41, 43, 112, 118
Kanbur, R. 8
Kesserler, R.C. 92

kinship *see* family groups

labour force 39–41
changing jobs 165, 166
child labour 2–3, 13, 34, 35, 38, 59–69
female *see* female workforce
gender analysis 72
work disabling illness 3–4, 34, 95–110, 156–9, 163–4, 170, 179–80, 184
working conditions 181, 184
working hours/patterns 2, 13, 35, 74, 80, 98–9, 104–105, 183, 184
labour market 39
employment insecurity 39, 104–105, 164
graduation in employment 39–41
inequalities in 72
land holdings 2, 35, 38, 98–9, 183
latrines, use of 140, 144, 145, 146, 180
legal issues 14, 50, 178
life expectancy 84
*see also* mortality rates
lineage groups (*goshti*) 177
as dysfunctional 46–7
literacy levels, adult 60, 138, 139, 145
*see also* education
livelihood clusters 2, 33–42, 183
analysis of 34–5, 41, 96
casual skilled 2, 3, 38, 41, 99, 104–105, 179, 183
casual unskilled 2, 3, 34, 35, 41, 98–9, 101, 179, 183
female headed households *see* female headed households
income levels *see* income levels
policy issues 183
self-employed 2, 3, 35, 41, 98–100, 179, 183
work disabling illness and 97–100
livelihood strategies 19–22
*see also* Urban Livelihood Study
livelihood system concept 161, 184
loans/lending 2, 10, 13, 34, 95, 98–9, 106, 158, 165, 167–8, 183
case studies in 168
government loans 180
interest levels 158
*see also* micro-credit programmes

male controlled households 112, 114–20, 182
child labour in 176, 177

financial shocks 162, 163, 166, 168
nutritional status 130, 156–9
male headed households 30, 31, 34, 35, 38, 53, 98, 99
male ill health 3, 87, 88, 91, 92
male literacy 138, 139, 145
*see also* men
malnourishment *see* nutritional status
marital instability 2, 43–58
    children, effect on 55–7, 178
    coping strategies 47, 49–51, 178
    deserted wives 25, 26, 27–8, 105
    divorce *see* divorce
    domestic violence 2, 46, 49, 117, 120
    effect of 54–7, 178
    lineage groups (*goshti*) and 46–7, 177
    negotiation/mediation in 50
    policy issues 177–8
    reasons for 45–7, 48, 177–8
    reduction in 177–8
    responsive strategies 51–3
marital status, of study group 25–8
marriage 43, 59
    dowries 45, 52, 59, 155, 177–8
    evidence of 50, 117, 178
    gender relations 118–19
    love marriages 43, 47, 177
    monogamous 25, 26
    polygamous 25, 26, 44, 45, 49
    re-marriage 44, 51–2
    as universal 43–4, 177
maternity leave 183
men 47
    deviant behaviour 45–6, 178
    female competition for 54
    gender bias 9, 71, 79
    as irresponsible 54–5, 178
    marital instability *see* marital instability
    nutritional status 9, 151–3, 156–9
    *see also* children; male ...
micro-credit programmes 175, 176, 180, 184
migration/mobility 24, 168–9
    refugees 154, 157
minimum wage 184
    *see also* income levels
money control *see* financial management
money management *see* household management
monogamous marriage 25, 26
monsoon season 134
moral economy concept 161, 170–71

morbidity measurement 84–5
    *see also* ill health
mortality rates 9, 83, 84
    children 79, 81, 83, 84, 90
Moser, C. 170

natal kin *see* family groups
National Food and Nutrition Policy 134
National Poverty Line *see* poverty line
natural disasters 13, 18, 134
Naved, T.R. 54–5
networking strategies 51, 72, 104–105, 109–10, 112
    patron/client relationships 105–106, 154, 155
    social networks 105–106, 161, 178
non-governmental organisations (NGOs) 71, 112, 134, 155, 158, 174–6
    foreign aid distributed by 175
    function 175, 176, 178, 183
    micro-credit programmes 175, 176, 180, 184
Nutrition Surveillance Project (NSP) 144
Nutritional Rehabilitation Units (NRUs) 155, 157
nutritional status 1, 20
    adult 4, 123–36, 151–3, 180–81
    body mass index (BMI) 4, 123–36, 150, 151, 180
    of breast fed children 151, 155
    case studies 153–9
    of children 4, 9, 118, 119–20, 137–8, 151–9, 180, 181
    factors affecting 123, 126, 127–8, 137–46
    female 9, 151–9, 180–81
    in female headed households 5, 130, 144, 151, 153–6, 180, 181
    housing conditions and 139–40, 144, 145, 146, 180
    income levels and 123, 126, 127–8, 134, 137, 141, 143, 145–6, 153–9
    intra-household distribution 4–5, 149–60, 181
    latrine use and 140, 143–4, 145, 146
    male 9, 151–3, 156–9, 180–81
    in male headed households 156–9
    policy issues 134, 146, 180–81
    seasonal variations 142, 144
    statistical analysis 138
    *see also* vulnerability

patron/client relationships 105–106, 154, 155
policy issues 2, 5, 22, 41
   child labour 176–7
   financial management 184
   health care 101, 110, 181
   labour market 182–3
   marital instability 177–8
   nutrition 134, 146, 180–81
   poverty alleviation 174–85
   women's issues 181–3
polygamous marriage 25, 26, 44, 45
   female acceptance of 49
population levels 59, 60
   urban areas 1, 19, 32, 173
poverty
   absolute 1, 7
   child poverty 2, 3
   debt 156, 157
   ill health and 1, 3, 83, 88, 92, 103
   impoverishment process 153–9
   nutritional status and 123, 126, 127–8, 134, 137, 141, 143, 145–6, 153–9
   vulnerability and 1–2, 7–16
   *see also* income levels
poverty alleviation
   institutional structure for 13–14, 22, 174–6
   policy issues 174–85
   success/failure rate 175–6
poverty gap 8
poverty levels 173–4
poverty line 7, 8, 19, 174
poverty measurement 1–2, 7–16
   capability theory and 2, 9, 14
   consumption measurement 7–8
   data collection 8
   entitlement theory and 2, 9–10, 14
   income measurement 7–8, 10
   within-household 8–9
poverty trap 13–14
price levels 9
   *see also* food expenditure
profit levels 165
Pryer, J. A. 100–101, 103, 123, 134, 137
public health issues 103

Rahman, S. 71
random cluster sampling 23
refugees 154, 157
risk/risk exposure 10–14
Rowntree, S. 7

rumours *see* factions/rival groups
rural areas, moving back to 108–109, 168–9

savings 2, 35, 115, 118, 120, 181, 183
   use of 107–108, 176
self-employed workers 2, 3, 35, 41, 98–100, 179, 183
Sen, A. K. 9, 14, 19, 55, 111, 120, 182
skill levels 2, 3, 35, 41, 99, 104–105, 179, 183
   unskilled 2, 3, 34, 35, 41, 98–9, 101, 179
   upgrading of 181
slum areas (bustees) 1, 19
   definition 23
social interaction
   lineage groups (*goshti*) 46–7, 177
   male/female 45
social networks 105–106
   importance of 161
   victim support 178
spiritual beliefs 158
Stichter, S. 79
Sudan 170

Tanzania 133
trade unions 184

unemployment *see* employment insecurity
United Nations (UN) 176
urban areas 19, 33, 173
urban growth 1, 19, 32, 173
Urban Livelihoods Study (ULS) 1, 17–32, 144
   background 17–22
   data collection 22
   methodology/design 2, 19, 22–32, 84–5, 96–7, 112, 124, 138, 149, 162
   population sample 24–31
   purpose 22
   qualitative studies 31–2
   quantitative panel survey 22–4
urban poverty levels 173

victim support 178
visiting rights 116
vulnerability 20, 33, 161–2, 170, 179, 184
   community 20
   defencelessness 162, 184
   external 161, 184
   individual/household 20

internal 161–2, 184
poverty and 1–2, 7–16
*see also* ill health; nutritional status

wages *see* income levels
water supplies *see* drinking water
women
  economic independence 51
  household management by 4, 111–12, 182
  marital instability *see* marital instability
  nutritional status 9, 151–9, 180–81
  policy issues for 181–3
  status of 71–2, 178
  subordination of 112
  violence against 2, 46, 49, 117, 120
  visiting rights for 116
  well-being 4, 53, 111–21
  widowed 9, 25, 26
  *see also* female ...
women's education 9, 181
  literacy levels 138, 139, 145

women's shelters 178
work based health care 181
work disabling illness 34, 95–102, 170
  case study 156–9
  coping strategies 3–4, 103–10, 179–80
  cost of 99–100
  effects of 95–6, 103–106, 163–4, 184
  livelihood clusters and 97–100
  measurement of 96–7
  policy issues 179–80
working conditions 181, 184
working hours/patterns 2, 13, 35, 74, 80, 98–9, 183, 184
  employment insecurity 39, 104–5, 164
  leisure days 74
  maternity leave 183
  *see also* labour ...
World Bank 7, 8, 175
World Declaration on Nutrition (FAO) 134
World Health Organisation (WHO) 144
Wratten, E. 83, 103